BEN JONSON'S THEATRICAL REPUBLICS

Also by Julie Sanders

REFASHIONING BEN JONSON: Gender, Politics and the Jonsonian Canon (*editor with Kate Chedgzoy and Susan Wiseman*)

Ben Jonson's Theatrical Republics

Julie Sanders
Lecturer in English
Keele University

First published in Great Britain 1998 by
MACMILLAN PRESS LTD
Houndmills, Basingstoke, Hampshire RG21 6XS and London
Companies and representatives throughout the world

A catalogue record for this book is available from the British Library.

ISBN 0-333-67662-9

 First published in the United States of America 1998 by
ST. MARTIN'S PRESS, INC.,
Scholarly and Reference Division,
175 Fifth Avenue, New York, N.Y. 10010

ISBN 0-312-21498-7

Library of Congress Cataloging-in-Publication Data
Sanders, Julie.
Ben Jonson's theatrical republics / Julie Sanders.
p. cm.
Includes bibliographical references (p.   ) and index.
ISBN 0-312-21498-7
1. Jonson, Ben, 1573?-1637—Political and social views.
2. Politics and literature—Great Britain—History—17th century.
3. Literature and society—Great Britain—History—17th century.
4. Political plays, English—History and criticism.   5. Jonson, Ben,
1573?-1637—Dramatic works.   6. Social problems in literature.
7. Republicanism in literature.   I. Title.
PR2642.P64S26   1998
822'.3—dc21   98-15378
                                                                        CIP

© Julie Sanders 1998

All rights reserved. No reproduction, copy or transmission of this publication may be made without written permission.

No paragraph of this publication may be reproduced, copied or transmitted save with written permission or in accordance with the provisions of the Copyright, Designs and Patents Act 1988, or under the terms of any licence permitting limited copying issued by the Copyright Licensing Agency, 90 Tottenham Court Road, London W1P 9HE.

Any person who does any unauthorised act in relation to this publication may be liable to criminal prosecution and civil claims for damages.

The author has asserted her right to be identified as the author of this work in accordance with the Copyright, Designs and Patents Act 1988.

This book is printed on paper suitable for recycling and made from fully managed and sustained forest sources.

10 9 8 7 6 5 4 3 2 1
07 06 05 04 03 02 01 00 99 98

Printed and bound in Great Britain by
Antony Rowe Ltd, Chippenham, Wiltshire

To John Higham
with all my love

Contents

Acknowledgements ix

Note on Editions Used xi

1 Introduction 1

Part I Republics – Fake and Genuine

2 Roman Frames of Mind 11

3 'Saying Something About Venice' 34

Part II Theatrical Republics

4 The Alternative Commonwealth of Women 49

5 Republicanism and Theatre 68

6 The Republic in the Fair 89

Part III Theatrical Commonwealths and Communities

7 The Commonwealth of Hell: *The Devil is an Ass* 107

8 The Commonwealth of Paper: Print, News and *The Staple of News* 123

9	Alternative Societies: *The New Inn* and the Late Plays	144
10	Local Government and Personal Rule in *A Tale of a Tub*	164
11	Conclusion: 'The End of [T]his Commonwealth Does Not Forget the Beginning'	180

Notes   188

Bibliography   223

Index   253

Acknowledgements

As ever, and perhaps especially so with a first book, there are many people without whom it would not have been possible. I hope the book itself is some thanks, if not necessarily thanks enough. Firstly there was, and is, my family – thanks for all the loans to buy books, all the love, and all the encouragement – to my mother Kay, my father Mike, and my brother Neil. Thanks too to my extended family, especially Anne and Geoffrey Higham who helped me buy a laptop computer at the vital moment, and Lynn Sanders for endless generosity and hospitality. I cannot thank Carol Harpster enough for those fondly remembered Californian days. I hope that my adopted family in Cambridge will forgive me for embarrassing them here, but love and thanks also to Susan James, Quentin Skinner, Olivia Skinner and Marcus Skinner.

Those who inspired me as an undergraduate were many, but especial thanks to my exemplary tutors at Girton College – Jonathan Bate, Juliet Dusinberre, Gillian Beer and Jill Mann. University, though, would have been a very different experience without the initial and ongoing guidance of the very finest teacher of them all, once of Girton herself, then of Chingford Senior High, now of St Felix's in Suffolk – to Sue Roberts, my love, thanks, and admiration always.

In academic life the list of acknowledgements is inevitably endless, but special mention must go to those who have been and I hope will long continue to be colleagues, role models, and the very best of friends – Kate Chedgzoy, Sue Wiseman, Bridget Bennett, Helen Stoddart and Ann Hughes. Both Sue and Ann have spent far more time than friendship should demand reading and commenting on drafts of this book. Their wisdom has been much appreciated and any remaining errors are solely mine.

Sections of this book have appeared in earlier (and occasionally extended) versions in the following journals. I am grateful to the institutions concerned for the permission to reproduce that material here: Chapter 9 previously appeared as '"The Day's Sports

Devised in the Inn": Jonson's *The New Inn* and Theatrical Politics', *Modern Language Review* 91 (1996), 545–60; Chapter 10 previously appeared as ' "The Collective Contract is a Fragile Structure": Local Government and Personal Rule in Jonson's *A Tale of a Tub*', *English Literary Renaissance*, 27 (1997), 443–67 and a small section of Chapter 7 appeared as 'A Parody of Lord Chief Justice Popham in *The Devil is an Ass*' in *Notes and Queries* 44 (1997) 528–30. Sections of Chapter 8 appear in 'Print, Popular Culture, Consumption, and Commodification in *The Staple of News*', in Julie Sanders, with Kate Chedgzoy and Susan Wiseman (eds), *Refashioning Ben Jonson: Gender, Politics, and the Jonsonian Canon* (Macmillan, 1998).

Others who have contributed to this book in very tangible ways include my colleagues in the Department of English at Keele (special thanks to the best of mentors Jim McLaverty for the advice and the biscuits) and those with whom I worked previously at the University of Warwick. Grateful thanks to the support staff and librarians at both institutions, as well as at the University Library, Cambridge and the British Library in London. Thanks too to Richard Burt, Martin Butler, Rowland Cotterill, Stephen Greenblatt, Peter Holland, Arthur Kinney, Gaynor Macfarlane, Jeremy Maule, Kate McLuskie, Christopher Pye and Blair Worden. Thanks, too, to my wonderful editor at Macmillan, Charmian Hearne. I cannot thank enough, personally or intellectually, my now-fellow Jonsonian (if he will forgive the presumption) Richard Dutton: I only hope this work does his influence and guidance justice.

Finally though there is the person to whom this book is dedicated. 'All that I am in arts and all I know'? Well, maybe not, but thank you for being there through it all. This one is for John, if he wants it.

Note on Editions Used

The availability of Jonson's canon in print is the subject matter for a book in itself. Unlike the situation of Shakespeare, there are no modern complete editions of Jonson to employ for easy reference. There is of course the monumental C.H. Herford and Percy and Evelyn Simpson (eds), *Complete Works* published by Oxford University Press in 11 volumes (1925–52) (henceforth Herford and Simpson) but this is largely present only in libraries, in old spelling, and now somewhat out of date in a critical sense. Until Oxford University Press's newly commissioned *Complete Works* to be edited by Martin Butler and Ian Donaldson emerges, Jonson scholars must resign themselves to an expensive lifestyle of multiple single copies and the odd selective but not comprehensive collection.

I have, with accessibility in mind, elected to use modern spelling in the quotations from Jonson found throughout this book and have therefore favoured recent editions of the plays, poems, prose and masques, where these are available. Where possible, therefore, I have used the two-volume Cambridge University Press edition of *Selected Plays of Ben Jonson*, ed. Martin Butler and Johanna Proctor (1989). For those plays not included in that selection I have, again where possible, used single Revels editions (Manchester University Press) and only as a last resort – in the case of *The Magnetic Lady*, *Every Man Out of His Humour*, *Cynthia's Revels*, and *The Sad Shepherd* – turned to Herford and the Simpsons. I should add that *Every Man Out of His Humour* and *The Magnetic Lady* are forthcoming with Revels. To assist the reader, the following is an outline of all editions used:

Plays

Every Man In His Humour (Quarto) – Herford and Simpson, Volume III

Every Man In His Humour (Folio) – Martin Seymour-Smith (ed.),

Every Man In His Humour (London: A & C Black (New Mermaids), 1966; repr. 1988)
Every Man Out of His Humour – Herford and Simpson, Volume III
Cynthia's Revels – Herford and Simpson, Volume IV
Poetaster – Tom Cain (ed.), *Poetaster* (Manchester: Manchester University Press (Revels), 1995)
Sejanus, His Fall – *Selected Plays of Ben Jonson*, Volume I
Eastward Ho (by Jonson, with George Chapman and John Marston) – R.W. Van Fossen (ed.), *Eastward Ho* (Manchester: Manchester University Press (Revels), 1979)
Volpone, the Fox – *Selected Plays of Ben Jonson*, Volume I
Epicoene, or The Silent Woman – *Selected Plays of Ben Jonson*, Volume I
The Alchemist – *Selected Plays of Ben Jonson*, Volume II
Catiline, His Conspiracy – W.F. Bolton and Jane F. Gardner (eds), *Catiline, His Conspiracy* (London: Arnold, 1973)
Bartholomew Fair – *Selected Plays of Ben Jonson*, Volume II
The Devil is an Ass – Peter Happé (ed.), *The Devil is an Ass* (Manchester: Manchester University Press (Revels), 1994)
The Staple of News – Anthony Parr (ed.), *The Staple of News* (Manchester: Manchester University Press (Revels), 1988)
The New Inn – *Selected Plays of Ben Jonson*, Volume II
The Magnetic Lady – Herford and Simpson, Volume VI
A Tale of a Tub – *Selected Plays of Ben Jonson*, Volume II
The Sad Shepherd – Herford and Simpson, Volume VII

Masques

All masque quotations are taken from Stephen Orgel, *The Complete Masques* (New Haven and London: Yale University Press, 1969; repr. 1975)

Poems and Prose

All quotations from poems or from *Timber, or Discoveries* and the *Conversations with Drummond of Hawthornden* are taken from Ian Donaldson (ed.), *The Oxford Ben Jonson* (Oxford: Oxford University Press, 1985)

1
Introduction

Ben Jonson was not a republican. Ben Jonson was not an absolutist. Ben Jonson desired a limited monarchy. Ben Jonson believed in republicanism. Ben Jonson did not counsel the abolition of monarchy. Ben Jonson sought to extend the rights of the monarch's subjects. All of these contradictory statements, and more, are true about the paradoxical figure of Ben Jonson, public theatre dramatist and court masquer.

Jonson's relationship to republicanism and to republics is hard to pin down. In this study I suggest that the plays he wrote during the Jacobean and Caroline reigns use language taken from the debates about the 'republic' and the 'commonwealth' that were current in early seventeenth-century England. Not only is it possible to trace the shifting discourses of English and European politics in Jonson's language, but it seems clear that he recognized the theatre itself as a 'republic' in another sense – as a place where audiences engaged with and to a certain extent participated in the different political positions articulated in Jonson's onstage worlds or 'theatrical republics'. I will, therefore, delineate a Jonson who, for example, moved *between* the domains of court and public theatre, and who, rather than becoming a King's poet, continued to meditate on politics and popular opinion even in (and possibly especially in) the last works of his career.

In this, the Jonson I outline differs to an extent from recent critical accounts which have contributed to an understanding of him that is court-orientated in its emphases. A particular engagement with New Historicism and its so-called 'cultural poetics' will be evident. Jonson has in many respects provided the archetypal figure for New Historicist constructs of power in seventeenth-century literature and yet in anything other than his guise as Jacobean court poet he has been strangely absent from many of the movement's seminal texts (in particular the ground-breaking work of Stephen Greenblatt).[1] The public theatre dramatist that is also Jonson has tended to be viewed from the vantage point of his career as a court masquer. Such a perspective is necessarily limiting and has led to a tendency to read the public theatre plays as paeans to the monarch and the court instead of as significantly juxtaposed and contraposed texts which contain, in my account of them, potential for more radical and subversive social and political critique.[2] In accordance with the interest of this book in varied forms of 'republicanism' (actual, theatrical, communal), different chapters adopt different critical approaches and techniques. Cultural Materialism, Gender Studies, and Performance Theory, as well as recent developments in historical studies of the early modern period, are all seen to offer ways of reconfiguring the Jonsonian canon and our critical perspective.[3]

In literary historical accounts of the reign of King James VI and I, Jonson has been represented as the 'King's poet'.[4] A significant date in the construction of this 'Jonson' has been 1616, when he published his Folio *Works*. That conscious intervention in print culture has been viewed by many critics as indubitable proof that Jonson had an absolutist's drive towards fixity. He sought, they claim, to embody his written words in the concrete form of print, altering those areas of his manuscripts with which he was dissatisfied, omitting substandard texts, and controlling and manipulating reader reception via material factors such as prefaces, prologues, epilogues, marginalia, and frontispieces.[5] Jonson did not cease to write in 1616 though, nor did he cease to write literature aimed at the public or popular sphere, but the stress on the printed aspect of his canon has skewed critical appreciation of this continued literary and political fluidity. The resulting portrait of Jonson has been a largely conservative one.[6] It has contributed to the presentation of a dramatist whose investments are in monarchy, patriarchy and literary control. The exploration of the language and the tropes of republicanism in Jonson's work here offers a rather more nuanced picture of the author, one that sees him investigating in more open fashion the politics of state, family and authorship.

No fixed or even stable definition of what Jonson understood by the term 'republicanism' will be offered. 'Republicanism' in the seventeenth century was itself a slippery and complex term. The modern understanding would appear to be that a republican is someone opposed to monarchy and to the existence of courts. In the sixteenth and seventeenth centuries the inflected meaning was more constitutional: a republic implied a mixed form of government. Feasibly, therefore, even a monarchy – a limited, accountable monarchy – might be republican in its politics.⁷ This complex presence of 'republicanism' in English early modern culture informs Jonson's writing and, in turn, the structure of this study's sections and chapters. Jonson's theatrical republics employ actual political paradigms such as Ancient Rome and contemporary Venice. They use urban locations to explore the potential 'republicanism' or populace-based politics of the city, and in turn employ the medium of theatre to explore these ideas in microcosm. They invest the word 'republic' with the widespread seventeenth-century meaning of 'commonwealth' to explore ideas of community. The three sections of this book reflect these variant forms of 'republicanism' on the Jonsonian stage.

The polysemic way in which a term like 'republic' or 'republican' shades into questions of commonwealth, common good and community in this period will be crucial for my purposes. I am not arguing that Jonson saw an English republic as a political option: Blair Worden has indicated that whilst the sometimes contradictory discourses of republican theory were current in early seventeenth-century politics there were no tangible aims to institute an English republic: 'There would,' he suggests, 'have been little point.'⁸ It is Jonson's engagement with those discourses, with the 'language' and ideas of republicanism that I am concerned with. In order to identify traces of that political debate in the Jonsonian canon, this book will employ the forms of close reading suggested by Richard Machin and Christopher Norris which 'do justice to the effort of writing' and look to terminology rather than any specific action or experience that terminology might seek to produce.⁹ Jonson's explorations of actual republics such as Rome in his Jacobean tragedies and Venice in *Volpone* will be considered alongside more theoretical explorations of concepts of republicanism and community, not least the theatrical community, in plays such as *The Alchemist*, *Bartholomew Fair* and his later Caroline drama. His use of the term and concept of 'republicanism' will be seen to differ according to these different contexts.¹⁰

Annabel Patterson has written recently of the 'republican agenda' of the early modern period, suggesting that there was a 'general understanding of republican values' at this time and that alongside this general understanding 'there was considerable, and fertile, range of opinion'.¹¹ She suggests that there is often a republican subtext even in seemingly apolitical contexts, which can be registered by the marking of certain 'ideologically freighted words' and related questions of liberty, freedom, absolutism, equity, equality, the popular, the populace, Common Law and Magna Carta.[12] These questions will be central amongst those we see debated within the context of Jonsonian drama.

An important initial question concerns the extent of Jonson's exposure to 'classical republicanism', by which I refer to the range of writings on the Ancient Roman republic (and attendant comparisons with the Empire), which historians have seen as such an important political and philosophical influence in the early modern period.[13] During the Renaissance these writings, by Livy, Sallust, Tacitus and others, were frequently filtered through the work of continental humanists such as Niccolò Machiavelli, Justus Lipsius, and Jean Bodin, and in turn took on a localized form within an English context. Blair Worden has remarked that 'The ideas of the English republicans are not easy to classify. ... Writing in order to shape events, they adapted their arguments and their emphases to immediate circumstances.'[14] This helps to explain why although 'there was admiration for classical (and aristocratic) republican virtue, there was no suggestion that England could or should become a republic'.[15] In a connected vein, by no means do I intend to present Jonson as a republican in any active political sense of the term but I do believe that he toyed seriously (and the oxymoron is intentional) with ideas of limited monarchy.

Jonson's treatments of actual, historical republics are explored in Part I, 'Republics – Fake and Genuine'. Renaissance Venice is a vital concern there. The singular figure of the Venetian Doge fascinated political Europe, representing as it did a form of controlled or limited monarchy within an ostensibly republican context; one myth fostered by Renaissance, republican Venice was that it was the direct descendant of the Ancient Roman Empire, a paradox in itself. Jonson explored the advantages and disadvantages of limited monarchy (open or covert) in a number of his plays (see in particular Chapter 2, 'Roman Frames of Mind'). He certainly had access to the range of writings that come under the heading of 'classical republicanism' and he was highly engaged with the new post-humanist politics and history stemming from Italy.[16] It was from sources such as Machiavelli's *Discourses* and the innumerable political tracts on the Venetian constitution that the language of republicanism in the seventeenth century largely derived, especially the concept of the '*stato misto*'.[17]

Venice was for the Renaissance a perfect paradigm of the

classical Polybian concept of a mixed constitution managed by a combination of the single ruler, an elected few, and the ultimate power of the many – the populace.[18] How real such a notion was in the closed oligarchy of the Venetian senate is a matter for debate but the myth was nevertheless a potent one.[19] The myth of Venice as a stable and peaceful constitutional state was propagated not only by the Venetian patriciate themselves but taken up and proclaimed in other Italian city-states, even ostensible rivals such as Florence: 'Throughout Europe during the sixteenth and seventeenth centuries it formed part of a language of republicanism which stood in opposition to increasingly absolutist theories of government.'[20] Questions of specifically Venetian republicanism will be argued for as crucial to a full understanding of Jonson's *Volpone* (see Chapter 3).

Dutch rebels, opposing Habsburg Spain in the United Provinces in the late sixteenth century, adopted the notion of the *stato misto*. The republican terminology these rebels increasingly employed during their lengthy and uneven revolt against Spanish rule was also hugely indebted to the political tracts stemming from and about republican Venice.[21] Mulier, examining the linguistic aspects of the conflict, observes:

> Certainly the language of classical republicanism, of which the myth of Venice was an embodiment, served, at times, purely rhetorical ends. But it was also incorporated into a number of political tracts as an analogy for the Dutch Republic, which was already being described as a mixed state by the beginning of the seventeenth century. In this way an attempt was made to clarify the undefined and tense relationship which existed between the stadtholder and the other parts of the structure.[22]

but adds that this was not necessarily an immediate occurrence; the republican vocabulary now associated with the revolt was not inevitable from the outset. The 'language of classical republicanism' mentioned here is essentially an invocation of ancient and civic liberties by the Dutch rebels, of the rights of the community as against the absolute power of the monarch, rather than a committed struggle to establish a republican constitution from the outset (since many of the Dutch magnates of the States-General were protecting their rights against Habsburg interventions).

The idea of a *stato misto* is an attractive but unstable idea that allows for greater stress on any one of the three elements involved, hence so often early modern republics were oligarchical in nature. The ideologies of republicanism and the language in which these ideas are defined in different contexts are crucial. In the Dutch instance popular liberties rather than an open democracy were being encouraged. The role of republican debate in English politics could be seen as following a similar path to the Dutch experience, from initial linguistic interest evolving only gradually into active republican politics. The House of Commons debates of the 1620s and 1640s employed republican terminology (often with reference to ancient precedent, including Magna Carta, and to the inheritances of Common Law) in order to facilitate discussion of subjects' rights in the face of what was seen by many as the abuse of prerogative by the monarch; but notions of citizenship and community rights were often invoked without the full force of the debate, or the full valency of the words being utilized, being recognized at the time (a comparison can be drawn with present-day debates in Parliament and the somewhat vague and manipulative use of terms such as 'community' and 'general public').[23]

Ben Jonson had a more than linguistic experience of the Dutch Revolt.[24] In 1591 he abandoned his stepfather's trade of bricklaying and joined the English army stationed in the Netherlands. Since the pay of a common soldier was only equivalent to that of a bricklayer, Jonson's biographer, David Riggs, suggests that this was a far from prudent decision and taken for other than material reasons.[25] Riggs, however, spends little time examining exactly what those reasons might have been; he records the episode as indicative of Jonson's innately aggressive character and swiftly moves on:

> To judge from Jonson's reminiscences [in the *Conversations with Drummond*],[26] he joined the army for psychological rather than material reasons. 'In his service in the Low Countries,' he recalled, 'he had in the face of both the Campes killed ane Enemie and taken *opima spolia* from him.' Once Jonson had killed his man, he returned home 'soone' – the wording of Drummond's notation suggests that he did not serve out his time – presumably because he had accomplished what he set out to do.[27]

There seem to be too many gaps in this particular account. It is certainly worth noting that Jonson's choice of descriptive vocabulary – *opima spolia* – is a Roman term and therefore a pointer to his awareness of the classical republican tradition in recalling this conflict; even in the group context of war he continues to flaunt his independence – educational and political.

Jonson's experience fed directly into his drama: there is a large number of specifically Dutch references embodied in the text of *The Alchemist* (1610).[28] It is the linguistic role of republicanism in the Dutch conflict mapped out here that I would argue had a huge influence on Jonson. The language(s) of republicanism offered not a viable political alternative but a means of discussing potential alterations and improvements that might be made, both politically and socially.

Throughout his career Jonson engaged with the semantic shifts that political language was undergoing. His 'republicanism' is a mark of his participation in the debate and that participation extends to his prose, poetry and drama. As well as registering and annotating direct republican references in Jonson's plays this book seeks to place Jonson's approach to theatre and its conventions within a theoretical context of republicanism, recognizing, as I believe Jonson himself does, the republicanism inherent in the dramatic genre itself with its co-production of meaning between writer, director, actors and audience. This is no absolutist medium, particularly so in the early modern period when playscripts belonged to acting companies and not to individual authors.[29] These and related issues are the concern of Part II, 'Theatrical Republics' (see Chapter 4, 'The Alternative Commonwealth of Women'; Chapter 5, 'Republicanism and Theatre'; and Chapter 6, 'The Republic in the Fair'). The terminology and conceptual notions of republicanism are seen to provide dramatic potential. I believe that Jonson experienced an everyday version of 'republicanism' in the very nature of the theatrical experience: in significant ways, therefore, Part II seeks to redefine the almost commonplace notion of Jonson's 'anti-theatricalism', which I regard as being not only a far more playful stance than has previously been suggested but also one that masks a more radical awareness of the potential of an audience to produce multiple readings and interpretations. A related sense of 'republicanism' in terms of flexibility, pluralism and multiplicity is traced in Jonson's printed matter. This study adopts a fresh approach to the 1616 folio printing of the *Works*, refusing to accord it the fixed and definitive position it has heretofore held in the Jonsonian canon.[30]

As questions of republicanism and audiences, republicanism and commonwealths, and republicanism and communities and the communal are found to be prevalent in Jonsonian texts and their performance, the study also constructs a theory of the communities of Jonsonian drama, finding in the late plays in particular a dominant concern with the role of the locality, not only in theatre but also in politics (see Part III, 'Theatrical Commonwealths and Communities'). Community politics are seen to be espoused by the treatment of the theme of fen-drainage in *The Devil is an Ass* (see Chapter 7) and Chapter 10 on *A Tale of a Tub* explores the effects and impacts of non-parliamentary 'Personal Rule' by Charles I in the 1630s on communities and theatre (Jonsonian theatre in particular). Other chapters in this section examine the role of the populace in this period of increasingly personal rule via a consideration of print culture and the press (in Chapter 8 on *The Staple of News*), and drinking-houses and private theatres (in Chapter 9 on *The New Inn* and other late plays), investigating questions of the rights of the localities and of parliament in the decade of non-parliamentary rule.

In his commonplace book, *Timber; or, Discoveries* (further textual evidence, if it were needed, of a seventeenth-century desire for a common ground, a common place, a commonwealth of learning) Ben Jonson remarks:

> I could never think the study of wisdom confined only to the philosopher: or of piety to the divine; or of state to the politic. But that he which can feign a commonwealth (which is the poet) can govern it with counsels, strengthen it with laws, correct it with judgements, inform it with religion and morals is all these.
> (ll. 1043–8)

The above quotation is more usually read as a sign of Jonson's Platonic ambitions, envisioning a poet-ruler as an extension of the philosopher-ruler of the *Republic*, yet in the context of this study we can see that Ben Jonson did indeed feign commonwealths and that through his theatrical republics he sought to counsel the political actors of his day.

Part I
Republics – Fake and Genuine

2
Roman Frames of Mind

Ancient Rome, republican or otherwise, loomed large in Jonson's creative and political imagination. Not only was he well-read in the writings stemming from that period, he was committed to scholarly reconstructions of classical Rome for both comic and tragic dramatic purposes. Rome fascinated him as both an aesthetic and political community, providing him with clear paradigms against which to measure his contemporary situation. Jonson used this comparative dynamic in different ways at different times – in alternately ambiguous and precise fashion depending on the context. In his 1601 'comicall satire' *Poetaster* he explored the aesthetic community or republic of letters of Augustan Rome, creating for dramatic purposes an ahistorical triad of writers vying for the 'Emperor's' favour – Ovid, Horace and Virgil.[1] In the later tragedies, *Sejanus, His Fall* (1603) and *Catiline, His Conspiracy* (1610–11), he employed Roman, and ostensibly republican, political communities for the purpose of comparison with his own age. This chapter will use the tragedies and a consideration of the source materials they were inspired by to account for this comparative dynamic and these distinctly 'Roman frames of mind' in Jonson's dramatic canon.[2] At different moments, and sometimes simultaneously in these plays, Jonson explores not only republicanism in both its theoretical and its elite political manifestations, but also engages in what has been described by Franco Moretti as a 'tragic deconsecration of sovereignty' or ideas of monarchy on the stage.[3] In turn, he explores ideas relating to the populace and to theatre audiences as political and politicized communities which raise questions about democracy in the political sphere. While I do not wish to elide in any overly simplistic fashion republicanism and democratic politics, what does become clear is that Jonson's Roman frame of reference for his plays is far from being removed or even abstracted from its republican context and that this fact has a determining effect on the nature and structure of his dramatic works.

'QUEASY TO BE TOUCHED': REPUBLICAN THEORY AND THE ROMAN TRAGEDIES

As playtexts, *Sejanus* and *Catiline* concern themselves with emphatically political subject-matter: the detailed representations of senatorial procedures and consul elections in *Catiline* alone bear witness to this. On an equally obvious level, the topographical and historical placement of these Roman tragedies necessitates authorial engagement with republican themes and with Roman politics in a more general sense. This might seem to be particularly the case in the later *Catiline*, the events of which manifest themselves during the time of the Ancient Roman Republic, but it is in fact the political eclipse of the Republic that we witness there: three years after the events dramatized by the play, the formation of the First Triumvirate would sound the republic's death-knell.[4] In truth, the events of both *Catiline* and *Sejanus* manifest themselves when there is contestation in Roman history; *Sejanus* takes place when the 'Principate' has been formed, transfiguring the republic into a covert absolutist state. Both plays deal with the attempted survival, or even viability, of republican terminology. Whilst they may cast their glance from opposite ends of the spectrum, they concern themselves with the collapse of the republic, and there is therefore an historiographical logic to their pairing.

Jonson was a scrupulous employer of his historiographical source material. *Sejanus* derives for the most part from the *Annals* of Tacitus, along with the works of Suetonius and Livy, and the plot of *Catiline* originated in Sallust's account of the conspiracy against the republic. Jonson's copies of Suetonius and Sallust are extant; a more doubtful attribution has been made of a copy of Tacitus's *Annals*.[5] Nevertheless, Jonson would have received training in reading Tacitus and the others during his childhood education at the Westminster School; that his tutor William Camden's own historical volume *Britannia* was translated by Philemon Holland, who also translated Livy for publication in England in 1600, serves to consolidate our understanding of Jonsonian exposure to these classical texts recounting Ancient Roman political history.

Jonson's 'republican' playtexts bear clear signs of engagement with their sources not only in terms of the furnishing of their plots, but also via their employment of secondary renderings of these texts in the works and translations of the Italian and the Dutch humanists. The Livy and Tacitus of Niccolò Machiavelli and those of Justus Lipsius can be counted as additional influences upon Jonson's political and dramatic ruminations and this can be evidenced through precise instances of vocabulary.[6] Jonson's copy of Guicciardini's translated *History of Italy* and his multiple-volume collection of Lipsius's political and religious writings are extant, though sadly no copy of Machiavelli is attributed to him.[7] The intention here though is not to carry out an exercise of glossing precise references in Jonson's work to those texts: Herford and Simpson have performed that task more than adequately. The objective is rather to consider the paradoxical role of 'republicanism' and political contradiction *per se* in Jonson's Roman tragedies. *Sejanus* and *Catiline* do not even share a political viewpoint on absolutism and republicanism; if the political dramas of the Elizabethan and Jacobean periods, such as these two tragedies, and Shakespeare's *Julius Caesar* and *Coriolanus*, constructed themselves partially as forums for the debate about republican theory that was circulating in contemporary political discussions (for undoubtedly in the course of these dramas numerous permutations of the republican debate are being explored), it does not follow that any single, coherent, seventeenth-century concept of 'republicanism' can be extrapolated from any of them.

We are dealing here with a complex process of textual filtration of ideas relating to republicanism that feeds into the texts, Jonsonian and otherwise; if Livy's *History* led to the darker ambiguities of Tacitus's *Annals*, then both in turn influenced Machiavelli's *Discourses*.[8] The work of the sixteenth-century Italians constituted a re-evaluation of the classical authors' historiographical stances. Attitudes to Caesar, Pompey, Brutus, Cassius, Coriolanus and Catiline were not fixed literary legacies: they were fluid, constantly undergoing reinterpretation, and alongside this, reinterpretations of 'republicanism' took place. Bruni, for instance, instigated a defence of Brutus as the liberator of Rome; prior to this, writers had come largely to praise Caesar and to denigrate his assassins. Machiavelli was one of those greatly influenced by this shift in attitude and, increasingly, Italian drama as a whole began to adopt a more sympathetic attitude towards the republican conspirators. Pescetti's *Il Cesare*, written in 1594, and taking as its source Plutarch's *Lives*, treats Brutus and Cassius with considerable empathy and may even have been known to Shakespeare when he commenced work on his own dramatic version of these events.[9]

If Machiavelli's reading of the assassination of Caesar was a potential influence on Elizabethan and Jacobean drama, then so too were his writings on Caius Martius Coriolanus, Sejanus, and Catiline. Chapter VI of Book III of the *Discourses*, which concerns itself specifically with the subject of the conspiracies of these men, would appear to be closely linked to Jonson's tragic dramas, in that it recounts not only Catiline's famous rebellion, but also the personal conspiracy of Sejanus against the Emperor Tiberius who had raised him from humble beginnings. It is nothing new to suggest that Machiavelli influenced depictions of political life in Elizabethan and Jacobean drama; but it is the Machiavelli of *The Prince*, the adviser to tyrants, as it were (however false a reading that is in itself of the text of *The Prince*), that has been concentrated upon to the neglect of the rather more populace-orientated texts of the *Discourses*.[10] Jonson, I am arguing, is responding to the Machiavellian texts in all their political complexity and not merely gesturing towards the Elizabethan Machevil stereotype so memorably portrayed in the prologue to Christopher Marlowe's *The Jew of Malta*. Machiavelli's 're-visions' of Livy and Tacitus are far from straightforward in their 'republicanism', however, and should by no means be used to 'prove' Jonsonian sympathies along those lines; Machiavelli, although often directly associated with Tacitus and neo-Taciteanism in the Renaissance, was ostensibly anti-Tacitean in that he felt the historian's portrait of the republic's decline into absolutist rule was unduly negative.[11]

A passage contained within the *Discoveries* confirms Jonson's awareness of Machiavelli as a political theoretician:

> A prince should exercise his cruelty not by himself, but by his ministers; so he may save himself and his dignity with his people by sacrificing these when he list, saith the great doctor of state, Machiavel. But I say he puts off man and goes into a beast, that is cruel. No virtue is a prince's own, or becomes him more than his clemency: and no glory is greater than to be able to save with power.[12]

The juxtaposition of this passage in the *Discoveries* with a consideration of the Emperor Tiberius, tyrannical centre of the political machinations of *Sejanus*, has not escaped critical attention.[13] Jonson read Machiavelli, then, and he read him astutely. William Drummond may have claimed in the *Conversations* that Jonson could speak no Italian but numerous translations into French and

English were available in illicit printings, and Jonson's scholarly use of Italian in other plays such as *Every Man In His Humour* and *Volpone* may anyhow offer a cogent refutation of Drummond's claim.

As Quentin Skinner has argued, Machiavelli's *Discourses* are a commentary on, or rather a critique of, Livy's *History*, revaluing the latter's account of Republican Rome in the light of other classical authors such as Cicero and Tacitus, and in turn applying its lessons to his native city-state of Florence, which by 1519, when the *Discourses* were largely composed, was advancing swiftly towards an era of Medici despotism.[14] Machiavelli was offering the classical example of the Ancient Roman Republic as a model for his contemporary Florence, a city which claimed direct descent from the Caesars.[15] The dualities and divisions which constitute the warp and woof of Jonson's dramatic texts seem almost to pre-exist in Machiavelli's writing: the schizophrenia of a politician who sought state solutions to everything and yet who recognized the successful exploitation of religion as an institution as a key to successful state operations.

Whilst it is often argued that Jonson, in selecting an Ancient Roman setting for his tragedies, was simply protecting himself from hazardous accusations of topicality, his appearance before the Privy Council on charges of sedition made by the Earl of Northampton and relating to *Sejanus* is proof that the topical friction of his texts did not escape the notice of its initial audiences. *Sejanus*, written on the cusp of the Elizabethan and Jacobean eras in 1603, would seem by its subject-matter to signal particular political relevance: Jonson is envisaging a new ruler in England and possibly negotiating through his drama some of the ways in which he would prefer to see that rule operate. The central scene in *Sejanus* which witnesses the historian Cordus defending authorial state freedoms could be seen as a direct plea for tolerance from the incoming monarch: the present James VI of Scotland and future James I of England. In turn, *Catiline's* language and imagery has been linked to the Gunpowder Plot and other conspiracies of the Jacobean reign.[16] The point is not that Jonson is eschewing topicality but neither is it that his Roman themes are mere shields for contemporary debate; they rather represent a complex fusion of past and present debates on how to govern a state or country. The paradigmatic Italy of Ancient Rome and of Renaissance Florence and Venice provided ample means to foster those debates.

It seems feasible that Jonson was engaged intellectually and creatively with Machiavelli as a 'patriot republican'.[17] The Italian theorist of state was undoubtedly cynical in his assessments, but was the author of crucial political documents. Machiavelli's own 'republicanism' was extremely complex but it looked to a populace-based, or at the very least, populace-aware, republican constitution. *Discourses* 56–60 in Book I deal with the advantages of popular government and Machiavelli goes as far as to compare the voice of the populace with the voice of God:

> Not without good reason is the voice of the populace likened to that of God; for public opinion is remarkably accurate in its prognostications, so much so that it seems as if the populace by some hidden power discerned the evil and the good that was to befall it.[18]

Many critics have, however, labelled Jonson's Roman tragedies as essentially 'royalist' tracts, condemning conspiracy and rebellion, and preaching centrism. Blair Worden has suggested that the plays demonstrate a fear 'not of monarchical government but its ill administration: not absolute government, but arbitrary rule'.[19] Even in the wake of this subtler account of Jonson's 'royalism', the Machiavellian and wider classical humanist framework I have been proposing suggests that the political dynamics of *Sejanus* and *Catiline* are not so clear.

In a stirring speech to the citizen army of Rome, at the beginning of Act V of *Catiline*, the good general Petrius states their motives for fighting:

> ... I am proud to have so brave a cause
> To exercise your arms in. We not now
> Fight for how long, how broad, how great and large
> Th'extent and bounds o'th'people of Rome shall be,
> But to retain what our great ancestors
> With all their labors, counsels, arts and actions,
> For us were purchasing so many years.
> The quarrel is not now of fame, of tribute,
> Or of wrongs done unto confederates,
> For which the army of the people of Rome
> Was wont to move, but for your own Republic,
>   (V.i.4–14)

In this way he overtly defines the war as a direct defence of republican beliefs and values.

Jonson's play is set during the time of the Ancient Roman Republic and charts the discovery and overthrow of an actual conspiracy led by Catiline against it. The event was regarded as a crucial incident in texts of classical history. Petrius's speech, however, is significant not only for its reiteration in military rhetoric of the traditional view of Catiline and his cohorts as 'unnatural' conspirators against liberty but because it is, ironically, the most effective outline of the practical attraction of Catiline's campaign to a high proportion of the Roman citizens: he mentions the troops disbanded since Sylla's conspiracy and who are seeking financial redress – something Catiline was astute enough to recognize and harness for his political purposes:

> One sort, Sylla's old troops left here in Fesulae,
> Who suddenly made rich in those dire times
> Are since by their unbounded, vast expense,
> Grown needy and poor, and have but left t'expect
> From Catiline new bills and new proscriptions.
> (V.i.22–6)

In terms of his Roman patrician background, Catiline's violent resort to conspiracy was paradoxical if not unique, and yet he did recognize real failings in the republic: not least the debt nexus. In this respect there was potential for any dramatist to portray him more empathetically (and it might be expected that a 'royalist' would champion his opposition to republicanism). Catiline's promises of new financial legislation held genuine appeal and yet Jonson appears to have knowingly suppressed these details until this belated stage in the drama precisely to resist a similar appeal to theatre audiences. The articulation of these fiscal policies is accorded not to Catiline himself. This distances the audience from the issues in hand and, although Petrius's voice is absented from the clamorous and potentially off-putting hysteria of Catilinarian rhetoric, these factors all combine to cancel out the potential for extensive audience empathy with Catiline. Whether this promotes a sense of Jonson as enacting his own defence of republican values in the play is another matter.

Catiline here seems designed to play the stereotypical role of violent disturber; he is self-centred and self-destructive, and knowingly so. His rhetoric at the play's commencement abounds with the terminology of the Faustian overreacher:

> It is decreed. Nor shall thy fate, O Rome,
> Resist my vow. Though hills were set on hills
> And seas met seas to guard thee, I would through;
> Ay, plow up rocks steep as the Alps, in dust,
> And lave the Tyrrhene waters into clouds,
> But I would reach thy head, thy head, proud city.
> (I.i.73–8)

Yet in the very next scene we register a distinct fall in Catiline's tone; as he organizes his wife and co-conspirators to electioneer on his behalf, we witness a colder, more cynical mind in operation. This is a shrewd strategist; an arch-pretender, one who can assume hyperbolic speech and action (witness the bloody sacrifice of the slave) when he deems such behaviour necessary. He is as double-edged and contradictory as the republic itself and this representational fact problematizes any reading of Jonson's plays as 'royalist' or even anti-republican. The plays explore, and often juxtapose, alternative political options without necessarily opting for one way over another.

There is an historiographical point to be made here: Jonson is in part rendering through his characterization of Catiline moral reservations about the almost seductive treatment of the conspirator in Sallust. Sallust himself did not adopt a necessarily coherent position on his subject-matter, although he did concede that social and political conditions could affect the individual. But Catiline's thespian qualities in Jonson's version are also contributing factors in another general theme in that they represent the way in which party politics and political ideologies are consciously constructed for particular effect.

In truth, the majority of Catiline's verbal excesses in the drama are displaced onto his truly hysterical co-conspirator Cethegus and by comparison appear relatively tame; Cethegus gives full vent to his spleen when retrospectively describing Sylla's conspiracy:

> Slaughter bestrid the streets and stretch'd himself
> To seem more huge, whilst to his stained thighs
> The gore he drew flow'd up and carried down
> Whole heaps of limbs and bodies through his arch.
> (I.i.235–8)

Throughout this scene, Catiline seems to be singing a duet in close harmony with Cethegus but this is only one of many pairings he will knowingly construct for himself in the course of the play; one of the most interesting being that with Cicero himself: the self-seeking patrician and the 'republican' *novis homo*, two men whose politics and political approaches are ultimately more akin than they might like to consider.

Catiline is not Cicero's only enemy within. Jonson could have read in Plutarch's *Life of Cicero* of rumours surrounding Caesar's involvement in the Catilinarian conspiracy; to allude to it was not therefore a radical gesture. Retrospectively, we can read Caesar as an empire-builder, but at the point in time which provides the context for this play he was too young to qualify for a position equivalent to Cicero's in the consulship. He was, however, haunted by the historical precedent of one who obtained the consulship prematurely, at little over 30 years of age in fact, and that was Pompey: this precedent alone explains Caesar's restiveness. What Caesar and Crassus do effectively is to play off all sides against the centre: they are careful time-watchers, as Crassus reveals in an aside:

> A little serves
> To keep a man upright on these state-bridges,
> Although the passage were more dangerous.
> Let us now take the standing part.
> (V.ii.12–15)

This republic (like that of Venice in *Volpone* and in a manner directly comparable to the Principate of *Sejanus*) is decaying into a world of individual self-seeking. Cicero, unmoored by his status as a social *arriviste* in Rome, cannot function successfully in this circumscribed environment and is therefore forced to define a political position for himself: what the doubleness of the Jonsonian portrait implies, however, is that his stance might just as readily have been anti-republican as pro. Republicanism in *Catiline* has become an attire, a guise which is easily assumable and yet equally rejectable. Behind the facade of the republican institution and procedures stand individual power-seekers, such as Caesar and Crassus, and the absolutist doctrines of one-person rule. Recognizing this in *Catiline* is scarcely difficult; defining a position for Jonson within this dramatic framework is more complex. It is perhaps fairest to suggest that the political schizophrenia of Jonson is embodied in the contradictions of the characterizations of Catiline and Cicero.

Jonson does not introduce us to Cicero until Act III of *Catiline*. By then we are able to measure him against the portraits of him we have already been offered by others. This alone may have an alienating effect upon our empathies comparable to that which I have suggested is in-built into the representation of Catiline; this renders us potentially more alert to Cicero's political self-fashioning and to the cynical operations of his orator's rhetoric.[20] Significantly, in his opening speech before the Senate, given in acceptance of his election to the Consulship (one of two places on offer – the other going to Antonius), Cicero resists the employment of the first-person pronoun, save in referring to the act of utterance itself: 'I speak this, Romans, knowing what the weight/Of the high charge you have trusted to me is' (III.i.7–8). In all other respects, he casts himself, somewhat like Brutus in Shakespeare's *Julius Caesar*, as a spokesperson for the general case, implying that he speaks for the 'common weal', or *il bene commune*, to use Machiavelli's term.

Yet, as so often in this play, the language has a double thrust to it; Cicero speaks of the weight of the charge pressed on to him by the senatorial elections and this equates him linguistically with Sylla's ghost whose prologue had opened the play in quasi-Senecan style, describing how the weight of the conspiracy he authored presses hard against the Roman Capitol:

> Dost thou not feel me, Rome? Not yet? Is night
> So heavy on thee, and my weight so light?
> Can Sylla's ghost arise within thy walls
> Less threat'ning than an earthquake, the quick falls
> Of thee and thine?
>
> (I.i.1–5)

The implicit sexuality of the image is important, but what Cicero's imagistic echoing of Sylla's speech does is to associate him, albeit in subterranean fashion, with the Catilinarian conspiracy.

As a self-made man Cicero has been posited as a potential political role-model for Jonson (an *arriviste* himself at the Stuart court). From neither literary nor governmental circles, like Sejanus, Cicero was charged with 'provincialism' by the Roman inhabitants (again this cross-play pairing of Cicero and Sejanus is politically intriguing, and as Geoffrey Hill has pointed out is one of the thornier problems of the Roman tragedies).[21] There was widespread resentment of Cicero's lack of links to an old family. The rapid rise to a position of stature in the Consulship, a position he obtained at the earliest possible age of 40, meant that he faced a double load of aristocratic resentment from his senatorial counterparts: Caesar, too young to qualify, expresses unadulterated envy: 'O confidence, more new than is the man!' (III.i.46).

As Katherine Eisaman Maus has indicated, just as Cicero drew an analogy between his political and cultural role in *De Finibus*: 'Just as I do not seem to myself to have shirked labours, dangers, or public service in the position in which I was placed by the Roman people, so I surely ought to strive as jealously as I can to make my fellow citizens more learne,' so Jonson admired the Roman moralists because they were upwardly mobile, 'self-made' men.[22] Maus writes:

> Jonson and many of his contemporaries admire the way the Roman moralists acquire political and cultural authority, and they desire to emulate them; they share the Roman desire to be of service to a secular power ... the Roman moralists tend to seize upon the self as a factor that persists through changing circumstances. In an unpredictable world, personal identity seems comfortingly continuous and inalienable.[23]

I would take issue with Maus's notion of Jonson as identifying with stability of self in Cicero. The Cicero of the moral/philosophical tracts was some ten to twenty years older than the Cicero of Jonson's play and it may be that Jonson effected a separation between the two in his mind. The characterization of Cicero in *Catiline* seems to embody the inherent doubleness of Jonson's approach to life, and the schizoid nature of Jonson's literary activities carries over into the drama; as the play progresses it becomes increasingly difficult to find endorsement for any single political theory or doctrine.

Cicero stresses in his acceptance speech how he will act for the benefit of the state in quelling the turmoil that is ripe within Rome's republican confines:

> I know well in what terms I do receive
> The Commonwealth, how vexed, how perplex'd,

In which there's not that mischief or ill fate
That good men fear not, wicked men expect not.
I know, beside, some turbulent practices
Already on foot, and rumors of moe dangers —
(III.i.47–52)

Crassus's aside alerts us to the potential for exaggeration here: 'Or you will make them, if there be none' (III.i.53). One important question that must be posed is whether Cicero fashions Catiline as a convenient political Other; indeed, whether the republic itself, declining as it is, requires a conspiracy to reconsolidate its position. There is a strong case to be argued for Cicero's invention, or at the least exaggeration, of the threat represented by Catiline, and indeed there appear to be a host of over-compensatory measures in his behaviour. Cicero has quite deliberately fashioned a political conservatism for himself; as a 'new man' without tie or allegiance, he is somewhat awash in the political seas of Rome, seeking the rock of party identity to which to cling. The important dramatic question in Jonson's play is the problem of determining whether Cicero holds any sympathy at all for the conspirators. Cicero's 'republicanism' is a limited, self-conscious affair which will alter, and which might with good reason be expected to do so: he is the new man moving against traditional institutions. Perhaps this provides us with a model for reading Jonsonian attitudes towards the political institutions he depicts in the Roman tragedies, as neither royalist nor republican in any fixed sense: his stance remains fluid and shifting.

In *James I and the Politics of Literature* Jonathan Goldberg constructs Ben Jonson as an unswerving royalist, although not necessarily of the first order.[24] He suggests that Jonson's limited brand of 'royalism' was insufficient to quell the monarch's anxieties and so James served sedition charges on the writer: 'Because Jonson's royalism stopped short of James's absolutism, the picture of absolutism in *Sejanus* troubled James.'[25] Goldberg does not seem to have gone far enough in this reading: Tiberius is scarcely a flattering portrait of a ruler. Cordus's *Annals*, under suspicion for their sympathetic portrait of Brutus and his co-assassins of Julius Caesar, are burned at Tiberius's edict. Cordus's lengthy central speech prior to his sentencing is no mere dramatic set-piece: what it engages with is the notion of an ideal state where the potential would exist for balanced debate, countenanced even by the ruler who might feasibly be criticized in the context of it. This would seem to be naive in a surveillance-based state such as Tiberius's Rome. Tyrants may not always have punished such writers but there are no records of their rewarding them either. Yet, Cordus's speech, bound up as it is with the touchy issue of censorship, cannot have failed to bear resonance for Jonson himself. He may even have reiterated Cordus's claims at the Privy Council hearing he was summoned to.

Few contemporary audience members could have failed to register the parallels between Tiberius's opposition to theatrical display and James I's own reservations about the iconographical power-shows indulged in by his predecessor Elizabeth I (this was of course a feature of his early years of rule and was to undergo a seismic shift in the form of the court masques commissioned from Jonson and Inigo Jones, but we need to remember that it was James's wife, Anne of Denmark, who initially sponsored these events, in opposition, some have argued, to James's mode of court government).[26] Franco Moretti, arguing that the form of tragic drama in this period contributed to the theatrical 'deconsecration of sovereignty', has suggested that the structural weaknesses of the English crown, fiscal, legal or otherwise, rendered it necessary for James, on his accession, to encourage the ideal construction of the monarchy onstage.[27] In many respects James's reluctance to 'perform' rule in this way was justified: some would argue that sovereignty is nothing but a theatrical form. A plausible representation of a king in a theatre might make the monarch seem more powerful in a dramatic context, but in a real sense it undermined any true power by impressing its fictionality upon the audience. Such representations were never in any sense 'real'; they devalued actual monarchy by their representation of it. Moretti suggests that a genuine shift in the representations of courtly power can be registered in the transition from Elizabethan to Jacobean tragedy: he notes a vacancy created by the disappearance of the tragic sovereign-hero. The new focus is on courts as 'the exemplary site of an unrestrained conflict of private interests'.[28] Jacobean tragedy increasingly performed the 'degradation of the cultural image of the sovereign' and eventually the complete absenting of it. *Sejanus* would seem to be an initial gesture towards this transition and *Catiline* a culmination of it. The absence, in all but epistolary form, of the Emperor Tiberius from the fifth act of *Sejanus* constitutes the crucial 'withdrawal of spectacle' that critics from Goldberg to

Womack have registered in Jonson.²⁹ Yet James I is no more Tiberius than Jonson was Cordus (although as Blair Worden has pointed out he saw little distinction between the role of poet and historian).³⁰ As a play *Sejanus* does not strive to be openly contentious in that it attempts to provide the balanced political debate Cordus recommends; in political terms, the play is being used to support antithetical discourses in ways that have already been suggested for *Catiline*.

Tiberius's portrait is the core of the first act of the play and in many senses it can be classed as a Tacitean portrait. The emperor is a man anxious to reveal himself only in the most ambiguous of terms: 'We can no longer/Keep on our mask to thee, our dear Sejanus;' (II.ii.278–9), and Tacitus was a historian anxious to highlight this ambiguity, usually to the detriment of the Emperor's reputation. By way of the *Annals* then, Tiberius was in historical terms already a figure subject to ambiguizing commentary. Like that of Cicero in *Catiline*, Jonson's portrait of Tiberius is a schizoid representation; this renders it problematic in terms of questions of the existence of 'republicanism' as a held belief in this play. Tiberius demonstrates an apparent nostalgia for an age of equality, or at the very least for genuine senatorial rule:

> We stand amazed, fathers, to behold
> This general dejection. Wherefore sit
> Rome's consuls thus dissolved, as they had lost
> All the remembrance both of style, and place?
> It not becomes. No woes are of fit weight
> To make the honour of the Empire stoop;
> (III.i.35–40)

and yet in the first scene he speaks of the absolute power of a prince. Tiberius certainly exhibits a lively interest in senatorial procedures (Tacitus too mentions his regular attendance at governmental meetings) but this can equally be viewed in terms of continued attempts to exert control over proceedings: the ultimate gesture of control surely being that letter. Even from Capri, even in his state of withdrawal, Tiberius determines the course of governmental events.

Sejanus had erroneously believed that by persuading Tiberius to leave Rome and withdraw from the political centre he could marginalize his imperial power:

        Sleep,
Voluptuous Caesar, and security
Seize on thy stupid powers, and leave them dead
To public cares, awake but to thy lusts.
The strength of which makes thy libidinous soul
Itch to leave Rome; ...
***
By this, shall I remove him both from thought,
And knowledge of his own most dear affairs;
Draw all dispatches through my private hands;
Know his designments, and pursue mine own;
Make mine own strengths...
                    (III.ii. 598–603; 613–16)

Unwittingly, though, Sejanus creates a more powerful symbol than he ever had to constrain when Tiberius was present in Rome; as with the Caesar of Shakespeare's play, the spirit proves more potent than the man. The Isle of Capri may suggest Tiberius's absence from both stage-proceedings and the political arena but in truth it is a world elsewhere that remains firmly within, and largely determines, the remaining field of discourse. In Jonson's dramatic telescoping of the events recounted in Tacitus, the power vacuum Sejanus encourages enables the rise of other imperial powers such as Macro and Caligula and paves the way for his own destruction at the violent hands of the Roman populace: 'The dismemberment of Sejanus symbolizes ... the impossibility of placing such power and authority in one man.'[31] The action of the people is also a violent blow against the tenets of absolutism. The sudden and frenzied eruption of the people into action when the play has thus far been confined to those individuals in power indicates, says Miller, 'that a people deprived of the right to play in affairs of state are finally more dangerous than a people who exercise the right – in a balanced republican polity, for example'.[32]

The republicanism of Ancient Rome, as it would largely have been understood by Jacobean audiences, was ostensibly hierarchical; it remained an elitist constitution, with membership and position restricted to the chosen few. This then is the oligarchical republic depicted in plays such as *Julius Caesar* and *Coriolanus*. In adapting Cicero's four speeches against the Catilinarian conspiracy for *Catiline*, Jonson shows a highly selective bent which on the surface appears to extract the populace of republican Rome from the play's direct concerns. He uses the first speech and only partially employs the fourth; in doing so, he entirely omits the two speeches delivered by Cicero to the Roman populace; the first and last speeches having been given in the Senate.[33] The reasons for this are doubtless partly to do with dramatic economy: the main scenes of accusation in the play occur in the Senate and establish a vital dramatic picture of Cicero as an orator and Catiline as a listener. It could also be said that this accords Cicero status on the stage equivalent to that of a monarch or absolutist ruler (we hear little after the initial mention of him of his co-elected second consul); the Senate operates as his court.

For dramatic effect, Jonson certainly required the presence of the conspirator at his own condemnation; this would not have been possible in a marketplace scene, and yet the dramatic world of *Catiline* is otherwise distinctly peopled. A sense of group activity is stronger than amongst the highly discrete and individualized community of *Sejanus*. This is in part a product of the historical basis of these two plays: *Catiline* being set during the time of the republic and *Sejanus* during a period of one-person rule, although that is not to make any advanced claim for populace-based republicanism in *Catiline*. Indeed the complex and double characterization of Cicero serves to directly confuse the issue of Jonson's political sympathies, and the importance of Catiline's patrician origins should never be underestimated. The republic of *Catiline* is not a *res publica* or 'public thing' in Dol Common's understanding of the term in *The Alchemist*: it is an elitist construction, as the limitations governing the nominations for the consulship and the resentment of Cicero as the *novis homo* indicate.

Admittedly, the large number of conspirators fashioned into a group on the stage of *Catiline* have more visible connections with a populace, and therefore, in turn, with any theatre audience, than the distinct and largely disparate individuals of *Sejanus*. In addition, *Catiline's* choric framework fulfils the function of promoting audience self-consciousness. The populace of Rome, but also by extension the theatre audience, is implicated by the collective pronoun employed by the Chorus:

> Now do our ears before our eyes
> Like men in mists
> Discover who'd the state surprise,
> And who resists?
>
> (IV.vii.20–3)

However, the energies unleashed in the shocking dismemberment of Sejanus are no longer a possibility in *Catiline*: in what is ultimately a far more conservative act, the populace here has been carefully contained and harnessed to the existing systems, even in terms of the play's dramatic structure.

Jonson's reservations about the practical viability of populace-based republicanism, also anxiously present in that detailed description of Sejanus's dismemberment, were grounded in the actual experiences he had in the Low Countries' war against Spain for independence. He not only witnessed the hardships of the conflict first-hand but afterwards in London he would also have heard the reports of public speakers there being attacked and often spontaneously hanged by furious crowds.[34] He was not producing dramatic calls to arms aimed at the London populace who would see his plays; that much is clear. Like his political mentor Justus Lipsius, he dealt with republican issues on a largely theoretical and hypothetical basis.

Jonson's plays are not manuals for political activism, but neither are they royalist propaganda that dismisses the politics of the masses (as might be believed from the readings produced by Goldberg and others). Though the republicanism that he deals with in the tragedies is largely theoretical and in practical terms highly elitist, this does not preclude him from exploring other political logics, such as the 'deconsecration of monarchy', figured most obviously in the absented shape of Tiberius in *Sejanus*, and the genuine possibility of populace political activity, realized both in a public and a theatrical sphere (witness Jonson's persistent negotiations with the audiences of his plays).

Annabel Patterson has looked at the problematic and problematized representation of the 'common people' in the plays of this period.[35] She poses the question as to whom exactly the term refers:

> While social historians today are quick to point out that terms like 'the commons', the 'commonalty', 'the people', or 'populace' were and are blanket terms that conceal large social and economic differences, and while the ranks of the gentry and even the aristocracy were not in practice impermeable, the fact remains that there was a clear line drawn conceptually (ideologically) between the gentry and everyone below, whether successful yeomen or merchants, wage labourers, apprentices, or, at the bottom of the scale, the rural poor.[36]

That, as Patterson records, 95 per cent of the 'commons' were actually excluded from having any voice in major state affairs in this period casts considerable doubt on any application of republicanism in a modern understanding of the word, that is to say as somehow indicative of a true democracy, to the 'commonwealth' being vaunted in any of Jonson's or Shakespeare's Roman plays. There was an ambiguity about sixteenth- and seventeenth-century conceptual notions of republicanism which was exactly parallel to the ambiguities of the Roman interpretation of the term.

In a sweeping statement at the beginning of an essay on the topic of the political multitude or 'many headed-monster' as was the traditional depiction, Christopher Hill claims that, 'Most writers about politics during the century before 1640 agreed that democracy was a bad thing.'[37] Whilst class hostility was a simple fact, Hill seriously underestimates attempts, even if only hypothetical, by the likes of Machiavelli and others to harness these social tensions for the benefit of the state. Book I Chapter VI of the *Discourses* is entitled, 'That Discord between the Plebs and the Senate of Rome made this Republic both Free and Powerful' (p. 113). There are of course limitations to Machiavelli's envisaged democracy: the cry seems for people simply to be acknowledged rather than for power ultimately to be invested in them, and the modern example he forwards of a functioning republic is the distinctly hierarchical set-up of contemporary Renaissance Venice (see Chapter 3); nevertheless the crucial role of the populace was acknowledged by certain schools of political thought in the sixteenth and seventeenth centuries.

The role of the populace in Jonson's Roman tragedies is therefore a complicated matter. The claustrophobic atmosphere of *Sejanus* is regularly remarked upon; events occur solely within the walls of the Imperial Palace, which is a dangerous labyrinth of corridors and spy-holes, where people are sent not only into the next room, but into the room beyond that in an attempt to preclude overhearing. What incidents do occur beyond the palace walls are heard only by report; Sejanus, Macro, Arruntius, Lepidus and others function within the parameters of a clearly-defined territory: within that space in which they consider power to be centred, although Tiberius's willed absenting of himself from Rome in his dramatic retirement to the Isle of Capri exposes the vacuum they inhabit. Tiberius carries fundamental power with him, as his continuing dictatorship of events via seemingly irrefutable edicts in letters demonstrates.

Within the palace confines Sejanus can convince himself erroneously of his potential to seize imperial power; once he steps outside of this charmed circle, however, he is torn apart by the unseen populace. This act mirrors with hideous repetition their earlier destruction of his self-important work of statuary:

> Sentence, by the Senate;
> To lose his head: which was no sooner off,
> But that, and th'unfortunate trunk were seized
> By the rude multitude; who not content
> With what the forward justice of the state
> Officiously had done, with violent rage
> Have rent it, limb from limb. A thousand heads,
> A thousand hands, ten thousand tongues, and voices,
> Employed at once in several acts of malice!
> (V.vii.826–34)

Such behaviour allows several characters to express conventional contempt for the citizenry of Rome, and this includes opponents of Sejanus, such as Arruntius, who, whilst vocal in the play in criticizing present corruption, are clearly far from envisaging a republican alternative: their aim is rather to preserve and protect the conservative and aristocratic status quo.

The Senate in *Sejanus* acts only under the pressure of profound stimuli: invariably the commands of Tiberius himself. They merely follow the initiative of others whom they perceive to be more powerful. The actions of the citizens then are simply a 'frighteningly logical extension' of the senators' own irrational behaviour.[38] Fundamental power, however, continues to rest with Tiberius, even in the midst of the crowd's uprising; this is a quasi-Foucauldian release of populace-based energies that reinstates the mainstream: 'In calling on the crowd to manifest its power, the sovereign tolerated for a moment acts of violence which he accepted as a sign of allegiance, but which were strictly limited by the sovereign's own privileges.'[39] There are, however, signs of the crowd's transgression, even violation, of these authoritarian limitations in their excessive and brutalized reaction: for this too Foucault made allowance: 'on this point ... the people, drawn to the spectacle, intended to terrorize it, could express its rejection of the punitive power and sometimes revolt'.[40]

Certainly the description of the destruction of the statue of

Sejanus and then of the man himself by the Roman citizenry is the only evidence of that social group's existence in the play: they are barely considered in any governmental discussion. Some critics have suggested that with such an elitist cast-list the play seems unlikely to be forwarding any republican theory, but this position is only tenable if the understanding is that republicanism in this period was necessarily populace-based. It is equally inaccurate to state that the populace is marginalized in *Sejanus*, ostracized as it were to a point of non-appearance beyond or behind the palace walls; for the off-stage power of populace action is immense within the context of the play. Stage absence (as Tiberius's letter proves) carries a potency of its own within the operations of this playtext. Absence enables ambiguity and unpredictability and within these modes lies access to power.

Sejanus can, paradoxically, be said to depict the fate of 'republicanism' in a monarchical context. Whilst the republican constitution itself no longer appears viable, its driving forces are awarded a certain degree of validity and importance. The corrupt empire of Tiberius does appear a grim fact; the impotence of characters who praise republican liberty is obvious.

In an opposite movement to that which commences *Catiline*, *Sejanus* begins with the opponents of tyranny – Arruntius and his followers who are 'rarely met in court'– only then introducing us to the objects of their despisal: Sejanus and Tiberius himself. For many, the delayed entry of these characters merely increases the audience's sense of their remarkable power once they finally do appear, thus emphasizing the inertia of their political opponents, republican and otherwise. Arruntius sees the problem as a lack of the *virtù* that was the guiding spirit of *Romanitas*:

>   Times? the men,
>   The men are not the same: 'tis we are base,
>   Poor, and degenerate from th'exalted strain
>   Of our great fathers. Where is now the soul
>   Of god-like Cato? he, that durst be good,
>   When Caesar durst be evil; and had power,
>   As not to live his slave, to die his master.
>   Or where the constant Brutus, that (being proof
>   Against all charm of benefits) did strike
>   So brave a blow into the monster's heart
>   That sought unkindly to captive his country?

Oh, they are fled the light.

(I.i.86–97)

Arruntius allies himself with the republicans of old, but it is with a heightened awareness of their anachronistic status in the political present. There is a nostalgia for past liberty and Arruntius adopts a truly Tacitean approach to history in recognizing that Roman institutions are mere pretences of republicanism; Tacitus's *Annals* describe Augustus's self-investiture with the title of 'princeps' in an attempt to quell the problems inherent in a decaying republic but that text has no illusion either as to the absolutist roots of such an action or its transformation and deformation under figures such as Tiberius.

Arruntius's 'republicanism' then, if it can even be termed such, consists of nostalgic references to a bygone era. For the present time his solutions are orthodox and conservative: in this he seems to adhere to Sabinus's statements against rebellion:

'Twere better stay
In lasting darkness, and despair of day.
No ill should force the subject undertake
Against the sovereign, more than hell should make
The gods do wrong. A good man should, and must
Sit rather down with loss, than rise unjust.

(IV.iii.161–6)

This reading of *Sejanus* would appear to consign 'republicanism' to the irretrievable past, and yet the role of the citizenry in the downfall of Sejanus himself would suggest a residual power in the multivalent figure of the populace: in a Foucauldian reading they have become powerful interveners in the political sphere from which the rulers have presumed to exclude them. It is through this understanding of the political energy of the people that the 'republicanism' of *Sejanus* (and by extension *Catiline*) can be traced and through it I believe we come to view the dramatic genre itself as potentially republican in its mobilization of audiences.

Exactly how republican notions are given dramatic form in these two plays is important and diverse. By comparison with the highly foregrounded individualism of *Sejanus*, the physical dynamics of *Catiline*, despite the singularity of the title, do seem decidedly more group-orientated. This is not simply because of the play's republican setting and large cast. The conspirators function together as a group and the group must be considered an important entity in Jonson's Roman tragedies. Carrying this fact to its logical dramatic extension, *Catiline* has a Chorus of Roman citizens. This is crucial to consider in terms of the play's functioning in that the use of a chorus implicates theatre audiences in the events via the medium of direct address and encouraged identification.

The Citizen chorus does not open *Catiline*: that rhetorical responsibility falls to Sylla's ghost. There are republican implications in this: Sylla had led the most recent conspiracy of Roman history (and Bruni, the Italian writer responsible for the reevaluation of Brutus had also led the movement to co-opt Sylla as the founder of the present Italian city-state republics) although this fact is suppressed by Jonson in favour of the language of violence and excess. This, in dramatic terms, successfully pre-empts the likelihood of any audience sympathies with Catiline's conspiracies. This is a complicated area – I do not wish to suggest that Jonson wanted to deny audience empathy with Catiline entirely, but the early speeches do seem excessively loaded in their content, packed as they are with bloody and violent vocabulary (and often highly sexually charged). The very problem of audience sympathies is, as our discussion of Cicero has indicated, one the play elects to engage with on an intellectual level.

Identification with one faction is not the issue here; indeed, if we share anything with the Chorus it is their more immediate state of confusion. They are aware of their vacillating opinions, and the political incoherence it engenders. Are they representative of the 'fickle multitude'? They are strikingly self-aware and judge themselves in a quasi-juridical manner which would seem to have its roots in Jonson's notion of an ideal audience of 'judging spectators'. The Chorus can never be entirely impartial since their fate is determined by the course of events but they do look out directly on an audience which has the capacity to be so. It is no small coincidence that the fifth and final act of the play has, unlike the other four, no closing choric commentary. The audience filing out of the theatre is now forced to decide alone; the power of judgement is firmly invested in them by this felt absence.

Is the populace and audience awareness of *Catiline* part of the new acceptance on Jonson's behalf of the energies of the public as a mass group and an instancing of 'republicanism"s availability as a mode of interpretation within his plays? Both *Sejanus* and *Catiline* depict the decay of the Roman republic and this in itself invites an analysis of its demise. The use of the Chorus incorporates the role of the populace into the play and, by extension, the audience as well. Jonson was deeply engaged with the question of the diffusion of authority, not only within a political, but also a dramatic, context: the difficulty of determining where the responsibility of interpretation lies, in speech, gesture, or the act of reading, is deliberately problematized by both of his Roman tragedies. As a result of this, both plays, and Jonson's canon as a whole, conduct a complex critique of absolutism – in political and creative processes. This is why Cato's succinct but wholly singular speeches are such a key factor in *Catiline*. Cato's language, like that of Cicero and countless others, is consciously constructed. Jonson is prepared to recognize that not only dramatic characterizations but public personae at large are equally self-fashioned. Split characters, and by this I mean not simply two-way identities but a form of disjuncture within the self, ambiguize the very notion of personality. The self is not a stable entity and therefore political systems devised around, or by, 'personality' are, as Machiavelli warned, destined to fail. Oligarchical republics are then flawed at their very heart as the civil war of *Catiline* and the ever more overt and deranged absolutism of *Sejanus* indicate.

I suggested earlier that the role of the populace in *Sejanus*, however small it may seem, in the sense that the single act it performs is the nihilistic one of Sejanus's dismemberment, is essentially republican in its life-forces. Jonson acknowledges in this explosion of populace-based power the futility of one-person rule. The political solution had to lie in limited rule (monarchical and otherwise) and in constitutional attempts to incorporate these people into the political sphere; but what Jonson also realized was that it was the dramatic solution. The dramatic genre, inherently republican by nature, had to allow for this same release of creative energy by the audience for the theatrical experience to be allowed its full potential.

3

'Saying Something About Venice'[1]

Jonson was as meticulous in his Venetian staging of *Volpone* as in his scholarly appropriation of classical sources for his Roman plays.[2] Whilst *Volpone* may not have had extensive accompanying notes like *Sejanus* and *Catiline*, nevertheless it offers a detailed rather than merely impressionistic depiction of the city of Venice at a particular point in its historical and political evolution.

The accompanying notes to the Quarto versions of his Roman tragedies constitute in part Jonson's citation of his sources, yet they also evidence the highly individual choices and selections he made in employing them. If, despite wholesale transposition of their prose, Jonson's use of Cicero, Sallust, Tacitus and others in *Sejanus* and *Catiline* was by no means unevaluative, similarly Venice underwent a literary and dramatic transmogrification in *Volpone*. The authorial and performative reshaping of the city of water was an intensely political act, informed at every turn by questions of Venetian and European constitutional development and also by the politics of dramatic convention itself.[3] It is now something of a literary-critical cliché that 'foreign' locations in plays of the early modern period were employed as shields from accusations of topicality and sedition, and therefore from the over-anxious penstrokes of the censor; however, our monolithic understanding of the term 'censorship' is undergoing critical scrutiny at present (the argument, in brief, being that the operation of censorship was by no means as uniform or predictable as we might previously have assumed) and as a result we must question the overdetermined reading of locations other than English.[4] Whilst, undoubtedly, *Volpone* signifies its connections with the increasingly urbanized London in which Jonson himself was resident, the play is most decidedly set in Renaissance, republican Venice.[5]

Jonson's Venice is realized by precise topography; its streets, *piazze*, and bridges are carefully identified by character and dramatist alike. There is a case that critics are 'not taken enough' with what Stephen Greenblatt describes as the complicated 'thingness' of this play; yet this for him connotes an empty centre, a 'deadness' which 'has all along been lurking just beneath the glittering surface of *Volpone*'s existence'.[6] The 'vertiginous swirl of words' which for Greenblatt constitutes an avoidance of depth, for Anne Barton threatens to engulf the play's characters in its suffocating density: 'Things in *Volpone*, the urban detritus of a civilization out of control, are perpetually on the verge of rising up to drown the people who wade and push their way through them.'[7] Barton's notion is in many respects more suggestive: there is even now something akin to suffocation in the crammed nature of Venetian architecture and civic design, its cramped back passages and numerous blind alleys. The city reflects the potentially stifling atmosphere of Volpone's bedroom.

The representation of Venice is not wholly reliant on surface details; the city is realized in all its political complexity: its ideological centre is revealed and explored during the course of events. But it is also an early modern republican state, the focus of European propaganda and myth, and, as such, endlessly recounted in constitutional texts; the model of government cited by Italian civic humanists such as Machiavelli and Guicciardini, Contarini, and Giannotti. It is, paradoxically enough, the home of the Doge, a quasi-monarchical figurehead, and of republican state pageantry; the politics of the city are part of the politics of the play-text.[8]

As Jonathan Goldberg has observed, this paradox was all too well understood in contemporary England:

> There is a point in considering the play's setting in some detail, for Venice – especially what historians call the myth of Venice – was richly appreciated in England, and Venice could be appropriated for absolutist dissimulations.... The history of Venice is tied to the revival of republicanism in the Renaissance, first in Florence, in the reunderstanding of Roman history and the exaltation of Brutus as hero and with him a new definition of the relation of antiquity to active participation in political life.[9]

The city-state *per se* has had enormous influence on the way we think and speak about politics: the latter word even derives from the Greek *polis*. Yet many city-states embody what one historian has termed the 'contradictions of freedom'[10]; many of the most famous Italian republics – for example, Florence and Venice – were, strictly speaking, oligarchies. A myth may well have grown up around the notion of Venice as the perfect mixed constitution (*stato misto* in Machiavelli's terms, themselves a gloss on the classical writings of Polybius and interestingly Jonson's personal copies of the works of Justus Lipsius contain commentaries on Polybian theory),[11] a blend as it was of Doge (monarchy), Senate (aristocracy), and Great Council (populace), but in essence it was an oligarchy since power rested in the hands of a closed group of approximately two thousand male nobles. That oligarchy clearly operates in *Volpone*, a play distinctly concerned with issues of rank and gender, of localism and centralism, and of the role of the individual within the (city) state.

Lewis Lewkenor's English translation of Gasparo Contarini's *De Magistratibus et Republica Venetorum*, entitled *The Commonwealth and Government of Venice*, had been published in 1599 and was familiar to Jonson. Herford and the Simpsons suggested that this text was likely to be Jonson's sole source for the political details of *Volpone*, yet Jonson was familiar with the contents of Italian expatriate John Florio's library of Italian textbooks in London: he utilized Florio's *A World of Words* to furnish his Venetian play-text with Italian terminology. Jonson's desire for accuracy and authenticity suggests that he would have sought access to a number of other texts on the subject of the Venetian republic. It was the mixed state of Venice that Thomas Coryat observed on his travels and whilst *Coryat's Crudities* appeared in print in 1611, the ideas contained therein had been circulating much earlier.

This sense of alternative sources on the Venetian political make-up becomes an interesting issue if we consider some of the details, constitutional and otherwise, of *Volpone*. In Contarini's text the *Avocatori* are prosecutors without powers of judgement. Lewkenor rather loosely translates this as 'judges or magistrates' and Herford and the Simpsons suggest that Jonson merely follows this inaccuracy in his depiction of the *Avocatori* of this play as judges. Other critics suggest the scene is modelled more on English than Venetian law, yet Jonson was not usually either this Anglocentric or impositional, as his detailed depiction of the ancient Roman republic in *Catiline* indicates. Possibly he was not importing an alien legal system into Venice but merely failing to be totally accurate in his dramatic rendering of the operations of Venetian law.

However, C.J. Gianakaris has shown that during a specific period in Venetian history, the *Avocatori* did exercise judicial as well as investigative powers.[12] They were not superior to the Council of Ten or the Senate but they did approach parity with these central bodies; even the Doge fell under their scrutiny by the fifteenth century, as then would a *magnifico* like Volpone – the precision of Jonson's text is telling here, confirming a specific concern with the Venetian republican moment. Gianakaris posits the work of Donato Giannotti as a possible alternative source for Jonson since his text on Venice is far less ambiguous on the role of the *Avocatori* than Contarini's. That Giannotti was also far more the inheritor of Niccolò Machiavelli's republican thinking than Contarini's more obviously aristocratic leanings lends weight to the argument that Jonson had a specifically republican as well as Venetian theme in this play.

Renaissance Venice, like Ancient Rome, was recognized by English political commentators to contain contradictory impulses – towards republicanism and populace participation, and yet simultaneously towards absolutism and imperial rule; this is why Venice itself looked to classical Rome for political precedent, and why Machiavelli juxtaposed the two systems in the *Discourses*, discussing absolutist and arbitrary rule alongside Polybian models of mixed government. Goldberg continues:

> The myth of Venice was particularly suited to the English political mind. Although nominally Venice was a republic, and although famed for its consultative, rational institutions, the myth took Venice out of time, placing it in an eternal present.... In Venice, contradictions cohere and the republican myth masks an oligarchic state.... What might be regarded as completely opposite systems of politics – absolute imperialism on the one hand, participative republicanism on the other – divine right and imperial Rome versus the councils of Venice – may not have been. The two meet in classical Rome.[13]

Sir Politic Would-be is generally understood to be a parody of the English ambassador to Venice, Sir Henry Wotton. Wotton was an acquaintance of Jonson and his dispatches from Venice (in the periods 1603–10, 1616–19, and 1621–23) were widely responsible for creating the English perception of *La Serenissima*, its rituals and its politics.[14] Sir Pol claims to have read Machiavelli:

> ... for your religion, profess none;
> But wonder, at the diversity of all;
> And, for your part, protest, were there no other
> But simply the laws o'th'land, you could content you:
> Nick Machiavel, and Monsieur Bodin, both,
> Were of this mind. Then, must you learn the use,
> And handling of your silver fork, at meals;
> The metal of your glass (these are the main matters,
> With your Italian), and to know the hour
> When you must eat your melons and your figs.
>   (IV.i.22–31)

Pol is an unremitting misreader of events and also of the very texts he claims a political and philosophical affinity with; he completely misses the complexities and nuances of Machiavelli's theorizing on the public management of religious belief and there is something haplessly naive in his parallel evaluation of a book on etiquette and hardline Machiavellian political theories.

Pol's wife is another of Jonson's political dreamers in *Volpone* and she is another reader of surfaces. Easily duped by Mosca's tale of Pol's adventure with a courtesan, Lady Would-be thoroughly fails to comprehend the double standards her jealousy reveals.[15] She fails to penetrate the multi-layered social and sexual politics of Venice: her make-up peels away all too easily in the steamy Venetian climate, leaving her amateur aspirations of social and political mobility, like those of her husband, unattractively exposed. It is Volpone, the fox himself, who initially at least proves best-equipped to penetrate the 'mask' of Renaissance republicanism; he 'aims at the subversion of the republic, the unmasking of the vice beneath the show, absolutist aims that he exemplifies and which his suitors and servants imitate ...'.[16] His seemingly 'casual' politics operate to unveil the patriarchal and self-serving ends of the admired Venetian republic.

Rank was certainly a determining feature even in the supposedly democratic Venetian republic. This proves pertinent in the trial scenes. Tellingly, Volpone addresses the *Avocatori* as the 'Fathers' of the state, thus subtly revealing the patriarchal system they represent and enact. The Fourth *Avocatore*, for all the supposed impartiality of his office, is tempted by the prospect of Mosca 'the *magnifico*' (and his newly inherited wealth as he understands it) as a possible husband for his daughter. When Mosca's low rank is eventually revealed his sentence is pronounced accordingly:

> You appear
> T'have been the chiefest minister, if not plotter,
> In all these lewd impostures; and now, lastly,
> Have, with your impudence, abused the court,
> And habit of a gentleman of Venice,
> Being a fellow of no birth, or blood:
> For which, our sentence is, first thou be whipped;
> Then live perpetual prisoner in our galleys.
> (V.xii.107–14)

Volpone only escapes similar sentence by dint of his rank: 'By blood, and rank a gentleman, canst not fall/Under like censure;' (V.xii.117–18) but he is incarcerated in the hospital of the *Incurabili*, permanently enclosed indoors, to suffocate in health for having feigned sickness until he is truly ill and lame from the restriction. The consummate performer is effectively denied an audience and that may of course be regarded as punishment enough. Yet Jonson allows Volpone to address the audience in the play's infamous epilogue and this can itself stand as a comment on the injustices of the republic's legal system: that the lower-class Mosca is silenced even by the stage whilst the *magnifico* can use (and abuse) the audience as a court of appeal. Volpone can step beyond the play's boundaries and continue to transgress whereas Mosca's performative skills have been effectively crushed and contained by an oligarchical republic's imbalanced version of discipline and punishment.[17]

Venice's almost schizophrenic existence as a glamorous European city and as a place of harsh sentences is quite literally bridged by the Ponti di Sospiri which joins the Palazzo Ducale and the damp, dank prisons where the republic's condemned prisoners were held. Michel de Certeau has stressed the ambiguity of the architecture of a bridge: 'it alternately welds together and opposes insularities. It distinguishes them and threatens them. It liberates from enclosure and destroys autonomy.'[18] Locations prove equally diverse and ambiguous in *Volpone*, not least in their urban ramifications. Jonson is examining in the course of the play what the sociologist Richard Sennett has called the 'public geography' of the great city.[19] It is in the great city that Sennett locates the potential for public life which he deems essential to the operation of a community or *res publica*: interestingly though, he dates the decline of that *res publica* from the Augustan period of Roman history.[20] Significantly for *Volpone*, that city-centred play, he also connects intrinsically the nature of the city and the nature of theatre: not least in their joint invocation of audiences:

> the theater shares a problem not with society in general, but with a peculiar kind of society – the great city. The problem is one of *audience* – specifically, how to arouse belief in one's appearance among a milieu of strangers.[21]

Volpone is concerned throughout the play with the arousal of belief (as indeed are those parodies of his aims and actions, the Would-bes). His problem in the Venetian republic proves to be exactly that of audience; danger creeps into his enterprise as soon as he ventures into the public space of the city squares – sites he utilizes for performance in the instance of the Scoto of Mantua sideshow which captures Celia's attention.

The various scenes in the play take place both indoors and outdoors, in the city-streets (carefully located), in the *Scrutineo*, the Senate House of Venice, and in various houses. The most recurrent house is that of Volpone himself, with its central visual focus of the bed. Jonsonian criticism has in the past treated Volpone and Mosca's abode (and I stress this co-habitation quite deliberately) as a 'politics-free zone'.[22] By extension, such judgements depoliticize Volpone's 'bed-trick', rendering it merely an antithetical alternative to the 'tricks of state' mentioned by Sir Politic Would-be. This is a misreading, not least because it denies Volpone the acknowledgement of his professional capabilities as a politician.[23] In truth, Volpone and Mosca's household has positioned itself as a site of liminal pursuits and beliefs, with all the threatening and dangerous connotations that such thresholds usually entail. Their abode is a point where limitations are tested and exploited.

Boundaries between the inside and the outside and between different kinds of property are clearly demarcated in this play. Jean-Christophe Agnew has written lucidly of the significance of the ancient marketplace as a threshold or *limen*, with obvious application to *Bartholomew Fair* and *Coriolanus* (where the word 'threshold' resonates and where Tullus Aufidius and Antium represent the liminal or marginal), but his ideas are equally valuable for a consideration of *Volpone* and the function of that play's various settings, political and domestic:

> Threshold rituals ... developed as ceremonial metaphors straddling the uncharted realm between the physical and the symbolic, the secular and the sacred, the past and the future. They ordered the passage from one stage of life to another, one state of mind to another, one household to another.[24]

Volpone straddles just such uncharted realms.

Venice was famous for its secularization of religious ceremony – the Doge regularly performed quasi-religious rituals such as the annual marriage of the city to the sea (a threshold ritual in itself; it is interesting to see how Venice's lagoon geography rendered it both liminal and secure). The opening scene of *Volpone* can be regarded as an extended threshold ritual; Volpone worships a distinctly secular God at his household shrine – Money – a sign, for Greenblatt, that God has been decentred in secular Venice: 'Open the shrine, that I may see my saint' (I.i.2).[25] As in *The Alchemist*, and in the genre of farce, the plot is propelled by the knocking on the door of various new characters, each in this instance performing a by now well-established bedside ritual before the supposedly declining and dying Volpone: a ritual performed not only to ensure his passage into the other world but to ensure their personal inclusion, preferably to the exclusion of others, in his anxiously anticipated will – another less than republican gesture.

Volpone and Mosca exploit this ritual for all it is worth; Agnew has stated that those involved in the 'transitional moment of ritual passage' are called 'liminaries' by anthropologists and that they are often masked or androgynous figures, or travesties of the surrounding social system. Such a description clearly fits both Volpone and Mosca and the other inhabitants of their liminal abode – Nano, Castrone, and Androgyno. But it is Mosca who perhaps most of all negotiates the equivocal region of the threshold. He answers the door; he travels into the street and to other households such as Corvino's; he is dispatched to put about publicly the greatly exaggerated news of Volpone's 'death'. Mosca is then a figure of urban recreation in its most active sense.

Described in the *dramatis personae* of the play as the *magnifico*'s 'parasite', Mosca the flesh-fly would seem to fit his title. A parasite feeds off his/her host, yet the term was not always so negative: initially it meant the guest who fed alongside the host. The prefix 'para' indicates something 'alongside', 'near' or 'beside', something 'beyond' or 'resembling', 'similar or subsidiary to'; the term then contains within it ideas both of proximity and distance; the label is itself an equivocation. J. Hillis Miller has described a parasite as 'something inside a domestic economy and at the same time outside it, something simultaneously this side of a boundary line, threshold, or margin, and also beyond it, equivalent in status and also secondary or subsidiary, submissive, as of guest to host, slave to master'.[26] All of these permutations relate to Mosca's role within the 'domestic economy' of Volpone's household. That household exposes the patronage network as a focus of nervousness and anxiety, not only in Volpone's exploitation of his clients through their attempted exploitation of him, but also through its complication of the servant–master relationship; that particular seemingly binary opposition becomes a site of tension: when Volpone decides disastrously to reveal his 'resurrection' from the dead, Mosca's desperate cry is revelatory of this: '(Why, patron!)' (V.xii.88).

Michael McCanles has demonstrated that Jonson was hugely influenced in his views on patronage by the works of Seneca, in particular by his accounts of patronage practices in the late Roman republic and the early Principate: an interesting choice of period in terms of Jonson's Roman plays, *Sejanus* (early Principate) and *Catiline* (late republic), but also in its application to *Volpone*.[27] McCanles suggests that Seneca redefined the supposed inequality between patron and client, recognizing a certain parity in the meeting of minds – clearly relevant for Tiberius and Sejanus, and for Mosca and Volpone.

Mosca prospers, albeit only temporarily, because he learns to use words with the same skill and artistry as his master, thus blurring the distinction inherent in the concept of parasitism:

> ... Oh! your parasite
> Is a most precious thing, dropped from above,
> Not bred 'mongst clods, and clotpolls, here on earth.
> I muse the mystery was not made a science,
> It is so liberally professed! Almost
> All the wise world is little else, in nature,
> But parasites, or sub-parasites.
>
> (III.i.7–13)

Mosca's predominant monosyllables here linguistically mimic his fly-like dartings across the various thresholds of this play. As a flesh-fly he possesses virtual invisibility in Venetian society; whilst he may bemoan his lack of education and privilege to Voltore, his lack of status empowers as well as restricts him:

> A thing in 'para', moreover, is not only simultaneously on both sides of the boundary line between inside and out. It is also the boundary itself, the screen which is a permeable membrane connecting inside and outside. It confuses them with one another, allowing the outside in, making the inside out, dividing them and joining them. It also forms an ambiguous transition between one and the other.[28]

Mosca then embodies the inherent contradictions and instabilities of the Venetian 'republican' state, blurring the very boundaries that might otherwise seem to define its existence. The *res publica* must control the private lives of its inhabitants in order to be truly successful: that is the Machiavellian conclusion, and it is one that by its very nature contradicts the republican image. The public and the private interact in a highly politicized manner in this play: the urban geography provides sites invested with political significance.

Writing on the theme of boundaries and frontiers, Stephen Greenblatt has observed that 'frontiers are places of highest tension, vigilance, delay',[29] stating that 'Often, though not always, the frontier is the point beyond which they speak languages, eat foods, and worship gods that are simply not your own.'[30] The problems of boundaries – be they determined (at the risk of sounding like Polonius) as national, linguistic, ethical, historical, constitutional, generational, geographical, racial, social, sexual, political, or religious – are all confronted in the remarkable text that is *Volpone* and it is Mosca who most obviously negotiates these dangerous frontiers.

Agnew has observed that the personal transgression of social boundaries invariably involved the multiplication of identities. This is certainly true for Volpone but also renders the act of crossing the threshold of his own front door and into the Venetian community such a dangerous one. Entrance into heterogeneity threatened the integrity of any individual and Volpone as an oligarch in disguise, as Scoto of Mantua, certainly compromises himself in this fashion. The dangers of protean identity become even more evident in the later courtroom scenes where Volpone virtually stages his resurrection. The house-to-street trajectory is then a significant one for many of the characters: Celia at the window throwing her handkerchief into the world of social interaction; Mosca playing the *magnifico*; Volpone's release of his 'bastard' housemates.

In *Volpone* these politically and socially charged thresholds are seemingly constantly sought out. Citizens seek access to other citizens' abodes and Volpone's desire to enter Celia's house after sighting her at a window is indicative of the general desire for penetration, social and sexual. An interesting question in this play is whether the inside or the outside is what ultimately betrays Volpone. In a simple reading of the play's architectural structure it would seem that it is in crossing his own front door that Volpone exceeds his narrow, personal threshold; the Scoto scene renders his disguises more public and therefore more vulnerable, more exposed. Ian Donaldson suggests that 'The theme of keeping to one's home is played over in many ways throughout *Volpone*.'[31] He examines the emblematic significance of Sir Pol's tortoise-shell disguise in V.iv. and suggests it provides a counterpoint to Volpone's 'uncasing' in the text. Pol turns inwards to read his own entrails, having previously been a surface reader of the details around him; Volpone's egotism is held accountable to the Venetian republic. Jonathan Goldberg observes that in Sir Pol we see a parody of Volpone: 'in him, we will see further into the ways in which the body is subverted for the sake of the state, ways in which absolutist rhetoric undermines republican values, ways in which parodic state secrets come close to the real thing'.[32]

Yet there is also a strong case for saying that Volpone, as a performer, is utterly dependent upon exposure of this nature (the arousal of belief) and that to remain permanently inside would constitute his own suffocation. Possibly what Volpone constantly seeks is an audience. Elsewhere in the play we see Celia's incarceration in her sadistic husband's house; she too looks to the outside for release in her own performance with the handkerchief at the window during the Scoto scene (a gesture surely intended to be read by the crowd).[33] Jonson's own relationship with crowds has been viewed as at best ambivalent; Richard Dutton suggests that he feared the fluidity of large crowds and the loss of control they entailed.[34] That risk and potential inherent in public performance (and attendant audiences) would appear to be being explored in *Volpone*.

The two trial scenes of *Volpone* are another inside location with a pre-arranged audience, and there the fox is once again driven, seemingly by internal desire, to expose himself; unable to stop at the one trial, greedy as he is for a second attempt, for more, for an excess of action, despite Mosca's sound advice after the first:

> ... We must, here, be fixed;
> Here, we must rest; this is our masterpiece:
> We cannot think, to go beyond this.
> (V.ii.12–14)

Volpone cannot rest still, a fact announced in his statement that 'Good wits are greatest in extremities' (V.ii.6). Such is the intense subtlety of this play that we must question whether Mosca does not deliberately tempt the eminently persuadable Volpone on to further exposure by this seemingly restrictive statement, just as he deliberately exposes the Celia scenes to Bonario.

Conscious theatricality is an important constituent of the Mosca–Volpone relationship and also of the Scoto of Mantua scenes at II.ii. The only prose scene amidst a wealth of vertiginous verse, this is where Volpone performs the part of a mountebank in the streets.[35] Scoto had in reality been the leader of a Mantuan *commedia* troupe which had performed for Elizabeth I in 1576. His name had also become a by-word for conjuring tricks and deceptions, so once again Volpone is teetering dangerously close to the edge in electing the signs and signifiers for his disguises that he does: it is almost as if the excitement lies in the risk of being found out. The *commedia* connections are significant; it is an improvised form of street theatre, still linked to the Venice *carnevale* today. Carnival is a time when boundaries are temporarily collapsed and disguises donned and Volpone indulges in carnivalesque behaviour of this kind. Early modern Venice apparently opposed many *commedia* troupes due to their subversive potential (they were frequently regarded as products of the subordinate classes), even setting spies amidst audiences – an interesting footnote to Sir Pol and Peregrine's spectatorship of the Scoto scene.[36]

Mantua too is important as a location. If Venice was inescapably in the Renaissance '*La republica*' then Mantua was under the quasi-monarchical rule of the Gonzaga family. Volpone is assuming the garb of an absolutist outsider, furthering the sense of his own liminality in Venetian society. Pol and his wife are interlopers of another kind, from England, unable either to converse in Italian or to understand Venetian customs. Peregrine's name signals that he too is a foreigner, not only a bird, but a traveller, wanderer, or an alien, according to the term's Latin etymology (to peregrinate is to travel). Early modern audiences were also English travellers to Venice albeit in their imaginations, and Jonson deliberately exploits both familiarity and distance on the part of audiences. Topical in-jokes (such as on the death of Stone the fool and the Wotton parody) are made, but new, and foreign, words and names abound and we are constantly made aware (often painfully aware) of being an audience and that the nature of our reception and response is crucial to the play's own arousal of belief. The collective constitution provides a legal and political analogue to the collective production that constitutes the dramatic text. The Venetian republic provides in essence a geographical and dramatic vehicle for contemporary political debate over republicanism but also for experimentation with dramatic conventions.

A city constantly gesturing towards self-definition is inherently theatrical. There is indeed a trick of state afoot in *Volpone*, a *raison d'être* for its locale and plot strategies. Lady Would-be's attempted seduction of Volpone by cataloguing her bibliography may not be so far from the mark as it at first seems since politically and dramatically Jonson himself may have been seduced by Florio's library of texts on the watery republic. He recognized the dramatic potential inherent in the decadent and decaying city and in its constitutions. Historians have always maintained that the myth of Venice was recognized as just that – as a piece of propaganda or a social construct.[37] The city's political realities lay elsewhere: in the self-conscious projections of the Doge and in the secret sessions of the Council of Ten where reputations and lives were frequently denounced. Ultimately for Jonson any truly republican realities rested in the shifting container that was the written word and that is where the republicanism of *Volpone* truly exists. In the play and in the theatre, Volpone the fox turns away from his sentencers (republican and accurate though they are) to plead for the audience's support and applause: applause which is invariably given. Like Prospero, Volpone is allowed to escape incarceration on the island of republican discipline by the nature of the theatrical contract – infinitely tolerant and equitable. He is allowed to transgress another boundary, that of the stage, and to blur the limits even of the theatrical experience.

Part II
Theatrical Republics

4
The Alternative Commonwealth of Women

This chapter re-examines a range of Jonson's female representations in his numerous stage-worlds, including those in *Epicoene* (1609), *Catiline* (1610–11), *The Devil is an Ass* (1616), a number of the masques commissioned by Queen Anne of Denmark (between 1605 and 1609), and his later Caroline drama. These representations are highly diverse in nature: Jonson's female characters range from the liberated to the oppressed, and they reside in commonwealths and patriarchies. The chapter seeks to politicize their import, particularly in the way that they function as communities of women, often as alternatives to those communities franchised by conventional and predominantly absolutist politics.

Jonson used classical texts, including those by Plato, to explore empowered and potentially autonomous female communities. Plato's *Republic* banished poets and accorded equality to women;[1] it claimed that gender differentiation was valid only in the area of sexual reproduction and therefore allowed women equal access to education and occupations. That said, Plato's text, in abolishing the family and establishing state nurseries in order to free women to pursue these newly allowed occupations, decreed that women and children be 'held in common', scarcely the edict of a proto-feminist.[2] The *Republic* though is not an exhaustive account of Platonic theories on poetry or women. Jonson would certainly have been aware of more positive poetic appraisals in both *Ion* and *Phaedrus* and possibly, although perhaps by default, in the *Symposium*, a text he used extensively in the composition of *The New Inn* (1629).[3]

Plato's views are no more embodied in the single text of the *Republic* than Jonson's are in any one play. In a number of his plays and masques, Jonson creates a female group, usually onstage, that dictates its own actions and behaviours free of patriarchal constraints. *The Masque of Blackness* and the *Masque of Beauty* have the Niger princesses who were, of course, performed by Queen

Anne of Denmark (who directly commissioned the masques) and her ladies in waiting. The *Masque of Queens* has both an antimasque of witches (a trope credited by Jonson to Anne herself although performed, because speaking roles, by professional actors) and the independent Queens of the masque proper. *Epicoene*, written for the public stage at much the same time as this feminocentric elite drama for the court, has the Ladies' Collegiate of Haughty, Centaur, Mavis and Trusty acting independently of their husbands, socially and sexually, and *The Devil is an Ass* has the Ladies' Academy of the ladies Tailbush and Eitherside which is a later variation on this.

The Devil is an Ass is ostensibly a play about a troubled marriage. Frances Fitzdottrel is married to an egotistical, greedy and brutal husband who is not only frittering away her money (signed over to him on their marriage-day) but also prepared to trade his wife's attentions in exchange for a cloak to wear to the theatre. This he does at the beginning of the play, enabling the gallant Wittipol to 'interview' (and effectively woo) Frances. Despite being sworn to silence by her husband in this exchange, Frances in time enlists Wittipol's aid in deceiving her husband into signing her finances back into her control. These events take place in the context of the economic marketplace of seventeenth-century London where projectors and goldsmiths join forces to beguile the hapless Fitzdottrel of his money by other means. The title refers to the framework of the play in which a junior devil is sent to London only to find a hell there worse than any he can find at home.

At one point in the play, Fitzdottrel sends his wife to the Ladies' Academy to gain tuition in how to be a duchess (he falsely believes he is to purchase a dukedom in the East Anglian fenlands: one of many fake schemes the projector Merecraft has inveigled him into). Significantly, the leaders of the Academy, Tailbush and Eitherside, claim familiarity with the Platonic republican precedent. Lady Tailbush, the female monopolist of this play, possesses a markedly politicized discourse as well as ambition:

> LADY TAILBUSH   If I can do my sex by 'em any service
> I've my ends, madam.
> WITTIPOL   And they are noble ones,
> That make a multitude beholden, madam:
> The commonwealth of ladies must acknowledge
> from you.
>
> (IV.iii.16–19)

Wittipol in female disguise as a 'Spanish Lady' at this point (this is how he has gained access to the 'Academy' and thereby to Frances) goads the women on to ever more extravagant objectives. Any sense of the potential for risk in their ambitions is dismissed by the women who blame the 'poets'.

Feminist criticism of the Jonsonian canon has also tended to blame the poet, for social conservatism, and frequently for misogyny. This chapter, by exploring the potent image of the female commonwealth on Jonson's stages, seeks to redress the balance.

I 'CONTENT TO LEARN IN SILENCE'

In a sermon, John Donne declared that woman 'must not govern' but must instead 'be content to learn in silence with all subjection';[4] this was a conventional view, often supported by scriptural reference, of female inferiority. Donne's emphasis is on duty and obedience; he regards the primary relation as that of Prince to subject and the secondary and tertiary as those of husband to wife (the order is significant) and parent to child. For him the love of a husband is unashamedly a form of political control and he views the relationship of the sexes as necessarily entailing submission and consent on the female side.

Embodied in Donne's texts are traditional notions of the supreme female grace being silence. The antithesis of this is to be labelled socially as a 'shrew'. *Epicoene*'s subtitle, *The Silent Woman*, has led many to accuse Jonson of similarly false expectations of women but this is a consequence of a critical refusal to look more closely at the operations of the play. Morose is a wealthy London citizen obsessed with expiating noise from his life. To that end, he marries a silent wife. But this cannot be taken as Jonson's endorsement of the conventional view of ideal femininity. Morose is tricked into this marriage and the silent woman proves to be no woman at all, but indeed a man, and part of an elaborate series of tricks by his nephew (who wants back the inheritance he has recently been cut out of). The 'silent woman' is, then, rarely silent and Morose's dream of a perfectly 'dumb' wife is exposed as a false social aim.

It has been argued that Puritanism affected female dramatic representation in the late sixteenth and early seventeenth centuries.[5] Puritan religious groups boasted considerable female membership; meetings and lectures offered women a context for existence outside of the household, expanding as it were their political threshold. The female collegiate of *Epicoene*, an 'alternative commonwealth' as Mary Beth Rose has so aptly termed it,[6] is a possible analogue to this, or even an extension of the thinking, fashioning as it does a wholly female gathering and decision-process.

Jonson does register the Puritan contribution to female education but in a somewhat qualified fashion. He has Dol Common reciting extensively from a controversial Puritan text by Broughton in the scene in *The Alchemist* where she is 'playing' a learned lady (in order to tempt the eminently persuadable Mammon into some sexual digressions). Editorial glosses tend to cite this as evidence of Jonson's scorn for the figure of the educated Puritan woman but are in danger of forgetting Dol in all of this. A Blackfriars prostitute she may be but she is clearly able to handle the complicated Broughton text and she also makes what are perhaps the most astute political comments in the play, recognizing the 'civil war' that threatens to fragment the 'venture tripartite' of the three cozeners who have established the fake alchemist's laboratory (see Act I).

The pursuits of the Ladies' Collegiate in *Epicoene* are similarly quoted as evidence of Jonson's disapproval of educated, independent women. Helen Ostovich's article on group aggression in Jonsonian drama has hinted at a more complex truth behind the characterizations of the collegiate membership.[7] Offering intriguing anthropological and behavioural explanations for the operations of group aggression amongst the frequently male gatherings of Jonson's plays (examining the jeerers of *The Staple of News*, the roarers of *Bartholomew Fair*, and the competing males of *The Alchemist* – amongst whom the female voice of Dol acts as pacifier), Ostovich argues that the mock-masculinity of the women's academy is a response to that behaviour: 'their mock-masculine aggressiveness parodies and crystallizes the pettiness of the male groups'.[8] Living apart from their husbands, the women rejoice in the reversal of all kinds of male expectations; they make passes at pages, lure lovers with gifts, and leer at men.[9] In the cruelly competitive society of *Epicoene*'s 1609 London, they perform their personalized version of one-upmanship. That is not to say that Jonson condones their actions, nor that he is expressing personal anxiety about independent women, but rather considering the socio-political implications of the Collegiate.[10] Nor are the portraits of the collegiate women constructed without empathy – their proactive sexuality is, for example, articulated as a poignant response to advancing old age:

> HAUGHTY ... ladies should be mindful of the approach of old age, and let no time want his due use. The best of our days pass first.
> MAVIS We are rivers that cannot be called back, madam: she that now excludes her lovers may live to lie a forsaken beldame, in a frozen bed.
> (IV.iii.46–51)

The Academy members are not actually seen until Act III, but the verbal build-up to their noisy entrance is considerable. Truewit describes and decries:

> A new foundation, sir, here i'the town, of ladies, that call themselves the Collegiates, an order between courtiers, and country madams, that live from their husbands; and give entertainment to all the Wits, and Braveries o'the time, as they call 'em; cry down, or up, what they like, or dislike in a brain, or a fashion, with most masculine, or rather hermaphroditical authority: and, every day, gain to their college some new probationer.
> (I.i.84–92)

The Collegiate is ultimately silenced by the sexual revelations of the final act but their sentence is certainly less harsh than Morose's. Epicoene infiltrates their ranks but not without some exhibition of sympathy. Competition over Dauphine does split them apart but the mere presence of male groupings such as the gallants suggests a need for female solidarity to be maintained. Jonson should be recognized as exploring the potential for female political configurations in the context of contemporary urban society and its masculine exercise of authority.

II THE PATRONAGE OF WOMEN/PATRONIZING WOMEN

In his depiction of the female Collegiate as free-thinking, self-financing, aristocratic women, Jonson was treading a dangerous line between humour and potentially offensive satire of his own eminent female patrons, amongst them Lucy, Countess of Bedford; Elizabeth, Countess of Rutland (Sir Philip Sidney's daughter); her cousin Lady Mary Wroth (daughter of Sir Robert Sidney, owner of Penshurst); and even Anne of Denmark herself. None of these women appears to have taken offence although Lady Arbella Stuart noted an apparent reference to herself and is said to have sought to censor the play. Her associations with Jonson did however continue after this and the Countesses and Lady Mary Wroth all participated as dancers in subsequent Jonsonian court masques, which suggests little genuine affront was taken. Both the Countess of Rutland and Wroth were themselves poets and Jonson expressed admiration for their work.[11] Indeed, he is recorded in the *Conversations* as being of the view that the Countess of Rutland 'was nothing inferior to her father … in poesy' (ll. 172–3), and in one of several striking poems he wrote in praise of Wroth, he declares that:

> I, that have been a lover, and could not show it,
> Though not in these, in rhymes not wholly dumb,
> Since I exscribe your sonnets am become
> A better lover, and much better poet.
> (*Underwood*, 28, 1–4)[12]

In Wroth and others Jonson had prime exemplars of well-read women and of astute theatre-goers; Jonson even dedicated his ultimate work of metatheatre, *The Alchemist*, to Wroth. Michael Shapiro has written an account of her use of the theatrical metaphor in her prose and relates this to her extensive experience of court performances in 1603–4, and 1608–9, when she may have seen or heard of up to forty plays.[13] Her 1621 prose romance, the *Urania*, is studded with theatrical references and structures, many of them clearly masque-derived. Jonson was, then, familiar with theatre-conscious female circles and that he chose to make his onstage female audience in *The Staple of News* astute spectators as well as stereotypical 'gossips' suggests that his assessments of female taste and intelligence cannot be so easily dismissed.

Epicoene, as already mentioned, was written in 1609 when assertive gestures at court by Anne of Denmark were particularly apparent; she was consciously fostering her own household and style.[14] Jonson had first written for Anne in 1605 when he won the coveted commission for the Twelfth Night masque. His *Masque of*

Blackness, with its twelve African daughters of Niger, danced by the Queen and her ladies, has been read by many scholars as an act of female aggression in the male-dominated Jacobean court.[15] Riggs sees the masque's content as a direct challenge being issued by the Queen against her husband's absolutist authority: 'the surface impression of license that inhered in the ladies' dark complexions was just as compelling as the King's power to whiten and cleanse'.[16]

Jonson's potentially feminocentric ventures into the masque form did not cease there. As a sequel to the *Masque of Blackness* he authored the *Masque of Beauty* in 1608, and in 1609 wrote the *Masque of Queens* also for Anne and her ladies. Anne played Bel-Anna, and her female attendants, amongst them the Countess of Bedford, and Lady Anne Clifford, took the parts of a selection of great queens, classical and historical. One of the female monarchs represented was Penthesilea, Queen of the Amazons, which is one of the titles with which Morose chides his voluble new 'wife' in *Epicoene* (III.v.59–61).[17]

A number of critics have also connected the themes and concerns of *Epicoene* with the 1605–6 masque *Hymenaei* which Jonson composed to commemorate the wedding of the young Lady Frances Howard.[18] Jonson's relationship with the Howard family had been fraught up to this point and he may well have accepted the commission for political reasons. The text combines themes of marital and political union. Ironically, Jonson would be recommissioned to write the masque for Frances's second marriage. The first had been annulled on the grounds of the groom's supposed impotence; the second would lead to scandal and a trial for murder.[19] It has been argued that as a result Jonson became 'embarrassed' by his involvement in these commissions: but his interest in Frances Howard did not cease there. Her demonization both by the general public and by the trial judges feeds into the witchcraft and possession accusations against another Frances, Frances Fitzdottrel in *The Devil is an Ass*, who is placed on trial for witchcraft by her husband when Wittipol proves successful in regaining control of her finances for her.

When Jonson was composing this Blackfriars-based play, the pregnant Frances was under house-arrest in the area and is likely to have been at the forefront of Jonson's alert political consciousness since her downfall also signalled the eclipse of the Somerset faction at court and the rise of George Villiers, the future Duke of Buckingham.[20] What is fascinating, however, is that in all of this he does not lose sight of the individual, and *The Devil is an Ass*, with its touching themes of marital rights and the power of friendship, evinces considerable sympathy for Frances Howard in 1616.[21]

Jonson's relationship to his female patrons and associates took, then, several forms and his depiction of the relations *between* the sexes must be seen in the light of this. He repeatedly analysed the failures and breakdowns of marriages in his plays, but this is not necessarily proof of any pessimistic belief that such relationships were impossible or even undesirable. That he expounds the need to create other spaces, domestic and institutional, in which to realize them is, I think, closer to the truth.

III 'THE GOBLIN MATRIMONY'

Marriage was frequently under investigation as an institution in Jonson's plays. Insistent in the printed text of *Hymenaei* is the idea of the coming together of disparate entities to form a coherent whole; the familiar Jonsonian trope of circles figures heavily, culminating in the 'one strong knot' of the bridal girdle. In *Epicoene* the circles are undone, the harmony reduced to a cacophony. The ending itself is an untying: Morose, in his agreement to be labelled legally impotent is 'undone'. The only form of knot mentioned in the play is that of Tacitus's writings but even this is referred to as 'an entire knot: sometimes worth the untying, very seldom.' (II.iii.64–5).

The language of *Epicoene* functions on negatives and nothings – with the familiar Renaissance pun on female genitalia, truly 'nothing' in the case of Epicoene. There are manifold cries of 'O!'. Haughty and her cohorts arrive as a veritable antimasque, revelling in the comedy of Morose's marriage to a 'silent' wife and reflecting on how all the crucial aspects of a wedding, such as a masque like *Hymenaei*, are missing: 'We see no ensigns of a wedding, here; no character of a bride-ale: where be our scarves, and our gloves?' (III.vi.80–2); 'No gloves? no garters? no scarves? no epithalamium? no masque?' (III.vi.100–1).

The fate of Frances Howard's first marriage might be said to bear out the falsity of sumptuous literary and visual epithalamia and Riggs argues that Jonson is commenting wryly on the theatrical illusion his masques were designed to achieve, papering as they do over the cracks, political and personal. Yet the space the genre provided for Jonson to create and foster female communities should not be underestimated: even this most courtly of forms contains 'republican' potential in that respect. For Queen Anne they provided an alternative vision of power to that symbolized by her marriage; for watching court women they surely contained that potential as well.

The marriages depicted on the Jonsonian stage are frequently rather unhappy arrangements. Many of his wife-figures fare badly; a semi-positive example might be the Littlewit partnership in *Bartholomew Fair* but by the close of that play Win the wife has been easily persuaded by Knockem that adultery is the best course. Proceeding onwards from the Stagekeeper's image in the Induction of a whore placed on her head, that play subjects women to brutal examinations of all kinds.[22] Placentia's devoted parents in *The Magnetic Lady*, in truth the parents of Pleasance, 'lov'd together, like a pair of Turtles,' (I.v.4) but are already long dead when the play commences.[23]

The brutality with which Corvino treats his partner Celia is deliberately difficult for any audience to reconcile with *Volpone*'s supposed comic genre; his attacking alliteration and plethora of syphilitic and venereal verbs and adjectives pour themselves over Celia (II.v.1–9, 15–18). Corvino's anger at her 'public' performance – 'You were an actor, with your handkerchief!' (II.v.40) – is expressed in violent terms:

> here's a lock, which I will hang upon thee;
> And now I think on't, I will keep thee backwards;
> Thy lodging shall be backwards; thy walks backwards;
> Thy prospect – all be backwards; and no pleasure,
> That thou shalt know, but backwards:
>
> (II.v.57–61)

The sodomitical taint of this language is plain; its vocabulary of restraint as well as its mention of devils, circles, and conjurors is a precursor of Fitzdottrel's discourse in *The Devil is an Ass* a decade later. Neither play condones male violence, be it verbal or actual (Fitzdottrel, in a shocking departure, actually strikes his wife onstage); this argues for careful characterization on Jonson's part, a nuance often missed in extravagant caricatured performances of both these roles on the modern stage.

In *Epicoene* the farcical marriage of the Otters predominates, alongside Morose's own ill-fated venture into the marriage-market. Captain Otter proclaims, through a haze of alcohol:

> Wife! Buzz! *Titivilitium.* There's no such thing in nature. I confess, gentlemen, I have a cook, a laundress, a house-drudge, that serves my necessary turns, and goes under that title: but he's an ass that will be so uxorious to tie his affections to one circle.
>
> (IV.ii.57–62)

but he is effecting a fatal misreading of the kind Corvino and Fitzdottrel perpetrate upon their faithful wives. Perhaps Otter's biggest mistake is not to realize that he has been set up by the gallants, and his wife is overhearing every condemnatory word. His description of the marriage is entirely inaccurate: not only is Mrs Otter its physical and vocal strength – as La Foole reflects, 'She commands all at home' (I.iv.32–3) – she is also its financial backbone, just as Frances is in her marriage in *The Devil is an Ass*. This reverses more general expectations of the husband as provider; Mistress Otter pays for the Captain's clothes, food and drink. We realize that he is the spendthrift of the relationship, for which reason she threatens at one point to stop his allowance as if he were a child not to be trusted with pocket money. Preferring the terms of absolutism to the subservient connotations of 'wife', Mistress Otter is addressed in her home as 'Princess' by her weakling husband.

In *Epicoene* marriage is at the mercy of Truewit's savage tongue. When Morose announces his marital intentions, Truewit unleashes a verbal diatribe against the institution:

> Marry, your friends do wonder, sir, the Thames being so near, wherein you may drown so handsomely; or London Bridge, at a low fall, with a fine leap, to hurry you down the stream; or such a delicate steeple i'the town, as Bow, to vault from; or a braver height, as Paul's; or if you affected to do it nearer home, and a shorter way, an excellent garret window, into the street; or a beam, in the said garret, with this halter;
> *He shows him a halter*
> which they have sent, and desire that you would sooner commit your grave head to this knot, than to the wedlock noose; or take a little sublimate, and go out of the world, like a rat; or a fly (as

one said) with a straw i'your arse: any way, rather than to follow this goblin matrimony.

(II.ii.21–39)

As with much of Truewit's condemnation of women, however, we should be wary of ascribing these extremist views to Jonson.[24] A parody of marriage is taking place both here and in other plays, but this need not constitute an attack on women: it could be viewed as articulating the need for routes for women outside of the confines of marriage. It is intriguing to say the least that Truewit goes on to cite masques as one of the current causes of women's corruption (II.ii.37); this places Jonson the author in opposition to, rather than in support of, this supposed 'true wit'.

The Devil is an Ass has the aforementioned Fitzdottrel relationship, but also the outspoken gallant, Wittipol, whose treatment of women is markedly different from Truewit's. Jonson once again resists type. In a remarkable departure from his Boccaccian source, he has his seducer cease sexual advances towards the wife at her request. Despite having earlier voiced the familiar arguments of *carpe diem* poetry:

> Flowers
> Though fair, are oft but of one morning. Think,
> All beauty does last until the autumn,
> You grow old while I tell you this.
> (I.vi.128–31)

Wittipol, in an inverse movement to Volpone's leap out of his sickbed, declares himself no ravisher but a true friend. Frances puts this to the test:

> My fortunes standing in this precipice,
> 'Tis counsel that I want, and honest aids:
> And in this name I need you for a friend!
> Never in any other; for his ill
> Must not make me, sir, worse.
> (IV.vi.24–8)

Her striking commonsense monosyllables may for some spectators fail to tally with her decision to remain within the (albeit newly defined) confines of such a sterile marriage, but perhaps the more significant event is the joint response of Wittipol and Manly:

> Virtue shall never ask my succours twice;
> Most friend, most man, your counsels are commands:
> Lady, I can love goodness in you more
> Than I did beauty; and do here entitle
> Your virtue to the power, upon a life
> You shall engage in any fruitful service,
> Even to forfeit.
>
> (IV.vi.35–41)

This is a different understanding of service to the Machiavellian version of Merecraft and Tailbush seen elsewhere in the play. Wittipol responds to Frances's virtue and in doing so both he and the aptly named Manly display their *virtù*; not that of the young male ravisher, but that of a man capable of an egalitarian approach to relationships, sexual and social.[25]

Together Wittipol and Manly set about retrieving Frances's fortunes from her husband's (lack of) control.[26] Intrinsic to many of Jonson's depictions of marriage appears to be the seizure of power in some form by the female half. This stands in direct contradistinction to the ecclesiastical homilies on marriage which tutor obedience and subservience to women. This is most directly figured in the Collegiate of *Epicoene*, where the ladies' assumption of control over their lives extends to biological operations, since they practise birth control and openly pursue their sexual partners and *The Magnetic Lady*, with its feminine conspiracy to 'hush up' Placentia's pre-marital pregnancy, is a further example of female power and initiative in the sexual commonwealth.

IV SHED SNAKESKIN IN THE HISTORY OF POLITICS

Sexuality brings its own sources of power for women; if this power is acknowledged by authors, readers and audiences then women's political relevance can never be entirely denied. A narrow definition of politics excludes women but this is not the definition being proffered by Jonson in his plays.[27]

The need for women in both the daily and political life of Rome is acknowledged from the very beginning of *Catiline* through the protagonist's employment of his wife and her female friends to woo potential voters for him. Fulvia also proves crucial to the fate of the conspiracy, and in her quest for unlimited money and sex resembles Catiline himself. Many have felt that Cicero's politic wooing of Fulvia to persuade her to reveal all not only demeans the politician but denigrates womanhood as being too easily persuaded to any cause by sexual wiles.[28] Cethegus scornfully regards women as capable only of 'smock-treason', equating the sexual and the political merely as a means of deprecating women, without recognizing that it is an area which invests women with hitherto unrealized power.

In his *Essay of Dramatick Poesie*, John Dryden declared of the Fulvia–Sempronia scenes in *Catiline* that they demonstrate 'the Parliament of Women, the little envies of them to one another; and all that passes between Curio [sic] and Fulvia: scenes admirable in their kind, but of an ill mingle with the rest'.[29] His opinion appears to be that women are manifestly fit subjects only for plays other than the serious Roman tragedy Jonson purports to be writing; however, his usage of the term 'parliament of women' opens up a wider spectrum of possibility.

Surprisingly, Barton's criticism of the play participates in this rather intolerant generic limitation on gender. She feels that the 'women's scenes' carry comedy dangerously close to the epicentre of the play, thus undercutting the dignity of both Catiline and Cicero, and somehow diminishing by their very presence the importance of state matters.[30] Barton speaks somewhat unforgivingly of how Fulvia, chatting first with her maid Galla and then with Sempronia, places in apposition air fresheners and state affairs, as though they were all somehow of equal importance; yet the very pettiness of her subject-matter placed in conjunction with the conspiratorial ideas of Catiline, Cethegus, and the others provides exactly the undermining effect that Jonson seeks to achieve. For Fulvia, state affairs are conducted as precisely that – affairs; she utilizes her sexuality to secure political and personal preferment, initially welcoming her previously jettisoned lover Curius back into her bed when he promises her the spoils of Rome, but then in turn casually betraying him for the more lavish incentives offered by Cicero.

That Fulvia's action of betrayal is also partially prompted by Sempronia's possession of a more primary role in the conspiracy is less a sign of the petty jealousies and ambitions of women than evidence of the limited social resources allowed them; it provides an analogy with the same 'little envies' that operate within the male political sphere of the Senate and the Consulship. Jealousy is after all a driving force in the Cicero–Catiline opposition, as each man vies to dominate the political discourse of Rome. As the Chorus declares of the republic:

> Her women wear
> The spoils of nations in an ear
> Chang'd for the treasure of a shell,
> And in their loose attires do swell
> More light than sails when all winds play;
> Yet are the men more loose than they,
> More kemb'd and bath'd, and rub'd and trim'd,
> More sleek'd, more soft, and slacker limb'd,
> As prostitute; ...
>
> (I.i.555–63)

Sempronia is a figure of political skill in this play; Galla describes her discourse as being all:

> O'the Republic, madam, and the state,
> And how she was in debt, and where she meant
> To raise fresh sums. She's a great stateswoman.
>
> (II.i.36–8)

She holds a high opinion of herself, claiming to be an orator and scholar the match of Cicero. Clearly educated, she speaks admirable Latin and Greek and is therefore credited with a 'masculine wit'. She also possesses accurate knowledge of political events: hoping to assist Catiline in the forthcoming elections for the consulship, she has been writing letters to that effect. Chapter XXV in Jonson's source, Sallust's *Bellum Catilinae*, does touch on both Sempronia's education and her masculine wit, but the political angle of her being a potential female ambassador appears to be a Jonsonian interpolation.[31] Sempronia is aware of all the competitors in the race but wrongly predicts that Cicero's nomination will be crossed by the nobility; this leads Barton to suggest that her learning is a pretence but Sempronia's understanding of 'common business' is, I think, central to her character.

In a subsequent scene, Sempronia reflects on the general

exclusion of women from active political life – in the narrow understanding of the term as meaning to be an ambassador or a spy – suggesting that much is sacrificed in terms of Roman achievement by this:

> I do wonder much
> That states and commonwealths employ not women
> To be ambassadors sometimes. We should
> Do as good public service, and could make
> As honorable spies, for so Thucydides
> Calls all ambassadors.
> (IV.v.8–13)

The play's events appear to endorse her counsel, since Cicero's discovery of the conspiracy against him hinges upon the double agency of Fulvia. This is not simply further opportunity for Jonson to berate the duplicity of womanhood; the point is rather that they are witnessed as being equal to men in the (political?) skills of calculation, possibly even exceeding them in that the men, excepting Cicero, fail to take this potential adequately into account.[32]

The example of Fulvia is intriguing for a number of reasons. As a prostitute she is making decisions about her sexuality (although in deeper sociological terms we may wish still to regard her career as circumscribed by patriarchal desire), and even though Curius declares that he will force her to sleep with him, her response is far from passive. In truth it is quasi-phallic since she draws a knife and Curius rapidly submits to her greater sexual power with an interesting choice of expression:

> Fulvia, you do know
> The strengths you have upon me; do not use
> Your power too like a tyrant; I can bear
> Almost until you break me.
> (II.i.293–6)

Curius's sense of personal weakness in the face of her sexual and seductive powers accords Fulvia a strength she is denied in the more overtly political world of senate and suffrage.

Much that has been written on the 'parliament of women' in the early modern period looks from a retrospective vantage point – that of the Leveller women's first petition to Parliament in 1649.[33] These women refused to be silent, no longer accepting that their husbands or fathers should speak for them in an act of ventriloquism, and the actions of Jonsonian characters such as the Ladies' Collegiate in *Epicoene*, or Frances in *The Devil is an Ass* are surely a precursor of this political change. Jonson may not have been a protofeminist but he inaugurated and advanced debates that would emerge with full verbal force during the civil war period.

V THEATRICAL ALTERNATIVES AND ALTERNATIVE COMMUNITIES

Building on the foundations provided by the operations of the Ladies' Collegiate in *Epicoene*, the female communities of Jonson's later plays frequently provide genuine social alternatives to the contemporary society reflected in the main plot, at least within the context of the theatrical performance. It has been noted that the female characterizations in these later playtexts are both more rounded and more mature:[34] commencing with Frances in *The Devil is an Ass* and continuing with Prudence in *The New Inn* right up to Marian in the unfinished *The Sad Shepherd*, Jonson offers intelligent and engaging versions of early modern womanhood.

Yet these plays have also been said to contain more stereotypical 'anti-feminist' depictions: the gossips of *The Staple of News*, Intermeans, the conspiratorial women of *The Magnetic Lady*, and Maudlin the witch in *The Sad Shepherd*. I want to consider the first two groups – both communities and acting ensembles – as examples of Jonson's interest in female communities.

The gossips of *The Staple of News* and the midwives of *The Magnetic Lady* are intriguingly etymologically linked: 'gossips' derives from the female godparents, 'god-sibs', or wise-women who attended the expectant mother's lying-in bed.[35] These *sage-femmes* were also often amateur midwives, certainly they lent their title to those in the profession.[36] It is precisely the potential, social and political, of these intimate female spaces of talk and reflection that Jonson explores in his group characterizations of women.

Ostovich has described the gossips in *The Staple of News* – Expectation, Censure, Mirth and Tattle – as 'ignorant she-critics' but this is not quite the whole story.[37] They are clearly astute theatregoers, if somewhat dated in their taste for fools and clowns. They have after all seen or heard of Jonson's *The Devil is an Ass*, a play I am arguing for here as a crucial intervention in his exploration of the female condition, and it is with the plight of women in this play that the onstage 'audience' of gossips frequently identify themselves.

When Pennyboy Junior, the prodigal son of *The Staple of News*, proposes to escort his new companion to dine in Picklock's lodgings in Ram Alley, Pennyboy Canter (his father in disguise) does his utmost to dissuade him:

> O fie! An alley, and a cook's shop, gross!
> 'Twill savour, sir, most rankly of 'em both.
> Let your meat rather follow you to a tavern.
> (II.v.115–17)

Ram Alley was a notorious London site of prostitution but Picklock protests that a tavern is an equally unsavoury location to take a Princess. A contentious and noticeably male-directed debate ensues over the fit place to escort a female; Pecunia's opinion is never asked. Canter's justificatory precedent for his choice is that Pocahontas, the Native American Indian daughter of the Virginia colony's tribal leader, who came to England in 1616, stayed in two taverns during that time. The rather ugly historical details of that sojourn reveal that Pocahontas was another female captive, of exploring English sailors; she was converted, baptized, and eventually married to an Englishman. In 1616–17 Pocahontas attended one of Jonson's Christmastide masques but died of ill-health before being able to return to her own country. The analogy with Pecunia is clear and tragic: they are both female captives, subjected to male readings, both during their lives and in historical retrospect, and the gossips are alert to this.[38]

They leap, verbally at least, to the defence of a number of women, actual and fictitious, who are the victims of male authorings in the play. All the emissaries (reporters) of the Staple news-office that forms the central location of this play are noticeably male – the only female assistance sought in the production of news is financial (Pecunia's name means 'money'). Pecunia is also known as the 'Infanta of the Mines'. Recognizing the topical reference to the Spanish Infanta, Isabella (Prince Charles's not-to-be bride in the failed Spanish Match of 1623),[39] in Pecunia's characterization, the gossips remark:

CENSURE Ay, therein they abuse an honourable princess, it is thought.
MIRTH By whom is it so thought? Or where lies the abuse?
CENSURE Plain in the styling her 'Infanta' and giving her three names.
(II. Intermean, 21–25)

Mirth, with a truly Jonsonian note of concern, warns Censure to 'Take heed it lie not in the vice of your interpretation' (II. Intermean, l.26), suggesting that she is overdetermining something obvious; yet the same warning can be reapplied to the male over-readings of Pecunia and indeed of the memory of Pocahontas. As Tattle says:

I would hearken and hearken, and censure if I saw cause, for th'other princess's sake – Pocahontas, surnamed the blessèd, whom he has abused indeed – and I do censure him and will censure him: to say she came forth of a tavern was said like a paltry poet.
(II. Intermean, 39–44)

Doubtless, we should be cautious about reading these women as a riposte to male stereotyping of women in the play since they too are male constructs, authored by Jonson himself. I would be equally hesitant about attributing to Jonson any protofeminist stance simply on account of the gossips' defensive dialogue, but read deeper as characters they do pose an interesting counterpoint to the usual charges of misogyny levied against his group representations of women.

That deeper reading of the Intermeans to *The Staple of News* enables the re-reading of that other conspiratorial and fast-talking female community of the later plays: the conniving midwives of *The Magnetic Lady*. Ostovich has suggested that through this gathering Jonson indicates: 'what happens when a household of women reappropriates maternity and motherhood in the course of their own pursuit of independent pleasure or profit'[40] and reads into this a negative response on Jonson's behalf to the disturbance this constitutes to the binary gender system operating in contemporary society. The plot of the midwife Mother Chair (her name suggestive of the birthing chair commonly used by female practitioners of medicine), Nurse Keep, and the Gossip Polish (again that title with its connotations of the potentially subversive female space of the lying-in bed is employed) is to conceal the birth of Placentia's child in order to conceal the deeper historical 'truth' of Placentia's identity as Polish's daughter and not the Lady Loadstone's inheritance-blessed and therefore desirable niece. This is, according to Ostovich, evidence of Jonson's fear of female ability to control sexuality in order to thwart patriarchy. However, her conviction that Jonson intends to portray this 'cabal of middle-aged women' in a solely pejorative light underestimates the scheming nature of the very examples of patriarchy that they thwart, such as the grasping financier Sir Moth Interest, the cynical lawyer Practice and the vapid courtier Sir Diaphanous Silkworm.[41] As with the Collegiate in *Epicoene*, the women seem almost to be forced by male aggression to form mirror-groups. Ostovich does suggest that the 'negativity' of the portrait of this conspiracy sits awkwardly in the context of Jonson's other female representations and for that very reason I would suggest a need to see them, and indeed the witch-craft of Maudlin in *The Sad Shepherd*, in the context of the patriarchal injustices Jonson seems equally intent on exposing.

Jonson's interest in community is not gender-biased, except in the recognitions he makes of contemporary womanhood's fate in a patriarchal society, domestic and political. We need to re-assess his depictions of marriage in plays such as *The Devil is an Ass* and of gatherings of educated or empowered women such as the Collegiates of *Epicoene*, the Gossips of *The Staple of News*, or the political interveners of the Roman tragedies, or even the female masquers of the Jacobean court, in the light of a revised understanding of Jonson's 'republicanism' and his interest in the active political participation of all sectors of society. In the mixed constitution of the stage, the alternative commonwealth of women certainly has a role to play.

5
Republicanism and Theatre

I 'A REPUBLIC OF WHOLESALE MERCHANTS'

Describing the evolution of the city-state in the early modern period, Richard Mackenney has observed that:

> London could scarcely claim to be a city-state, for it was the seat of a monarchy which in the early seventeenth century aspired to govern by divine right. However, as late as 1617, a Venetian observer – who could be expected to know what a republic was – described the city as 'a sort of republic of wholesale merchants.'[1]

The Venetian observer was speaking just seven years after Ben Jonson wrote *The Alchemist* and unwittingly captures the essence of that play and the central role within it of the London city location.

The Alchemist is set and was performed in the Blackfriars region of London, an intriguing location in that it had until very recently been part of the so-called area of the 'Liberties' due to the monastic status of the land on which the theatre was situated. It was part of the city and yet on its very margins, and, until very recently, outside the strict jurisdiction of the London sheriffs.[2] The open-air public theatres were mostly grouped in the Liberties, with all its attendant notions of licence and licentiousness and Steven Mullaney sees this in a textual light:

> The Liberties of the City were social and civic margins, and they also served as margins in a textual sense; as places reserved for a 'variety of sense' ... and for divergent points of view – for commentary upon and even contradiction of the main body of their text, which in this instance would be the body politic itself.[3]

If we consider the structure of Jonson's 1616 Folio which, emphasizing personal authorship, acknowledged in its copious marginalia issues of influence and source, we can see that Jonson was a writer more than alert to such ideas. The metadrama and vibrant stage communities of *The Alchemist* are exploitative of this power of the margins.

Yet the Blackfriars theatre for which the play was written was an indoor private theatre: a theatre for which tickets were more expensive due to their seated and covered location. This would suggest a potentially more elite audience for any production than would have been found in the open-air auditoria and that immediately complexes any understanding of the populist nature of this playtext; the audience for *The Alchemist* might as easily be the sector of the society that sought to regulate the likes of Face and Subtle as those to whom their antics turned a mirror.

Discussing what he describes as 'the inscription of ideological values on civic space', Mullaney discusses how 'the margins of the city were themselves a crucial part of its symbolic economy, ... they served as a more ambivalent staging-ground, as a place where the contradictions of the community – its incontinent hopes, fears, and desires – were prominently and dramatically set on stage'.[4] This statement conjures up the world we see created onstage in *The Alchemist*: the setting of the Blackfriars house, its careful location in recognizable London streets, the divergent dreams and desires of the visitors to the establishment of Subtle, Face, and Dol – in short, Lovewit's house. The play does concern itself with the differences within this collectivity, its disparate desires, and its contradictions – and in its linguistic *mélange* its contra-dictions, and yet it was playing them out within the city walls, the very city walls over which Dol and Subtle will escape at the end of the play.

The play's location is then politically charged in similar ways to the Venice of *Volpone*. The Blackfriars is an area of London that was in sociological transition and Jonson uses the transitional space of the 'private' Blackfriars theatre (and the term was as ambivalent as 'private' space proves to be in this play and in other city-texts by Jonson such as *Volpone*) to explore the changes underway.[5]

The alchemical laboratory established in the Blackfriars is socially and culturally significant not solely due to its inhabitants but due also to its visitors, not least the plague itself which in 1610, the date of *The Alchemist*'s composition and setting, had been raging around the vastly overpopulated streets that made up early modern London. The statistical evidence of London's size and demographics has been well-documented elsewhere but it is worth stating that the influx of people of diverse trades and backgrounds to the capital in the early years of the seventeenth century is reflected in the *dramatis personae* of this play.

Richard Sennett has proffered multiple definitions of a city: as a settlement where strangers are likely to meet, where the problem of a public audience always exists, where few have a notion of each other's history or background, and where, therefore, the immediate frame of the moment is what they must base belief upon.[6] For these reasons city culture is dependent upon public enactment and interpretation, and the temptation to falsify and conceal is omnipresent. The theatrical analogies here are self-evident and highly relevant for the cross-section of society in *The Alchemist*. It is now a critical commonplace to say that this play above all others in the Jonsonian canon proffers representations of London and theatre, and of London as theatre. The seminal essay on this subject is Robert Smallwood's, which depicts the accuracy of the location detailed in the play as a partial parody of the trend for such topicality in contemporary theatre:

> Plays which pandered to (or in satirical specimens of the genre, mocked) the local patriotism and class-consciousness of their audiences were a natural development from the history plays of the previous decade which had flattered national patriotism and race consciousness.[7]

Smallwood sees *The Alchemist* and Jonson's earlier collaborative text *Eastward Ho* (1605) as examples of the satirical strain. Recent research on the history plays of the 1590s has suggested their proximity in concern to the city comedies; both are theatrical representations of the new notion of the market-exchange (the notion of service and reward) which characterized urban relations.[8]

New definitions of service and the relations between social spheres had a definite impact upon theatre. Jean-Christophe Agnew suggests that

> The theater not only mirrored new social relations within the visible framework of the old, it improvised – as a matter of its own constitutive conventions – a new social contract between itself and its audiences and a new set of conditions for the suspension of disbelief that became over time the preconditions of most modern drama.[9]

He continues, significantly enough for *The Alchemist*, 'the stage then furnished its urban audience with a laboratory and an idiom within which these difficulties and contradictions could be acted out'.[10] By the end of *The Alchemist* we realize that the laboratory itself has been a product of our personal suspension of disbelief when Lovewit describes the actuality behind his front door:

> Here I find
> The empty walls, worse than I left 'em, smoked,
> A few cracked pots, and glasses, and a furnace,
> The ceiling filled with poesies o'the candle;
> And 'Madam with a dildo', writ o' the walls.
> (V.v.38–42)

The play's 'realism' is itself a consequence of dissemblance; the real communal act of *The Alchemist* is an imaginative one.

The unities of time and place are preserved to a remarkable extent in *The Alchemist*: the play's duration mirrors that of the plot's chronology and all the characters are envisaged as inhabitants of the immediate Blackfriars area; that site was not only that of the theatre in which Jonson's play was first commissioned and performed, but also the address of the dramatist himself (at least for a time) as we know from the dedicatory epistle to *Volpone* (1606). *The Alchemist*'s topicality was a tactic Jonson was to repeat to similar effect in *Bartholomew Fair*.

Many critics have noted how Jonson's meticulous attention to topical details implicated the original audiences both as Londoners and paying clients; Jeremy's epilogue is usually quoted in this respect:

> though I am clean
> Got off, from Subtle, Surly, Mammon, Dol,
> Hot Ananias, Dapper, Drugger, all
> With whom I traded; yet I put myself
> On you, that are my country: and this pelf,
> Which I have got, if you do quit me, rests
> To feast you often, and invite new guests.
> (V.v.159–65)

However the alignment of audience and cast, framed and highlighted though they are by the Prologue and Epilogue of this carefully structured play ('Our scene is London, 'cause we would make known,/No country's mirth is better than our own' (Prologue, ll. 5–6)) should not blind us to the careful individualizations and demarcations which operate within the *dramatis personae*. This is very much a community with all its attendant tensions, paradoxes and contradictions, and in his localized setting Jonson makes perhaps his most egalitarian (republican?) dramatic gesture.

II THE MIXED STATE OF SUBTLE, FACE, AND DOL

By the 1590s, London, which had previously been zoned into different occupational ghettos, was witnessing a breakdown of its divisional boundaries. In *The Alchemist* we have a whole blend of pursuits in coexistence, although it is interesting to note that the sustainability of the alchemist's trick is dependent upon the prevention of these strangers' paths ever crossing. As one character enters, another is invariably hurried offstage, in a theatrical style now suggestive of the farce genre with its constantly opening and closing doors. When the strangers do eventually meet and swap stories then the charade visibly collapses, as in Act V when the clients all gather around the locked door to Lovewit's abode.

The stage 'republic' Jonson fashions is highly diverse. Even though Dapper the clerk's character and particular section of the tale are based on the real experiences of one Thomas Rodgers, neither he, nor Abel Drugger the grocer, constitutes a cultural stereotype. Drugger is scarcely the financially consumed mercantilist elsewhere evident in early modern popular drama; with his gentle request for advice on the positioning of the shelves in his store he presents an almost sweet visage for nascent capitalism. If the individual portraits of the play are highly localized, it is also worth considering how local loyalties affected audience response. Like the contemporary audiences, Jonson's characters are mostly Londoners – including Subtle, Face and Dol. Sir Epicure Mammon is a gullible outsider, a knight of the shire, as too are Kastril and his sister Dame Pliant (her name perhaps indicating her susceptibility to her new environment). The *dramatis personae* refers to both the female characters of the play (there are only two) as male possessions; Pliant is Kastril's sister and Dol Common is Subtle and Face's colleague (already we are given the hint that Dol is not an entirely equal partner in the supposedly joint-stock company). Dol is highly subject to male readings of her nature. The Blackfriars community begins to look distinctly patriarchal from these angles, casting considerable doubt on any republican claims that it might make.

Both Subtle and Face seem anxious to attach various possessive epithets to Dol Common; so much so that an audience may begin to wonder whether she is the goods held in common by their partnership:

> SUBTLE   Royal Dol!
> Spoken like Claridiana, and thyself!
> FACE   For which, at supper, thou shalt sit in triumph,
> And not be styled Dol Common, but Dol Proper,
> Dol Singular: the longest cut, at night,
> Shall draw thee for his Dol Particular.
> (I.i.174–9)

Dol's profession as a prostitute does render her a common thing in their eyes; her body can be purchased and possessed by anyone with the necessary capital.[11] She is indeed the republican epitome of a 'public thing', the *res publica*: she says famously at I.i.110, 'Have yet some care of me, o'your republic.' Essentially, though, Dol is defined by the imperialist and patriarchal strategy of naming (Adam, not Eve, named things in Eden; Columbus re-named his New World 'discoveries').[12] That a woman should be so obviously denigrated by the joint-stock company's male membership (and that I have already referred to Subtle and Face as a 'partnership' is an indication of the dichotomies present) is something which is signified from the start in Dol's nomenclature. Like Pecunia, her aristocratic counterpart in *The Staple of News*, Dol is vulnerable to the allegorizations and interpretations of the men around her. For Sir Epicure Mammon she is the focus of his sexual ambitions; he may promise her a 'free state' but the offer is couched in the language of sexual and patriarchal absolutism. The few times that Dol is allowed to play characters above her station – the mad lady citing Broughton, the Faery Queen in the display for Dapper – it is made very clear that she is only 'playing', that such theatre poses no real threat to the social hierarchy. Any subversion implicit in the assumption of such roles is cynically undercut by Face's observation:

> Why, this is yet
> A kind of modern happiness, to have
> Dol Common for a great lady.
> (IV.i.22–4)

as indeed it has been previously by Dol's collusion, admittedly for the purposes of a quiet life, in these male readings:

> Oh, let me alone.
> I'll not forget my race, I warrant you.
> I'll keep my distance, laugh, and talk aloud;
> Have all the tricks of a proud scurvy lady,
> And be as rude as her woman.
> (II.iv.7–11)

To all intents and purposes Dol is Face's 'fond, flexible whore' and yet it is she who has many of the 'good thoughts' of the play. She makes perhaps the most astute, certainly the most accurate, observations of the play; she predicts, in an extraordinarily prescient statement for 1610, civil war between Subtle and Face. She also warns Mammon of the dangers of his dreaming in an absolutist state, albeit initially altruistic and democratic in its aims:

> I could well consent, sir.
> But, in a monarchy, how will this be?
> The prince will soon take notice; and both seize
> You, and your stone; it being a wealth unfit
> For any private subject.
> (IV.i.147–50)

As Dol Common she is also representative of the populace, the plebeian element of this oligarchical republic, the *stato misto*. To her falls the role of mediator or peacemaker during the opening squabble between Face and Subtle, 'Gentlemen, what mean you?/Will you mar all?' (I.i.80–1). She reminds the over-presumptuous Subtle of the democratic intentions of their republic:

> You will insult,
> And claim a primacy in the divisions?
> You must be chief? As if you, only, had
> The powder to project with, and the work

> Were not begun out of equality?
> The venture tripartite? All things in common?
> Without priority?
>
> (I.i.130–6)

The powder she refers to is that used in the alchemical experiments but the word again emphasizes the theatrical aspect of their joint enterprise. The notion of a 'project' is quasi-theatrical (think of Prospero's masque-project in *The Tempest*) but it is also the language of monopolies. The democratic aspect of the venture has been called into question from the outset, not least in light of the terms of deference Dol applies to her male colleagues: 'Sovereign' (Subtle) and 'General' (Face); and Richard Burt has suggested that the professionalization of the early modern theatre created an atmosphere in which joint-stock companies became little more than personal monopolies.[13] A social hierarchy operates in this city-state and Dol envisages all too clearly, with a Machiavellian notion of the inbuilt decay of all political institutions, that the senators themselves will be the downfall of this republic: 'Will you be/Your own destructions, gentlemen?' (I.i.104–5). This republic is visibly disintegrating when the play commences; Dol asks, 'Do not we/Sustain our parts?' (I.i.144—5), only to be told by Subtle, 'Yes, but they are not equal.' (I.i.145). The theatrical metaphor persists: 'Why, if your part exceed today, I hope/Ours may, tomorrow, match it.' (I.i.146–7).

Dol knows the consequences of absolutism. She may warn Mammon of the perils of his free-state ruminations but for her the threat is contained in the all-too visible signs of state authority in seventeenth-century London: the stocks, the scaffolds, and the gibbets of the hangman:

> Rascals,
> Would run themselves from breath to see me ride,
> Or you t'have but a hole, to thrust your heads in,
> For which you should pay ear-rent? No, agree.
> And may Don Provost ride a-feasting, long,
> In his old velvet jerkin, and stained scarfs
> (My noble Sovereign, and worthy General)
> Ere we contribute a new crewel garter
> To his most worsted worship.
>
> (I.i.166–74)

It is apt that Dol, who has fretted from the beginning that the master of the house might return and 'mar all', or that the neighbours might discover 'all', should be the one to announce that very occurrence in Act V.

Subtle and Face compete for the position of absolute monarch in this city-state, Subtle adopting the title of 'Sovereign', Face more cynically adopting the 'republican' cover of 'General'. Each claims praise for 'authoring" the other. Subtle claims the credit for rescuing Face from his life of cobwebs and subservience 'below stairs' in an act of alchemical transcendence:

> Thou vermin, have I ta'en thee out of dung,
> So poor, so wretched, when no living thing
> Would keep thee company, but a spider, or worse?
> Raised thee from brooms, and dust, and wat'ring pots?
> Sublimed thee, and exalted thee, and fixed thee
> I'the third region, called our state of grace?
> (I.i.64–9)

whereas Face is all too quick to remind Subtle of his humbler origins: the occasion for some fine Jonsonian descriptive passages:

> But I shall put you in mind, sir, at Pie Corner,
> Taking your meal of steam in, from cooks' stalls,
> Where, like the father of Hunger, you did walk
> Piteously costive, with your pinched-horn-nose,
> And your complexion, of the Roman wash,
> Struck full of black and melancholic worms,
> Like powder corns, shot, at th'artillery yard.
> (I.i.25–31)

The incessant competition of the 'venture tripartite' mirrors other rivalries in other Jonsonian stage republics: Sejanus and Tiberius, Cicero and Catiline, and Volpone and Mosca. Each of these plays, like *The Alchemist*, is concerned with a 'pseudo-republicanism' that shields the real operations of power.

For all their onstage warfare (the play after all commences mid-quarrel), Subtle and Face come together with perfect comic timing to stage the explosion of the laboratory in IV.v. The perfectly synchronized experiment is a further example of the theatrical awareness of Subtle and Face. What is remarkable about their volatile relationship is that in public, in performance, it coheres perfectly. The querulous opening scene might even be that of two lead actors battling over the spotlight; we enter in the midst of a bitterly contested debate over primacy in the action. It may also constitute an egotistical clash over who should perform the roles of stage manager and director – and that distinction is crucial for the theatre's own social hierarchy. The paradox of the stage republic is being played out before our eyes.

III YOU GET WHAT YOU P(R)AY FOR: THE BLACKFRIARS COMMUNITY

The traditional perception of touring acting companies as little more than vagrants has been well documented;[14] city authorities feared they might encourage disorder and this fear was embodied in various acts of prohibition and censorship. Theatre's impact on society was often regarded as being akin to contagion or an epidemic, an image given a frighteningly real dimension with the numerous outbreaks of plague in this period. These outbreaks necessitated the closure of the playhouses which, as densely populated buildings, increased the risk of infection and therefore the rapid spread of disease. This particular touring company seeks a more permanent theatrical base for its shows and discovers the perfect venue in the form of Lovewit's plague-vacated London residence. This house of course happens to be in the Blackfriars region of the city, within the vicinity of a theatre, and therefore of a theatregoing public. This is a joint-stock company of actor-sharers, able as Face says (I.i.185–8) to take a fortnight's break without falling apart.

This joint-stock acting company is popular; they attract a large cross-section of London society to their door. This notion of a target population for their activities is deliberately wide in its application and could even be a reference to the socially representative *dramatis personae* of the play. It could also refer to the audience in the theatre watching any given performance of *The Alchemist*. Smallwood stresses the deliberate collapse of real and fictive boundaries in this play, effected especially by the contemporaneous Blackfriars staging. Whilst there are a great number of 'illusion breaking remarks' (the phrase is Smallwood's) of the kind so expertly explored by Anne Righter (Barton) in *Shakespeare and the*

Idea of the Play[15] (for example, the references to cues and costumes, and to the borrowing of a Spanish disguise from a recent production of Kyd's *The Spanish Tragedy*),[16] the overriding sense is of something more complex than mere theatrical self-consciousness in operation.

Steven Mullaney has described the theatrical rehearsal as

> a period of free-play during which alternatives can be staged, unfamiliar roles tried out, the range of one's power to convince or persuade explored with some license; it is a period of performance, but one in which the customary demands of decorum are suspended, along with the expectations of final or perfected form.[17]

The sense of a rehearsal dominates when *The Alchemist* opens with Subtle and Face in mid-argument. The feeling is almost that we have invaded a tense rehearsal situation where the lead actors are clashing over egotistical and artistic desires which have possibly been held delicately in check until this very moment. There is an element of display and a testing of linguistic skill on both men's behalf. The partnership of Face and Subtle coheres with stunning effect before its various audiences; indeed it seems almost to thrive on account of this strategy of clashing. As soon as Dapper enters the scene, the bitter wrangling seems to disappear, as completely as their personal histories have been obliterated, for anyone but themselves, beneath the new guises of the Alchemist and his Captain. This also conforms to Richard Sennett's formula, that the city and the theatre are spaces where we meet with strangers who know little of our personal history and therefore invite innovation and performance; the free play indulged in by Face and Subtle is at the expense (quite literally) of their visitors.[18]

For all their arguments, Face and Subtle clearly lay considerable store by their partnership, or rather they have to, since in a strange way each is reliant upon the other. In acting terms, these two performers have to spend a remarkable percentage of play-time onstage and, even more significantly, together. Their lines spin off from one another; their exits and entrances are dependent upon each other's cues, and their timing is a matter of implicit trust with all the door-openings and disguises which the plot entails. A knowledge of the script-learning methods of early modern theatre, for which we do have extant documentary evidence, where actors were given prompt-books containing just their own lines and their cues, with no coherent or complete rendition of each scene, enhances this idea of the lead actors' mutual dependency. In this play without the ability of these two actors to work off each other the alchemical scheme and indeed the entire drama would collapse; their relationship offers a kind of metaphor for performance.

Homogenizing though the effects of performance are for this company, there is also the indisputable sense that once that performance is set in motion a degree of control is sacrificed. Complete control is now qualified by the potential for audience interpretations; the clients provide various reasons why Face, Subtle and Dol must think on their feet. The analogy with the authorial position is clear; Jonson too in any performance sacrifices, both to the audiences and to the performers, part of his ability to determine the meaning and outcome of his plays. The contradictions of Jonson's authorial stance are crystallized here; the tyrannical democracy of the Jonsonian drama is embodied in the contradictions of *The Alchemist*.

It is Dol who is most frightened by the judgemental audience throughout the high-pitched opening scene. Several times she attempts to quieten her male colleagues for fear they might be overheard:

> Will you have
> The neighbours hear you? Will you betray all?
> Hark, I hear somebody.
>
> (I.i.7–9)

In Act V we will learn that the neighbours have indeed heard everything and, as if to reinforce the points made in the previous paragraph, produced their own variant readings of the situation.

If the very fact of the play's theatricality is contained in its vehement denial of the same, then so is the ending of this play contained in its beginning. In a play so dependent for its impact upon audiences, upon reactions of surprise, and a predominant sense of chance and improvisation, there is also a remarkable sense of inevitability – not least about the neighbours' remarks, and the master's return – despite Face's assurances that they should 'fear not him': 'While there dies one a week,/O'th' plague, he's safe, from thinking toward London' (I.i.182–3).

There is a battle for authority between Subtle and Face. Both claim ultimate responsibility and credit for having dreamed up and organized the alchemical scheme. Both therefore demand a larger cut of the spoils. The careful balance between the organized and the impromptu in this play – its 'organized chaos' – highlights the need in any theatrical community (or, indeed, any republic) for a decision-maker, however collective the activity, and however communal the intentions or results.

Another battle for authority stems from the play's two Anabaptists. Jonson's careful demarcation of this pair is rarely explicated; he is not offering a generic portrait – just as Drugger is no stereotypical grocer, neither are Tribulation Wholesome and Ananias Puritan stereotypes. The specificity of their faith as Anabaptists (an extreme wing of Puritanism) has already been emphasized. Tribulation is undoubtedly the more worldly of the two; in many respects, with his practical politics, he represents a potential rival to Face and Subtle's schemes. He is the one character who sets out from the very start to cozen the cozeners, although Pertinax Surly soon follows suit.[19]

The best directors are those who allow the actors to reach their own decisions. The conscious evasiveness of the control figure is a fascinating one and has its political paradigms, not least in Machiavelli's guideline to being a pragmatic prince. In Chapter XVIII of *The Prince*, entitled 'How princes should honour their word', he stresses how 'one must know how to colour one's actions and to be a great liar and deceiver. Men are so simple, and so much creatures of circumstance, that the deceiver will always find someone ready to be deceived.'[20] The Machiavellian notion of behind-the-scenes control seems to constitute Tribulation's less-than-wholesome working theory: the less you are visibly enacting control, the more likely it is you will achieve the very depth of power that you seek.

Ananias is by comparison extremist and exclusivist in his attitudes, battling to come to terms with his more prosaic and pragmatic pastor:

TRIBULATION   Good brother, we must bend unto all means,
              That may give furtherance to the holy cause.
ANANIAS   Which his cannot: the sanctified cause
              Should have a sanctified course.
TRIBULATION   Not always necessary,

> The children of perdition are, ofttimes,
> Made instruments even of the greatest works.
> Beside, we should give somewhat to man's nature,
> The place he lives in, still about the fire
> And fume of metals, that intoxicate
> The brain of man, and make him prone to passion.
> (III.i.11–20)

The fire of Lovewit's house is more literal than theological hellfire; it is the furnace of the clients' imaginations that Subtle and Face so politicly fan. They fully comprehend the naiveté of the populace and how 'The common people are always impressed by appearances and results.'[21] Both Face and Subtle possess the qualities of rule, both are certainly fine actors, but as the play progresses it becomes increasingly clear that whilst Subtle is more obviously performing for their public, it is Face who is engineering events.

It seems that leadership can never be successfully shared by Face and Subtle in a truly cooperative venture; instead, one or the other must at any given moment dominate (and both must always dominate Dol). Jonson's theatrical ambitions were somewhat akin; his printing of the 1616 Folio proved that he did not freely relinquish texts into the public, pluralist domain and yet he positively welcomed audience interaction in the very structure of his drama. There is a Machiavellian awareness of the flaws inherent in the republican structure evident here.

There are absolutists in *The Alchemist*, but Ben Jonson is not one of them: Tribulation Wholesome is. He demands the 'restoring of the silenced saints' (III.i.38) and dreams, with some encouragement from Subtle, of being a 'temporal lord' on earth; he silences Ananias's spiritual objections and is so set on earthly power that he will sell the orphans' goods for the purposes of achieving it, claiming that 'Casting of money may be lawful' (III.ii.153). Tribulation has a rival for supremacy though in the bulky figure of a new Jacobean knight, Sir Epicure Mammon, who has purchased his way to position and now hopes to complete his social climb by purchasing the elixir.

IV THE MASTER OF THE REVELS: ABSENTEE MONARCHS AND ABSOLUTISTS

Sir Epicure Mammon's voluptuous mind ensures that he projects his dreams far beyond the confines of the place he inhabits, far beyond the grimy haunts of Blackfriars, towards the New World, and even the New Jerusalem. His nomenclature signals both economic and sexual consumption and his ambitions are similarly all-encompassing. Critics have abstracted Mammon into being a generic representative of knighthood, of the corrupt and hedonistic Jacobean aristocracy, and even of innate avarice. What in truth renders him so interesting in the theatre is his utter originality, and in particular his remarkable style of speech, as voluptuous as his dreams in its use of imagery and punctuation.

Mammon is, in expression at least, another absolutist, if not a monomaniac. He has an act-opening at II.i. (in that he is like Tribulation Wholesome, a companion absolutist at III.i.) and mistakenly believes that this is his play (he is akin to Volpone in that). His dream is really one of possession. If capitalism was inextricably bound up with the ventures of travellers to the New World, then Mammon's dreams also make it clear that he shares with them their will and ability to cross immense distances in search of profit;[22] the distances he travels are entirely imaginative but the immense confidence of these travellers is something he clearly shares.

Alchemy appears to create a comparable sense of wonder in Mammon to that experienced and articulated by New World voyagers:

> This is the utopian moment of travel; when you realize that what seems most unattainably marvelous, most desirable, is what you almost already have, what you could have – if you could only strip away the banality and corruption of the everyday ...[23]

Eastward Ho, Jonson's collaborative playtext, co-written with Chapman and Marston, aligns those characters who have New World ambitions, such as the mushroom knight Sir Petronel Flash, with those who claim knowledge of alchemy, such as Francis Quicksilver. The central scene of that play (III.iii) intriguingly lifts accounts of the Elizabethan colonies and settlements in Virginia and their attendant lust for gold from Richard Hakluyt's *Principal*

Navigations to expose the mercenary and morally dubious motives of characters such as Sir Petronel and Quicksilver in their attitudes to life in general.[24]

Mammon's initial stage-entrance in *The Alchemist* is vocalized in the rhetoric of sixteenth-century and seventeenth-century travel writings:

> Come on, sir. Now you set your foot on shore
> In *novo orbe*: here's the rich Peru:
> And there within, sir, are the golden mines,
> Great Solomon's Ophir! He was sailing to't
> Three years, but we have reached it in ten months.
> (II.i.1–5)

The bathos of this is self-evident; Blackfriars comes a rather poor second to Peru, as England does to the New World: 'Yes, and I'll purchase Devonshire, and Cornwall,/And make them perfect Indies!' (II.i.35–6).

Mammon's rituals of possession are entirely speech-enacted; he displays what Paul de Man would have termed the 'errancy of language' in his wayward hyperboles and translations of experience. Even punctuation, usually a constraining force, seems excessive here.[25] The unnaturalness of Mammon's desire for gold is unmistakable: the Blackfriars *conquistador* becomes increasingly consumed by the related lust. Initially at least, it may seem that Subtle and Face are the more likely *conquistadors* since they embroil Mammon in the 'grossly unequal gift exchange' that for Greenblatt characterizes the literature of exploration. They offer glass beads for pearls as Columbus did to the Indians. To begin with, Mammon harbours dreams of altruism as well as possession, as Subtle details:

> He has, this month, talked as he were possessed,
> And, now, he's dealing pieces on't away.
> Methinks I see him, entering ordinaries,
> Dispensing for the pox; and plaguy houses,
> Reaching his dose; walking Moorfields for lepers;
> And off'ring citizens' wives pomander-bracelets,
> As his preservative, made of the elixir; ...
> If his dreams last, he'll turn the age to gold.
> (I.iv.16–22, 29)

It is Mammon's companion, Surly, who plays the absolutist:

> Faith, I have a humour
> I would not willingly be gulled. Your stone
> Cannot transmute me.
> (II.i.77–9)

Increasingly, however, Mammon's venture becomes self-serving and self-indulgent; London begins to seem too small for his projections, despite being one of the fastest-growing European cities:

> My only care is
> Where to get stuff enough, now, to project on,
> This town will not half serve me.
> (II.ii.11–13)

Whilst he may claim the intention of employing his wealth in pious matters, Mammon's catalogue of good works is persistently invaded by lustful desires:

> I shall employ it all, in pious uses,
> Founding of colleges, and grammar schools,
> Marrying young virgins, building hospitals,
> And now and then, a church.
> (II.iii.49–52)

Although in an admittedly rather different fashion, like Shakespeare's Gonzalo in *The Tempest*, Mammon contradicts his own quasi-republican outlines: 'The latter end of his commonwealth forgets the beginning' (*The Tempest*, II.i.158). He effectively loses sight of everything stable in his (to use Agnew's phrase) 'fraternization with impossibilities'. His loss of control in the face of Dol's lengthy recitations from Broughton merely pre-empts his loss of control and power following the explosion of the laboratory and his hopes. In Act V we find him pleading to Surly to, 'Play not the tyrant' (V.iii.4), subjected as he is to the gamester's 'I told you so' discourse. For Mammon it has been purely a dream of possession; his absolutism has also disintegrated, his final line echoing this realization: 'What! In a dream?' (V.v.83). He may still argue that the loss is ultimately the commonwealth's, but his free state was always one where it was envisaged he would be ruler and freeholder.

Mammon wants only gold, and he even begins to define himself as a second Jove – in doing so, aligning himself with the current monarch, James I:

> Now, Epicure,
> Heighten thyself, talk to her, all in gold;
> Rain her as many showers, as Jove did drops
> Unto his Danaë; show the god a miser,
> Compared with Mammon. What? The stone will do't.
> She shall feel gold, taste gold, hear gold, sleep gold:
> Nay, we will *concumbere* gold. I will be puissant,
> And mighty in my talk to her!
>
> (IV.i.24–31)

Mammon's choice of Ovidian myth to exemplify his point is telling. As one of James's new 'mushroom' knights, his claims to status have distinctly fiscal foundations; that he should therefore choose to be Jove entering Danaë's tower as a shower of gold is entirely congruent with the driving motivations of his character – money and sex. Mammon's dreams of metamorphosis are as hopeless as the quest for the elixir; he is beguiled rather by the theatrical transformations of Subtle, Face and Dol.

In the theme of deceptive metamorphosis in the play, John S. Mebane has traced a series of parodic references to supposedly republican political values:

> The theme of deceptive metamorphosis is ... connected to Jonson's satire on Renaissance utopianism and millenarianism. As soon as he establishes the theme of false transformation and role playing he moves into the description of the relationship between the con artists as a republic or a commonwealth. Their 'venture tripartite' is a political arrangement. ... The important point is that the commonwealth the three clowns have established is ordered in accordance with the egalitarian ideals that Renaissance thinkers often associated with the lost Golden Age.[26]

Subtle's and Face's most dramatic metamorphosis takes place in the tradition of theatrical denouement in the final act. Act V signals a rapid turnaround not only in events but also in perspective in *The Alchemist*. Suddenly, after a continuous and almost claustrophobic indoors setting in the same room of Lovewit's house for the first four acts, we and the play are thrust out into the cold of the Blackfriars street.[27] As an audience we are thus identified with the neighbours who are recounting tales of noises they have heard emanating from the house. We have heard the same; those noises constitute the dialogue of the play, although our interpretations might differ. Peter Holland has written of the careful delineation of each of these neighbours, making particular reference to the remarkable (because unremarkable) figure of neighbour six, whose highly individual voice and small personal history ('About,/Some three weeks since, I heard a doleful cry,/As I sat up, a-mending my wife's stockings' (V.i.32–4)) ensure that any homogenized reading of the neighbours as a generic whole is expertly avoided by Jonson.[28] In acknowledging the crowd Jonson does not ignore the essential differentiations within the group.[29] The identification of audience and neighbours would seem a very public gesture – carrying the play into the streets and recognizing its implications for the populace; yet the device of bringing the audience into the final act and often directly onto the stage was a technique derived from Jonson's more royally connected pursuit of masque-writing. In masques, the noble spectators often participated in the final dance or movement. This public theatre gesture towards masque structures casts Lovewit, the returning master (a figure of Plautine origin), less as the 'everyday man ... who is the spectator of the common scene'[30] than as the monarch himself. James I, like Lovewit, would have vacated London during times of serious epidemic; the plague having initiated and induced in Elizabethan times the 'tradition' of summer country progresses when the heat meant the risk of infection in the city was at its zenith. Lovewit's evidential concern for self-protection would seem to echo this:

FACE   The house, sir, has been visited.
LOVEWIT   What? With the plague? Stand thou then further.
                                                                    (V.ii.4–5)

Lovewit regards himself as something of an indulgent master; we have already explored (see Chapter 2) ways in which Jonson appeared to plead for comparable indulgence, especially towards authors, from James I. If Face is the author of events, then Lovewit certainly treats him with great leniency, tolerating his role-playing and even accepting some of his material rewards, with the self-serving claim: 'I love a teeming wit, as I love my nourishment'

(V.i.16). He may refer to Face as 'My brain' but what is perhaps most shrewd is the way he manages to turn his late arrival to personal advantage, even planning to marry the rich widow Pliant himself. His return is entirely possessional in its gestures, 'The house is mine here' (V.v.26), and befits the actions of an absolutist manipulating his subjects in order to further consolidate his rule. It is Lovewit after all who gives the orders to Jeremy (Face) in the final scene – 'Fill a pipe-full, Jeremy' (V.v.141) – by naming him thus he stresses the limited social application of the guise of Face, however powerful we as an audience may have perceived that persona to be. Similarly it is Lovewit who gives Jeremy leave to speak the epilogue – as indeed James would be expected to give Jonson leave to perform his part in society, that of writer and social critic. Lovewit enacts then the effective role of dramatic censor or Master of the Revels;[31] he declares, 'I will be ruled by thee in anything, Jeremy' (V.v.143) but this is a carefully calculated show of indulgence, akin to the Jacobean displays of clemency that Greenblatt recounts in *Shakespearean Negotiations*.[32] Lovewit claims:

> That master
> That had received such happiness by a servant,
> In such a widow, and with so much wealth,
> Were very ungrateful if he would not be
> A little indulgent to that servant's wit,
> And help his fortune, though with some small strain
> Of his own candour. Therefore, gentlemen,
> And kind spectators, if I have outstripped
> An old man's gravity, or strict canon, think
> What a young wife, and a good brain may do;
> Stretch age's truth sometimes, and crack it too.
> Speak for thyself, knave.
>   (V.v.146–57)

Face does speak and tries to accord his newly subordinate, or more precisely resubordinated, position in the drama to the rules, less of social hierarchies, than of theatrical convention: 'My part a little fell in this last scene,/Yet 'twas decorum' (V.v.158–9); he ends the play by casting its moral reflections back out onto the theatre audience(s), thus questioning the extent of Lovewit's absolutism if not offering any precise definition.

Critical accounts of Lovewit vary; some choose to see him as the common, non-comic, non-performing type, normative almost in his retention of a single character, but this ignores his own pragmatic assumption of the Spanish disguise. I think he is a far shrewder character, one of absolutist tendencies in his control of events and use of language in the final act, and one who must bring into doubt any straightforward reading of this play as pro-monarchy and anti-republicanism.

Our sympathies as an audience are not with Lovewit at the end. His Act V return seems somehow too belated to be deserving of the rewards he so rapidly appropriates. In a play of participation he has consciously avoided interaction with the group (although he may be seen as the best improvisor of all). Our sympathies may not be with the dissolved venture either; their fractious collective scarcely constitutes a piece of pro-republican propaganda. The Blackfriars community has in effect been splintered by its collective efforts, perhaps because those efforts were simply not communal enough, or perhaps because such fissures are inherent in any given 'community'. Face, Subtle and Dol have relinquished their initiatives, Mammon and the Anabaptists have lost their investments (secular and temporal), Surly his dignity, and Dapper and Drugger have been humiliated beyond the call of duty. It is left only to the audience to cohere in the act of applause – democratic, egalitarian, republican applause.

6

The Republic in the Fair

The site and situation of the playtext of *Bartholomew Fair* (1614) have strong implications of community and the communal. To what extent however can we trace a 'republic' amidst the booths of Jonson's fair? Whilst there are inherent problems in associating the 'real' Bartholomew Fair with that contained within Jonson's dramatic representation, the annual Smithfield fair on 24 August in the ever-expanding *polis* that was early-seventeenth-century London attracted a diverse and populous gathering – diverse in terms of rank, profession, objective, and personality – and that diversity is also a feature of the stage 'population' of Jonson's play. By extension, it might appear logical to see Jonson's play, like the 'real' fair, as representative of popular culture and popular concerns, but these need not necessarily be democratic nor indeed republican (and these two terms as I have been at pains to suggest are not interchangeable).

A fair could be seen as a space in which it is possible to achieve a greater social democracy, a 'commingling of categories usually kept separate and opposed'.[1] Jonson's diverse stage population in this play would seem to mirror this social effect. Unlike the actual Bartholomew Fair, however, Jonson's dramatic version also looked courtwards through its actions, a fact which problematizes any simplistic reading of its 'popular' or 'populist' concerns. In exploring the 'republic in the fair' in this chapter, then, we will have cause to explore how and why the community of Jonson's play, its 'population', is situated within a debate *between* popular culture and court taste which renders it, like so much of the Jonsonian canon, perilously ambivalent in its politics, and how 'republicanism' to the extent that it exists in the play exists in the theatrical moment rather than in Jonson's politics *per se*.

Bartholomew Fair has often been made an exception in discussions centring on the Jonsonian canon. It is regarded as a 'unique' play, the play in which we find Jonson at his most 'genial' in his infamous altercations with the public theatre audiences, the play in which he is at his most populist and popular in his exercise of dramatic strategy.[2] The polyvocal, highly populated stage of *Bartholomew Fair* is taken to be less elitist, less selective, than other Jonsonian communities.[3] Not surprisingly, the term 'carnivalesque' is often evoked in these literary critical constructions: Jonson's 'celebration' of lower-class, frequently 'grotesque', social interactions is seen in quasi-utopian, sub-Bakhtinian terms as a subversive celebration of the 'popular'.[4] It would seem feasible that this play constitutes a likely site for republican politics, actual or aesthetic, real or theatrical.

The community depicted by *Bartholomew Fair* is, however, far from being a fixed or stable entity and this fact establishes some degree of resistance to any straightforward 'Bakhtinian' reading of the text as celebratory of plebeian or popular culture. That said, the Cultural Materialist re-appropriation of Bakhtin and his theory of the carnivalesque in order to talk about strategic containment by the authorizing power(s) of both author and monarch does not prove the perfect model either in its application to this play.[5] The 'safety-valve' theory of carnival is repulsed by *Bartholomew Fair* in some fascinating ways. The essence of this drama has, I believe, to be seen as something rather more complex than a carnivalesque celebration of London society or a containment of it by the ruling hegemony.[6] Notions of community and communal harmony are subjected to a biting critique within the play, but so too is absolutist authority.

The Fair can in one sense be seen as the epitome of 'contained subversion', although only ironically since the play as a whole self-consciously parodies the 'disguised duke' genre popular in contemporary Jacobean theatre.[7] The 'real' Bartholomew Fair was a symbol of disorder but was ultimately licensed and regulated; yet this *Bartholomew Fair* is a drama, and (ostensibly) a public theatre drama, and that in itself licenses any performance to behave very differently from 'real life' – a deregulating concept.

Marriage, that ultimate act of social licensing, is a central theme in *Bartholomew Fair*, but, as is typical of the Jonsonian canon, it does not carry with it the harmonizing potential that it does in, say, Shakespearean comedy; marriage here is pared down to its skeletal form of a social contract as partners are matched and mismatched in games of aversion and avoidance throughout the day. Quarlous's 'razed' marriage licence, with Grace Wellborn's name hastily removed to allow for the inclusion of Dame Purecraft's, reduces marriage to a fiscal contract, a financial transaction like any other effected at the Fair – indeed, possibly more mercenary.[8] Quarlous makes no effort to conceal the fact that he is marrying for money; that in order to do so he can illegally employ legal means – that is, the marriage licence, stolen, like so much else, from Bartholomew Cokes – is simply further evidence of the corrupted state of the hallowed marital institution. Licensed activities are, then, in a state of deregulation in *Bartholomew Fair*.

Marriage's status in the play as a ritual or ceremony effects its own analogies with theatre. As Benjamin Bennett has written in relation to the work of Hugo von Hofmannsthal: 'Like marriage itself, the "Zeremonie" in the theater is a symbolic act within society by which the absurdly arbitrary act that is society is reaffirmed and revitalized.'[9] The role of Jonson's theatre audiences in that act of theatrical reaffirmation and revitalization of society will be seen as being crucial to any 'republican' reading of this play. As in the case of the Roman tragedies, an argument is not being made for Jonson as a republican dramatist as such, but as one whose plays, due to the nature of the theatrical experience itself, contain, and enact, the potential for republican interpretation; that potential is realized in, and released by, the audience dynamic that contributes to the production of meaning at any given performance.

The contributory role of any audience is formally recognized by Jonson himself in the Scrivener's drawing up of the Articles of Agreement in the astonishing Induction to this play. If these Articles recognize the contractual and consensual aspects of the theatrical experience, so the participation or otherwise of Jonson's characters in the fair proves representative within the play of their stance on questions of community – political or otherwise. Grace Wellborn adamantly denies any politic intentions with regard to her choice of a suitor; if it was money she desired then marriage to Cokes would seem a less appalling prospect than it does: 'these are not my aims; I must have a husband I must love, or I cannot live with him. I shall ill make one of these politic wives!' (IV.iii.16–19). It is Grace who has been most reluctant from the beginning to participate in the fair, partaking in none of Cokes's desires to experience all of its sights and sounds. She prefers to close her eyes to the harsh commercial realities it embodies, casting herself instead as the heroine of some arcane romance. In truth, love, or rather sex, at the fair is being debased to the level of just another transaction carried out amidst the booths; 'pig' and 'punk' are the guiding authorities of the gathering and, in this respect, Ursla the pig-woman is undoubtedly the fair's human representative, its body 'politic'.[10]

What Grace aspires to ignore is the contractual basis of all we do, be it at the fair, at the theatre, or in society itself; she positively prefers to abide in the fictive realm of romance where men duel for her love laden under extravagant *nom-de-plumes* (the names they select – Argalus and Palamon – are taken from Sir Philip Sidney's pastoral romance *Arcadia* and Shakespeare and Fletcher's contemporaneous play *The Two Noble Kinsmen* (1613–14) respectively and it is worth noting that this aspect of the plot directly invokes the predominant courtly taste for romantic genres of literature: Jonson's play is glancing towards Whitehall, although the parodic nature of the reference may still support claims for the populist concerns of *Bartholomew Fair*).

The fair in the play has been seen as an analogue for the theatre and for London itself. The 'real' Fair was one of the various ceremonies and festivals conducted throughout the London year that helped to consolidate the city's civic identity by associating it with the physical body of the community.[11] Yet the fair was necessarily marginal, placed as it was at Smithfield on the outskirts of the city, in order to reduce its polluting effects (the meat market was regularly held there and this geographical placement helped to contain the resultant offal and ordure on the city boundaries). The fair was also marginal in that it performed a kind of commentary upon normal civic procedures. In this way too analogies can be drawn between it and the space of the Liberties on the other side of the city proper: the site of the public theatres including the Hope in Southwark where *Bartholomew Fair* saw its first performance. It should, of course, be stressed that no disingenuous claim is being made here that Jacobean public theatre was necessarily anti-authoritarian or subversive in its stances simply because of its topographical placement. Richard Dutton has, however, spoken recently of the 'unprecedented, quasi-democratic dimension to Elizabethan and early Stuart literary culture, that of the public playhouses of London'. He emphasizes that the phrase 'democratic' is necessarily relative in its usage, but that nevertheless even those playhouses which were under licence to the authorities were party to a 'more broadly-based "readership"' at this time.[12]

The first performance of *Bartholomew Fair* took place at the Hope on 31 October 1614; the second performance took place before King

James at Whitehall on the following day: no further performances are known of until 1661. These bare facts have led to much speculation with Keith Sturgess suggesting that the Hope performance, since the house itself, part-theatre, part-bear-pit (as the Induction to this play makes clear), had been opened so recently, was a mere dress rehearsal for the staging at court.[13] That last theory would endorse a 'contained' reading of the play and its interest in carnival culture, seeing the anarchy of the fair as diffused by the controlling ideology of the elitist commission and performance, although it would not explain the absence of subsequent productions until the Restoration (when of course the play of interpretation being brought to bear on 'Jonson' and his plays had undergone another seismic shift).[14]

The aforementioned Articles of Agreement were clearly designed with the Hope performance in mind and the linkage of the Liberties and Smithfield in the play's conception is, I would argue, equally deliberate. The alternative prologue for the court could suggest simply that there were two very different performance contexts envisaged for the playtext.[15] The space which that creates for speculation as to the separate and distinct reception(s) of various aspects of the play within the two locales is a crucial one and one which contributes to the antithetical readings it continues to produce amongst critics. It should be added that the version as we have it of the 'public theatre' *Bartholomew Fair*, whilst it can be read for popular inflections, may not be an entirely stable entity itself: its *dramatis personae* would have called for half as many players again as we know the company of the Lady Elizabeth's Men (who we know to have performed the play on this occasion) usually contained. It has been suggested that the Lady Elizabeth's Men were enlarged by amalgamating at this time with the theatre-less boys' company the Children of the Queen's Revels for whom Jonson had authored *Epicoene*. This fact at the very least renders this an unusual and scarcely archetypal public theatre performance, so we should be wary of reading out from the *Bartholomew Fair* experience at the Hope to other contemporaneous public theatre plays in our search for 'republican' potential. Once again the play, and possibly Jonson, adopt a mediatory role between obviously populist or dissenting voices and the authorized edicts of the court.

Rather than offering an untrammelled celebration of popular culture, or a blatant attack on the King, the play functions as a complex and subtle negotiation between the two spheres and between their separate cultural forms. The ballad scene featuring Nightingale is central in the play because it negotiates precisely that crucial centre space (aesthetic and political) where different discourses and ideologies collide. The polyvocality[16] of *Bartholomew Fair* has led many critics to describe it as a population writ small, more specifically as a microcosm of early modern London.[17] But the community of *Bartholomew Fair* is surely also just that, the community of *Bartholomew Fair*, which provides, on its own grounds and on its own terms, one of Stanley Fish's 'interpretive communities'.[18] That is not to discount Jonson's ability to take into dramatic and intellectual account the social transitions that were occurring in contemporary London – the new influx of rural poor, sudden suburban expansion, resultant overcrowding, the emergent *nouveaux riches*, and increasingly fervent movements of Puritanism and capitalism (not always unconnected) – but it is to stress the inalienable right of the play-community to be self-representative, and it is for this reason that I am also resisting too close an identification of the 'real' and the fictive Bartholomew Fairs in this discussion of Jonson and republicanism. The 'republicanism' of this play, such as it is, exists primarily in the theatrical experience of *Bartholomew Fair* because it is born out of the intrinsic dynamic of that experience.

It is the Justice of the Peace who presides over the fair, Justice Overdo, who persistently refers to its population as a 'commonwealth' or 'republic', within which he regards himself, of course, as the ultimate licence-giver and authority (his speeches resound with the term 'warrant'). Overdo no doubt regards himself as a 'commonwealthsman', but such a singular and absolutist assertion of the doctrine of power places a question-mark alongside his understandings of 'republicanism'; his would be an *ottimati*-led republic, along the lines counselled by Guicciardini rather than Machiavelli in sixteenth-century Italy, and not of the radical populace-based variety Annabel Patterson has striven, occasionally somewhat manipulatively, to find support for in Jacobean drama.[19] Overdo, in his parodic role of the 'disguised duke', sees himself as a representative of the state, even invoking Jamesian rhetoric to reinforce this position (the topical allusion of Overdo's speeches to James I has been well-documented).[20] Of course, he cannot help but suggest the King's own tendency towards hyperbolic self-comparisons with Jove, this being a central conceit of Jacobean iconography and the masque genre: 'Neither is the hour of my severity yet come, to reveal myself, wherein, cloud-like, I will break out in rain and hail, lightning and thunder, upon the head of enormity' (V.ii.4–7). Undoubtedly Overdo attempts here to create the kind of anxiety effect by which Jacobean law was frequently consolidated;[21] but, in truth, his position in the magistracy links him more obviously to local civic authority of the kind Jonson would explore in greater depth in *A Tale of a Tub* in 1633 than to the monarch. Overdo is a product of the city not the court, and his mediatory role in the play (functioning as commentator on the fair for audiences) renders him in effect the London recorder – a civic role which exposes him to our judgement and to his constituency's election.[22] By directing his audiences towards an understanding of this fact, Jonson encourages them to question the absolutist nature of Overdo's authority. At best, a constitution with a limited monarchy is sought by the fair community.

Constitutions are written contracts and this wider sphere of reference for the play should never be underestimated: the Articles of Agreement drawn up between audience and playwright in the Induction may be a synecdoche for the social contract between a monarch and his/her subjects, suggesting the need to accord those 'paying' subjects certain rights:

> It is further agreed that every person here have his or their freewill of censure, to like or dislike, at their own charge; the author having now departed with his right, it shall be lawful for any man to judge his six penn'orth, his twelve penn'orth, so to his eighteen pence, two shillings, half a crown, to the value of his place – provided always his place get not above his wit.
> (Induction, ll. 99–106)[23]

Jonson though was not the author of political tracts; he viewed himself as neither a political spokesperson, a precursor of Hobbes, nor a theatrical pseudo-monarch. However, he did see parallels to be drawn between questions of authorial right and the potential tyranny of either dramatist or acting company over a text and the debate over the prerogative, limited or otherwise, of the monarch him/herself: questions of democratic rights were prevalent in both domains. Once again we are talking here about republicanism in a dramatic context.

Language can be seen as yet another process of transaction underway at the Fair. The multiple dialects of *Bartholomew Fair* are one version of the linguistic transaction – the 'game of vapours' representing an extreme under which the exchange is no longer productive. Gillian Beer has discussed the fiscal meaning of 'utterance' in the Middle Ages:[24] utterance is the bringing of wares for sale; the production of meaning therefore requires both a buyer and a seller (the linguistic game is one of 'vapours' since no dialogic transaction actually takes place). Conversations may produce dominant exploitative salespersons, like Lantern Leatherhead duping Bartholomew Cokes, and theatre itself is sold to audiences, requiring their presence in varying numbers for the production of meaning. The game of vapours is also indicative of the multifarious tensions the fair only just holds in balance: the game at its extremity threatens to explode into violence and self-destruction. In the *Discourses* Machiavelli suggested that the holding in tension of two warring factions was the nature of a successful republic, since otherwise that republic was likely to produce tyranny and dictatorship in its struggle for democracy.[25] Jonson astutely recognizes these political truisms in the communities of his comedies as well as in his more clearly Machiavellian-influenced Roman tragedies.

The acting company was itself a sociopolitical 'republic', liable as it was to protracted power struggles as we saw in the case of *The Alchemist* (see Chapter 5). What the 'Articles of Agreement' indicate is Jonson's awareness that any performance is dependent upon the nature, composition, and reception of any one audience, on any one day. The specificity of the fair's occurrence or 'happening' is extended to the theatrical event. A certain group of individuals is held together, ostensibly by the dramatic text and the particular ramifications of its performance, under the collective title of audience for a limited period:

> the theater of the Renaissance more closely resembled an occasional discretionary compact struck between performers and audience. The transaction consisted of two 'partners' who agreed in effect, to authorize one another for the determinate duration of the play and, at the same time, to immunize one another from any extratheatrical consequences that would follow from a literal or, for that matter, a ritualist reading of their collaborative fiction.[26]

The theatrical contract drawn up at the outset of *Bartholomew Fair* establishes that 'even meaning becomes a commodity, something to be haggled over in the transaction between stage and gallery'.[27] Yet there is something more intrinsic to Jonson's artistic, as opposed to mercantilist, persona under debate here: the paradoxically liberating and yet self-negating recognition by the author that any reader or spectator produces an autonomous response to his/her work. Jonson credits the 'productive and emancipated spectator' that performance theorists such as Susan Bennett have described as a product of the contemporary theatrical experience.[28] As John Creaser has persuasively argued, 'Jonson's dramaturgy is founded not on distrust but on confidence in the audience' and herein I would argue lies its 'republican' potential.[29]

Jonson himself wrote in the *Masque of Queens* that 'a writer should always trust somewhat to the capacity of the spectator. . . .' (ll. 95–6). Yet that trust could be betrayed by the unpredictable and volatile group context of the audience as the treatment of Jonson's tragedies and some of his later plays testified. The mix or blend in an audience was important since the responses of others could prove infectious (and the topical plague references in a number of Jonson's plays – *Epicoene*, *The Alchemist*, and *Bartholomew Fair* amongst them – touch on this fact). Our responses, in society and in the theatre, are constantly guided by others; in this respect audiences were regarded as an analogue to the 'fickle multitude' of popular political consciousness and chided in pamphlets and plays alike for their aptitude to ebb and flow in opinion. Not only were dramatists, texts and players at risk, however: the very act of participation in an audience was also inherently dangerous for its constituent members who in some sense sought this paradoxical 'comfort of strangers' (similar ideas are at play in *Volpone* in the protagonists' constant drive outwards into the *polis* and away from the *oikos*). Certainly the fellowship of the Fair may have this troubling instigation; Nightingale and Edgeworth seek the comfort of strangers for alternative reasons – Nightingale, a ballad-singer, selects the busiest thoroughfares in which to sing, thus enabling Edgeworth, a thief, to ply his trade amid the confusions and convenient distractions of the crowd. The audience though makes a political undertaking in cohering (or not) in the activity of theatregoing as opposed to fairing – even if only in the gesture of social tolerance that it constitutes.

If the fair strips linguistics down to a mere transaction, then Jonson was also aware of language's contagious qualities. Poetry is described in these diagnostic terms by Overdo when he is an onlooker to the friendship and professional alliance between Edgeworth and Nightingale:

> I have followed him all the Fair over, and still I find him with this songster; and I begin shrewdly to suspect their familiarity, and the young man of a terrible taint, poetry! With which idle disease, if he be infected, there's no hope of him in a state-course. *Actum est* of him for a commonwealths-man if he go to't in rhyme once.
>
> (III.v.4–10)

This is Touchstone's theory of poetry, as the most 'feigning'; language as artifice is always foregrounded in audience consciousness of the fair. Jonson acknowledged that this reflected back onto his own trade; he was aware of how perilously close he, as a writer, trod to fraudulence and deception. Overdo sees the art of poetry as disqualifying writers from political office – specifically those offices representative of the people, the commonwealth or common weal; Jonson though is surely encouraging audiences to deduce the opposite and to conclude that poetry and ballads are political undertakings, relevant to the state. Nightingale's lyrics are aesthetically calculating and they have the firm objective, albeit illegal, of robbing Cokes; his craft is scarcely art for art's sake.

This heightened state of self-perception provides an explanation for the aforementioned centrality of the scene in III.v. where Nightingale and Edgeworth collude via ballad-making to rob the naive spectator that is Bartholomew Cokes. Cokes is easily drawn to the songs that Nightingale is 'selling' (and again we have words as the mainstay of a financial transaction: Shakespeare employed a similar situation with Autolycus's songs in *The Winter's Tale* (1610-11)).[30] But Nightingale's songs are no mere witty distraction: their lyrics warn against the prevalence of thieves and cutpurses in society: 'It hath been upbraided to men of my trade,/That oftentimes we are the cause of this crime.' (III.v.96–7); yet again Cokes fails to register the tell-tale signs that language offers him.

Purchasing goods, wares, and (fickle) friendships on sight as he goes, Cokes is a gloriously amusing example of conspicuous consumption. At the close of day, he finds himself bereft of everything, even his initial companion and prospective wife. Although presciently aware that his forename establishes or even endorses some vocative affinity between himself and the Fair, he fails to complete his reading of this signifier: for his surname is London slang for a fool and this is indeed what the fair and its community make of him. As a member of the rural gentry, Cokes cannot discourse fully in the city's urban (and perhaps urbane) language(s) and this leaves him open to abuse, persuasion, and deception. Quarlous, as astutely as ever, notes that Cokes is 'a rogue in apprehension' (I.v.153).

Not that *Bartholomew Fair* allows the audience to adopt any oversuperior stance towards Cokes for very long. The play's own signs (like those of London by which Wasp describes Cokes as being so entranced) are deliberately oblique, and readers and spectators are liable, even encouraged, to lose their way amidst its labyrinthine configurations of characters and plot development. Even the reassuringly distinguishable Jonsonian 'traits' are shifting sands in this context. Barton has written tellingly about Jonsonian nomenclature and it is true that defining and identifying names often humiliate or humble their characters into understanding, and indeed being understood, but nomenclature is never entirely reliable. Despite a wife-character called Win and a prospective suitor called Winwife, the wife being hunted is initially Dame Purecraft and subsequently Grace. The Fair is prone to blind us with its colour and variety, and therefore we can never differentiate ourselves morally from Cokes. Our judgemental capacity and authority are undermined as much as Overdo's.

Little wonder that Cokes misreads and poorly translates the signs and signals of the fair when his brother-in-law, the justice, persistently partakes of similar misapprehensions. Overdo's occasional soliloquies may hit on the truth but it is always unwittingly, as, for example, when explaining his disguise as 'Mad Arthur of Bradley', he declares:

> Would all men in authority would follow this worthy precedent! For, alas, we are public persons, what do we know? Nay, what can we know? We hear with other men's ears; we see with other men's eyes; a foolish constable, or a sleepy watchman, is all our information.
>
> (II.i.31–6)

Is misunderstanding of this nature the process that generates the individual in a community, notably so in the fair or the theatre? Benjamin Bennett poses the question 'of whether it is our individuality that involves us in misunderstanding, or a prior process of misunderstanding that creates our individuality'.[31] Chance and misunderstanding are seemingly crucial for the practical and linguistic operation of the fair. Cokes is not the only one susceptible to the ballads; Overdo is also in this instance an unquestioning observer, enjoying the 'paltry piece of poetry' and investigating little further than his own pleasurable responses. However, as Nightingale's lyrics warn him, his authority is no protection from the harsh realities: cutpurses have no qualms and will rob near scaffolds or at court (both sites of the execution of the monarch's power):

> At plays and at sermons, and at the sessions,
> 'Tis daily their practice such booty to make:
> Yea, under the gallows, at executions,
> They stick not the stare-abouts' purses to take
>   Nay, one without grace,
>   At a far better place,
> At court, and in Christmas, before the king's face.
>   (III.v.142–8)

This has intriguing connotations for Jonson's perception of his own role as masque-maker (frequently Christmas masque–maker) to the court of James I. Significantly enough, Cokes wishes to employ Nightingale as the 'poet' to his wedding 'masque'. This can be seen as rendering Cokes a parody of the monarch as patron, commissioning texts the full import of which he barely realizes. This in turn, however, politicizes the masques that Jonson had been composing in the years leading up to *Bartholomew Fair*; he might also have been committing criminal acts 'before the king's face', countenanced or otherwise. *Bartholomew Fair*, in its transposition from public theatre to court performance with just a day's grace between them, for all its alternative prologues, may also have been pushing the possibilities of what could be said and done before the king.[32]

Ballads were literary remakings – often the retelling of folk tales – with lyric and tune being handed down through generations; but they allowed for reinterpretations within each new context.[33] As convention rearranged, the ballad has definite parallels with *Bartholomew Fair* and the theatre at large. Dramatic potential includes the joint possibility for renewal and change. The fair is an annual event, repeated and yet subject to endless vicissitudes during a single day. Expectations exist but are invariably confounded; the fair, like the Jonsonian text, is a complex, multifarious thing to 'read', and liable to produce a multiplicity of meanings and intentions.

Jonson flirted with verse, prose, and a combination of the two, in his plays. *Bartholomew Fair* is a vibrant example of a prose-drama, possibly because this was the most evocative means of suggesting 'everyday speech', the quotidian language of the fair or marketplace. It may also be considered an egalitarian theatrical gesture. The prose of *Bartholomew Fair* is notable for its large propensity for dialogue scenes. The lengthy soliloquies of Justice Overdo are an exception and the ignorant commentary they provide underlines his need to discourse with others if only to reassess his interpretations. Quarlous's long speech at I.iii. is a rare moment and therefore intriguing. His rebuke of Winwife for wooing elderly widows in an effort to secure personal fortune strikes a brutal and rather angry note amid the humorous events and repercussions of the fair; there is a strange intrusion, albeit momentarily, of the darker side of affairs:

> thou must visit 'em, as thou wouldst do a tomb, with a torch, or three handfulls of link, flaming hot, and so thou mayst hap to make 'em feel thee, and after, come to inherit according to thy inches.
>
> (I.iii.84–8)

The hypocrisy of this is evident in retrospect when we consider the nature and motive of Quarlous's coupling with Widow Purecraft, but disease is again on the agenda. Linguistically this is a complex stage in the play's proceedings; the tone and the vocabulary seem markedly different; the critical cliché of *Bartholomew Fair*'s 'geniality' is clearly not the whole story of this community.

The fair operates on, and is operated upon by, its internal and external visitors in different fashion. Ursla is the 'body of the fair'; its 'enormities' pivot around events at her booth, where the synecdochical pig is roasted, and which would have been positioned onstage to resemble the old hell-mouth of medieval mystery plays. Women characters seek the refuge of her booth to urinate in her chamber pot and she herself constitutes a warped earthmother figure, her maternal instincts perversely reenacted in her relationship with the fair freak, Mooncalf. Although her body is the subject of various exclamations on leakage and escape – sweat, disease, urine, physical and sexual excess, all are invoked in the process[34] – she is less infected than infectious: 'Out upon her, how she drips! She's able to give a man the sweating sickness, with looking on her' (II.v.129-31). She remains essentially unchanged by the day's events; her role is one of catalyst as opposed to actuant or victim.

Cokes though is ultimately a victim of himself; as a result of his traumatic experiences at the Fair it is doubtful that he discovers himself in any altered condition:

> I ha' lost myself, and my cloak and my hat; and my fine sword, and my sister, and Numps, and Mistress Grace (a gentlewoman that I should ha'married) and a cut-work handkercher she ga'me, and two purses today. And my bargain o'hobby-horses and gingerbread, which grieves me worst of all.
>
> (IV.ii.97–103)

That the latter items grieve Cokes worst of all is an indication that his priorities are still all wrong. He is still misreading the signs, still blissfully unaware of the deceit practised upon him by Leatherhead and Joan Trash. The surface of life is what impresses him most. This is evidenced when he borrows the admission fee to see the puppet play, having lost all his money to Edgeworth's swift hands; despite its being a loan, Cokes insists on paying well over the odds in an ostentatious and ridiculous display of social status: 'Twopence? There's twelvepence, friend. Nay, I am a gallant, as simple as I look now, if you see me with my man about me, and my artillery again!' (V.iii.47–50). In a similar vein, he fails to realize that Leatherhead is not only the salesperson who duped him earlier in the day, but that the 'puppet-master' is deliberately simplifying the play's subject-matter for him and for the others whose interpretive record has proved similarly poor.

Leatherhead is tampering with his classical-mythological subject-matter, the story of Hero and Leander, to fit the discourse to the demands of his audience. In an obvious parody of the 1590s penchant for Ovid-influenced epyllia,[35] Jonson now locates the story by the Thames and not the Hellespont, writing his reductionist version in the classical metre of alexandrines and heroic couplets. Cupid is busy getting Hero drunk so that she will fall into bed with Leander. Interpretations of Jonson's motives here are various; many take this as confirmation of his objection to the theory that theatre needs to aim at the lowest common denominator, that to please the audience is the be-all and end-all. In that reading, the 'grotesque' rewriting of the courtly epyllion allows the court to laugh at the depth of popular tastes. This, however, underestimates the subversion already present in poetic versions of the story such as Christopher Marlowe's.[36] Leatherhead's character may be a partial satire on Inigo Jones's preference for the spectacular in the masques he co-designed with Jonson, and since the spectacular was included to satisfy courtly audiences the puppet-show can be read in reverse, as a parody of court taste designed to appeal to the urban populace.

The puppet play endorses the fact that language is a financial, commercial commodity at least in a theatrical context. It is a discursive enterprise for which audiences pay, as the detailing of the payment of admission fees suggests: 'Clearly the price of admission is an important ritual in the cultural event of theatre.'[37] The ticket price, the seating location, all these aspects of theatre-going can denote the operation of class-systems in our modern era, of rank and hierarchy in Jonson's.[38] In the Induction Jonson made gleeful reference to the overtly trusting nature of investors in the theatrical transaction, in that they pay out in full before even viewing the goods. The Induction also states that it is 'lawful for any man to judge his six penn'orth, his twelve penn'orth, so to his eighteen pence, two shillings, half a crown, to the value of his place' (Induction, ll. 102–5) – the right of judgement is relative to the price of admission. Thus status can buy access to the discourse of judgement and authority; such are the inequalities of the legal system. There is a recognition by Jonson here of the undemocratic basis of the supposedly democratic experience of public theatre as well as the Law.[39]

Bartholomew Fair is a play that engages with the concept of republicanism in more than just its communal ambience. The structure of the play and its exploration of the theatrical experience are factors in its engagement with questions of absolutism, limited monarchy, and democracy. In reading or responding to the overlapping communities of the play we should however bear in mind the warnings of the historian Ian Archer that 'just as there are dangers in exaggerating the "control" element in explaining the stability of Elizabethan [and Jacobean] London, so also do we run risks if we push the "community" arguments too far.'[40] *Bartholomew Fair* is neither a celebration of monarchical control, nor is it an overtly subversive account of the London populace. Jonson was, however, self-critical enough to see how the operations of those overlapping communities and neighbourhoods, and their inbuilt tensions, could usefully be applied to the dramatic creation, and its creator, in relation to questions of authority and the discourse of power.

As the experience of *Bartholomew Fair*, both as reading matter and in performance, indicates, Jonson is too readily seen as orthodox, as a supporter of the dominant ideology. Whilst not arguing any simple oppositional and extremist case for 'Jonson the republican' here, his careerist contributions to the court penchant for masques suggest a far more complex relationship with the structures of power than 'absolutist' or contained readings of his plays imply. Any writer's need for patronage made him/her accountable to those in authority or of higher social standing; yet Jonson persisted in his interrogation of questions of legality and social equality. That Jonson felt able to pose these questions through his drama was a mark of the innovation and courage (and perhaps that aforementioned social mediatory position) which for us is represented by his political and aesthetic experimentations.

Part III
Theatrical Commonwealths and Communities

Part III

7

The Commonwealth of Hell: *The Devil is an Ass*

The Devil is an Ass (1616) is partially a summary of Jonsonian dramatic innovation to date and for that reason links with many past plays are evident: *Volpone, Epicoene, The Alchemist* and *Bartholomew Fair* are perhaps the most obvious points of reference. Jonson is providing this summation not as a farewell to theatre but rather as a statement of his theatrical present: 'such a dramatist am I at this given moment in 1616'. That intense topicality of the play feeds into its political themes and concerns, a number of which have recently been excavated by critics.[1] The play touches on contemporary scandals such as the John Darrel trials for false religious exorcisms and the Frances Howard murder trial (through the storyline involving Frances Fitzdottrel – see Chapter 4), and political grievances such as monopolies through the characters of Merecraft and Lady Tailbush. In doing so it touches on particular anxieties about the Jacobean policy of fen drainage, the treatment of which serves to highlight the Jonsonian interest and investment in questions of community which this third section as a whole will explore in Jonson's later drama.

Since in the post-1616 dramas by Jonson it is in the creation and exploration of stage communities that we will most visibly trace the 'republicanism' we have heretofore been ascribing his playtexts, I should define the ways in which the term 'community' is being employed here. In many respects, we are talking about a series of communities, often overlapping ones, that involve the varying frameworks of social relations: neighbourhoods, gathering points such as fairs, alehouses, or theatres, villages, towns, cities, but also the structures of local and national government. Ian Archer's definition of community is helpful: 'Community is here defined as a locality or social organization (that is not necessarily defined by locality) characterized by social interactions, the density and frequency of which will determine the degree to which a community exists.'² Institutions such as the parish or the city company or guild can also play important roles in the creation of communities. Communities, as Jonson indicates, are not necessarily inclusive entities: rank, gender, and profession may all be implicated in the formation of exclusive social groupings. So the representation of 'communities' need not necessarily constitute a 'republican' political agenda: indeed, it may reinforce an opposing idea about the impossibility of any such constitution in a fractious and fractured society. These are the ideas I would suggest are under debate in Jonson's post-Folio plays, those from *Bartholomew Fair* onwards.³

The communities of *The Devil is an Ass* are many and varied. Most obviously we have the contrasted societies of London and Hell: a contest in which the latter appears as a poor imitation of the scheming society of the former. As a result of this comparative strategy, the word 'devil' takes on an Empsonian complexity within the text.⁴ Satan is a devil and therefore a devil can be the ultimate master, the director of events; but Pug too is a devil, in the sense that we today employ the phrase 'poor devil', as an expression of sympathy or pity: he is a 'petty puisne' devil, a junior member of the 'commonwealth of hell' who is sent to the Hell of seventeenth-century London for the day in the resurrected corpse of a hanged criminal. Dispatching his junior devil to London, Satan makes it clear that the only places he will feel at home are the taverns where the former court jesters and licensed fools have been 'exiled'. Pug finds himself at the receiving end of intrigues he supposed himself to be initiating, as Satan envisaged when he warned Pug at the outset that he was 'not for the manners, nor the times:' (I.i.120). London proves trickier and more self-serving than the 'commonwealth of hell'; there Pug encounters far superior devilry to his own anachronistic brand of work, causing him to cry out: 'You talk of a university! Why, Hell is/A grammar school to this!' (IV.iv.170–1); 'All/My days in Hell were holy-days to this.' (IV.iv.222–3)⁵

Other communities exist within the urban London context of *The Devil is an Ass*; as in Jonson's other London plays, the capital city is a multivalent entity. The guilds and professional companies are represented by Gilthead the goldsmith and his son Plutarchus, who yearns for that other group identity to be found in the shape of the citizen militia. The law is represented by the ambivalent figure of Justice Paul Eitherside and a corrupt constable or two. We have monopolists and adventurers, financially-driven groupings or communities, and gendered gatherings such as the ladies' 'academy' at Tailbush's house (a reworking, as we have seen, of the Collegiate of *Epicoene*), the male society of gallants such as Wittipol and Manly (a more empathetic reworking themselves of the Clerimont, Dauphine, Truewit triad of *Epicoene*), and of course the theatrical community, both of the Blackfriars theatre which Fitzdottrel attends and of the given Blackfriars audience for the play proper. That wider community of this play is the most important in Jonson's dramatic scheme. The metatheatrical aspects of *The Devil is an Ass* contribute to the play's general drive to create a heightened state of awareness about the conditions of existence and reception in the London spectators. Jonson is inviting the various communities of his contemporary London to identify themselves (and their actions) with the play's events.

The London of *The Devil is an Ass* is by no means a republican state and yet it clearly contains certain elements of life that were regarded as crucial to the formation of a republic by political theorists. Foremost amongst these (in the writings of Machiavelli and Francis Bacon for example) was a citizen militia. It is to membership of this particular grouping that the goldsmith's son, Plutarchus, aspires. Gilthead named his son in a fit of literary inspiration:

> That year, sir,
> That I begot him, I bought Plutarch's *Lives*,
> And fell so'in love with the book as I called my son
> By'his name, in hope he should be like him
> And write the lives of our great men!
> (III.ii.21–5)

The goldsmith intends that his son should write of the lives of great citizens, that is, the contemporary London equivalent of classical Greek and Roman republican heroes, and Plutarchus is indeed a great defender of citizens' rights in the face of aristocratic criticism and debauchery; he criticizes the way in which poverty-stricken aristocrats marry wealthy citizens' daughters and so produce a 'mongrel breed' (similar to those fears expressed by Audrey Turf and her father in *A Tale of a Tub*). But Plutarchus's name also means 'reign of, or origin in, gold' and in this too he remains true to the mercantile values of his rank. The central scene in which the Gilthead-Plutarchus plotline is introduced provides a central encounter between London's paradoxical mercantile and 'gentle' values and raises the question that this play as a whole agitates: that if ancestry and lineage no longer dictated the achievement of state office then perhaps money would win out. Meritocracy and the nature of 'true nobility' were also central to the debates centring on republicanism and classical humanism which Markku Peltonen has so persuasively argued were a feature of Jacobean political discourse.[6]

Plutarchus is scarcely a defendant of meritocracy; he is after all easily won over by Merecraft's seductive discourse to the notion of life as a captain in the militia and Jonson's pejorative opinion of that institution is clear from complex poems such as 'A Speech according to Horace', where the opening lines mimic the boasts of volunteer citizen-soldiers. If Everill, Merecraft's scheming sibling, is representative in this scene of a debauched aristocracy then mercantile values do not appear to proffer any utopian or truly republican alternative.

The citizen militia is merely one small cog in the complex urban mechanism that was Jacobean London. Social 'performances' of other kinds are also detailed in this play, not least those associated with religion, possession and exorcism, the spurious nature of which are explored by Jonson via Fitzdottrel's attempt to 'frame' his wife as an enchantress via the feigning of possession in the final act of the play. Stephen Greenblatt first observed the link between emblematic theatre and Catholicism.[7] He demonstrated how the Jacobean authorities were involved in trying to 'empty out' or evacuate the supernatural element from the rituals of possession and exorcism, in the process reducing them to containable theatrical performances. This was a policy enacted upon Jesuits and Puritans alike and not simply an anti-Catholic gesture. These attempts at evacuation led to the notorious 'show trials' of the period which sought to expose the 'stage taint', to use the Greenblattian term, of the unofficial spectacle that public displays of possession constituted and the most famous written accounts of these are to be found in the work of Samuel Harsnett.

In 1603, when he was chaplain to the Bishop of London, Harsnett wrote a detailed record of the trials of a group of English Catholic priests who had, as outlaws, performed a 'series of spectacular exorcisms';[8] his account was based on the sworn statements of the accused and entitled *A Declaration of Egregious Popish Impostures* and it has long been recognized that Shakespeare used the text in *King*

Lear (1605), not least in the scenes relating to Edgar's 'possession'. The following year, Jonson too employed Harsnett in his own reductive portrait of the legal system in *Volpone* (V.xii).

Greenblatt has described Harsnett's *Declaration* as part of the 'attempt by the established and state-supported Church of England to eliminate competing religious authorities by wiping out pockets of rivalrous charisma'.[9] Charisma was not a purely Catholic domain: in 1599 Harsnett had also authored a text entitled *A Discovery of the Fraudulent Practices of John Darrel*. In the 1590s the authorities had grown deeply concerned about the activities of a charismatic Puritan preacher, John Darrel. Through fasting and prayer he had assisted in the exorcism of Thomas Darling, who was popularly known as the 'Boy of Burton'; Darrel had gone on to further 'success' in the case of the mass possession of the 'Seven in Lancashire'. Alarmed, the authorities sought a means of exposing Darrel; in 1598 they found their means, William Somers, aged 21 and a musician's apprentice in Nottingham who was being exorcised by Darrel in yet another series of public spectacles. Evidently under great pressure from the aforesaid authorities, Somers 'confessed' to imposture and, in a complicated trial, that by Harsnett's own account featured various recantations and reconfessions, Darrel was himself 'exposed' as a charlatan. The trial's own vocabulary was predominantly theatrical – it spoke of theatre, plays, acting and dumbshow – and Harsnett exploited this feature in his written account, where he describes the exorcisms as stage plays and 'tragicomedies'.

The connection between the devil and the theatre is similarly exploited in *The Devil is an Ass* where we have a feigned possession, engineered by Merecraft and company, supposedly on Fitzdottrel's behalf: this in a play where all the 'marvelous possessions' ventured by the charismatic Merecraft are themselves 'acts' and counterfeits. Merecraft has clearly read Harsnett – his texts are a literary source he cites – and the precedent invoked for his actions is clearly that of John Darrel:

> roll but wi' your eyes,
> And foam at th'mouth. A little castle-soap
> Will do't, to rub your lips: and then a nutshell,
> With tow and touchwood in it to spit fire.
> Did you ne'er read, sir, little Darrel's tricks,
> With the boy o'Burton, and the seven in Lancashire,

Sommers at Nottingham? All these do teach it.
And we'll give out, sir, that your wife bewitched you –
(V.iii.2–9)

These 'possession' scenes expose the specious inter-translatability of all practices involving either the claim to possess or to decode inspiration. In the context of both *Volpone* and *The Devil is an Ass* the theatricality implicit in the presentation of the law and its claims is also exposed. In *The Devil is an Ass*, the Justice of the Peace Paul Eitherside (his very name implies translatability) is utterly convinced by Fitzdottrel's performance: ' 'Tis a clear conspiracy!/A dark, and devilish practice!'(V.viii.56–7), although as a party with vested interests in many of Merecraft's monopolies, it is easy to see why Eitherside might be inclined to such a reading.

Jonson expressed specific interest in the figure of the Justice of the Peace and the questionable operations of the law in a number of his plays (*Bartholomew Fair*, the 1616 Folio version of *Every Man In His Humour* and *A Tale of A Tub* to name a few),[10] but there is further topical significance to the figure of Sir Paul Eitherside, JP in *The Devil is an Ass*. Leah Marcus has suggested that his character in part represents two judges who were close associates of Lord Chief Justice Edward Coke – Sir Humphrey Winch, Justice of the Common Pleas, and Sergeant Randal (or Ranulph) Crew. These two had been involved in the notorious trial and execution of nine Leicestershire women falsely accused by a 13-year-old boy, John Smith, of witchcraft in 1616.[11] Merecraft himself makes specific reference to these events:

> Sir, be confident,
> 'Tis no hard thing t'outdo the Devil in:
> A boy o'thirteen year old made him an ass
> But t'other day.
> (V.vi.47–50)

King James himself had exposed the boy as a fake during his summer progress of that year, thus saving the lives of a further six accused women; the tale became the dominant theme of London gossip by the autumn and Jonson's play exploits this fact. Crew and Winch, and by association Coke, were duly disgraced.

Read in this way, Eitherside can be seen as an exposé of the law and a consolidation of royal prerogative of which Coke was a notorious opponent, but this perhaps belies the greater subtleties and critiques which Marcus also sees functioning within this play. In his cogent argument about the multifarious topical references of *The Devil is an Ass* Robert Evans suggests that Eitherside constitutes a direct parody of Coke and in particular his highly ambivalent role in initially supporting, and then abandoning, Alderman Cockayne's notorious project to curtail the Merchant Adventurers' monopoly on the exportation of cloth to Europe (essentially for his private gain) in the years leading up to 1616. There are certainly a number of satirical references to aldermen in the play.[12]

Peter Happé's recent edition of *The Devil is an Ass* endorses the reading of Eitherside as Coke but there is a further figure to add to those justices and judges of whom the confused JP can be said to be a creative dramatic amalgam. In addition to Harsnett's written account of the Darrel trial, Darrel's own sworn statements were recorded in a collection under the title, *The Triall of Maister Darrell, or a collection of Defences against Allegations Not Yet Suffered to Receive Convenient Answer* (1599); in one of these he directly addressed the presiding Justice. The judge on this occasion was the same Justice Popham who was later, as Lord Chief Justice, to preside over the trial of the Gunpowder Plot conspirators. Jonson's own involvement in events leading up to this trial have been dealt with by critics, not least by his recent biographer David Riggs, who records how, having been seen drinking with Robert Catesby only weeks prior to the plot's abortive carrying out, Jonson assisted the authorities in tracking down those implicated.[13] As a known Catholic, Jonson was no doubt under some duress to assist in this manner, and it is fascinating to learn that he himself had experienced an earlier run-in with Chief Justice Popham when in 1601 an anonymous informer had accused him of writing libellous material into his play *Poetaster*. The lawyer Richard Martin saved Jonson from any legal proceedings on that particular occasion but it proves that the dramatist's dealings with Popham were both numerous and complex. Admittedly Eitherside's role is a relatively small one in the play's proceedings and his responses are on the whole equivocal (as his nomenclature suggests) or merely confused but perhaps there is therefore convenient opportunity for a covert swipe at the, by then, deceased Judge Popham?[14]

What lends considerable support to critical speculation of this nature is that Jonson makes it clear that Eitherside is intimately involved in the financial venturing and corrupt projections of both

Merecraft and Lady Tailbush. This implicates him not only in the scandalous cosmetics trade, and the ridiculous manufacture of toothpicks for the court, but also in schemes for the drainage of the Fens in East Anglia. Those schemes are outlined by Merecraft and through them he convinces Fitzdottrel that he might become the 'Duke of Drowned land'. Popham was himself engaged directly in some notorious fen drainage schemes. In 1605 he 'undertook' (and that is a phrase which, along with its cognates, 'undertaker' and 'undertake', resonates throughout *The Devil is an Ass*) to drain the fenland at Upwell in Somerset. He put into motion similar schemes for Cambridgeshire – indeed the channel known as 'Popham's eau' was abandoned at his death in 1607. Such observations carry us into the direct locality of Fitzdottrel's dreaming in *The Devil is an Ass*. Indeed the Cambridgeshire plans and projections were in the process of being revived, amidst hopes of boosting seriously depleted crown coffers, in 1616 when the play was composed, stirring perhaps for Jonson memories of an old adversary, who was after all described in an anonymous letter to James I as 'covetous and bloodie', since he had ruined the livelihoods of and in many cases 'dispossessed' the fenland locals.

There is a danger of overstating the weight of significance carried by the specific fen-drainage project in the play, but it is crucial in any discussion of the play's interest in notions of community. What is clear even from reading a revisionist version of history such as Kevin Sharpe's *The Personal Rule of Charles I* – an effort, after all, to retrieve the monarch's damaged reputation during that period of non-parliamentary government (1629–40) – is that in the early modern period, fen drainage was a long-term focus of grievance.[15]

Often seen as a contributing factor to pre-civil war tensions in the Caroline 1630s, fen drainage has far earlier historical roots. Back in 1589, Humphrey Bradley, despite his name a Netherlander, had presented a treatise to Elizabeth I's chief minister proposing the reclamation of land from water, thus creating a whole new county in the area of the fens. The Queen declined interest but in 1600, a few years prior to her death, she signed an Act of Parliament for 'the recovering of many hundred thousand acres of marshes'. The Stuart kings focused with renewed determination on these schemes with hopes of reviving an ailing and often near-bankrupt Treasury. Although Kevin Sharpe is anxious to stress that their motives were not entirely profit-driven – it was hoped that new agricultural land would result, allowing far greater and more efficient crop-production in a period of soaring populations – in retrospect we tend to record the agricultural exhaustion of previously fertile soil and the devastation of essential wetland habitats by farming monocultures.[16]

In the early seventeenth century the aim was undoubtedly to employ new engineering techniques, mostly deriving from the Low Countries, to the benefit of the average person.[17] In the 1610s through the 1650s republic there was a veritable flood of Dutch engineers into Britain; naturally enough, social consequences were registered due to the habits of these Continental Puritans. Merecraft uses them as an example of frugality when castigating Everill for his social excesses:

> This comes of wearing
> Scarlet, gold lace, and cut-works! Your fine gartering!
> With your blown roses, cousin! And your eating
> Pheasant, and godwit, here in London! Haunting
> The Globes and Mermaids! wedging in with Lords
> Still at the table! and affecting lechery
> In velvet! Where you could ha'contented yourself
> With cheese, salt-butter, and a pickled herring
> I'the Low Countries? There worn cloth, and fustian!
> (III.iii.22–30)

Some of Jonson's own 'Catholic' lifestyle is suggested here in Everill's pursuits, but the suspicion of the Dutch 'invaders' should also be registered.[18]

In a fascinating book on water engineering, its history and its continuing responsibility to the community, Jeremy Purseglove observes:

> For the flood to yield up its riches, two things were required; a competent engineer and plenty of capital. To obtain the latter, there emerged a peculiarly modern group of business men who called themselves 'undertakers' or adventurers. An undertaker was one who contracted to 'undertake' a drainage scheme: an 'adventurer' was one who 'adventured' his capital on such an undertaking. The security of both was the premise of a large proportion of the land after the drainage operation had been successfully completed.[19]

This is Merecraft's discourse – 'He shall but be an undertaker with me'(II.i.36) – however he may choose to adorn its surface with 'natural' metaphors:

> Sir, it shall be no shame to me to confess,
> To you that we poor gentlemen that want acres,
> Must for our needs turn fools up, and plough ladies
> Sometimes, to try what glebe they are;
> (III.iv.44–7)

>   I have considered you
> As a fit stock to graft honours upon.
> I have a project to make you a duke, now,
> That you must be one, within so many months
> As I set down out of true reason of state,
> You sha' not avoid it.   (II.i.24–9)

In the latter example, even Merecraft's agricultural metaphor has an artificial, contrived aspect since he employs the idea of grafting rootstocks onto plants to create certain strains of fruit; the metaphor was employed throughout the Shakespearean sonnet sequence but here refers specifically to the rather unnatural world of the honours system. It implicitly constitutes a criticism of James's notorious policy of the creation and sale of titles.

Amidst all his Aristophanic cloud-cuckoo-land projections, Merecraft's real aim is to secure other people's money and investments:

>   He shall not draw
> A string of's purse. I'll drive his patent for him.
> We'll take in citizens, commoners and aldermen
> To bear the charge, and blow 'em off again
> Like so many dead flies, when 'tis carried.
> The thing is for recovery of drowned land,
> Whereof the Crown's to have his moiety,
> If it be owner: else, the Crown and owners
> To share that moiety, and the recoverers
> T'enjoy the tother moiety for their charge.
> (II.i.40–9)

His first entry onstage is wonderfully emphatic, bustling and assertive:

> Sir, money's a whore, a bawd, a drudge,
> Fit to run out on errands: let her go.
> *Via pecunia!* When she's run and gone,
> And fled and dead, then will I fetch her again
> With *aquae vitae*, out of an old hog's head!
> (II.i.1–5)

Encouraging Gilthead to make Plutarchus a captain in the London militia, Merecraft acknowledges the prevalence of the military metaphor in literary accounts of sexual encounters when he tells him to collect toy soldiers:

> Get him the posture book and's leaden men
> To set upon a table, 'gainst his mistress
> Chance to come by, that he may draw her in
> And show her Finsbury battles.
> (III.iii.38–41)

His strongly-stressed monosyllabic thrusts at II.i. are suggestive of a sexual attack on money (an idea that will undergo further exploration in *The Staple of News* a decade later):

> While there are lees of wine, or dregs of beer,
> I'll never want her! Coin her out of cobwebs,
> Dust, but I'll have her! Raise wool upon egg-shells,
> Sir, and make grass grow out o'marrow bones,
> To make her come.
> (II.i.6–10)

Coining out of cobwebs and dust recalls the alchemical schemes of Subtle and Face in Jonson's 1610 play; Merecraft is indeed a conjuror of finances, engaged in the performance that is money and investment. His very career entails the suspension of disbelief on the part of adventurers involved in his fiscal negotiations. Adventuring is necessarily a joint enterprise but one in which Merecraft seeks to have absolute control. The connections with other performative rituals, be they religion, exorcism or the theatre, are not so far-fetched.

Merecraft must make Fitzdotterel believe that he can tame the flood, although he has said that no man is a state of perpetuity in the natural world. Initially however he claims to have a far better researched project than fellow undertakers:

> Yes, which will arise
> To eighteen millions, seven the first year:
> I have computed all and made my survey
> Unto an acre. I'll begin at the pan,
> Not at the skirts as some ha' done, and lost
> All that they wrought, their timber-work, their trench,
> Their banks all borne away, or else filled up
> By the next winter. Tut, they never went
> The way: I'll have it all.
>
> (II.i.50–8)

Merecraft intends to avoid land-slippage or shrinkage by commencing centrally and not at the margins (indicative perhaps of his philosophy on life). In truth, many of the complex schemata advanced in the early seventeenth century for the purposes of drainage were, literally, swept away, reclaimed by the ever-encroaching waters. Fitzdotterel will also lose the other land he has claimed, that belonging to his wife, Frances; the land was secured over to him as part of her dowry, but Wittipol and Manly have won her back its economic management, albeit by underhand means, 'My land is drown'd indeed'(V.viii.160).[20]

Critics frequently point out that Fitzdotterel's gullible nature is signalled by his name: a dotterel is a type of plover, a bird which is by all accounts easily caught (the bird-names of Volpone's clients are similarly suggestive of their predatory instincts). A dotterel is also a wader-bird, particular to the East Anglian wetlands, especially so in Jonson's time: the same bird's movements, wading across the marshes, are mimetically represented by the invading strangers, the adventurers, of Andrew Motion's 'Inland', a poem explicitly about the drainage of the Cambridgeshire fens in 1618, the plans for which were being advanced at the time of Jonson's play.[21] Whilst the London setting for *The Devil is an Ass* is crucial for reasons already stated, the East Anglian sphere of reference is often reduced to a critical footnote, yet, like Merecraft's drainage schemes, Jonson has placed this at the pan of his play and not the skirts.

The dispossession of the local villagers that was the consequence of schemes such as Merecraft's is not really the theme of Jonson's play although he was interested in the operations of the local community. Nor is *The Devil is an Ass* a play that directly accuses the Crown of absolutist or dictatorial policies in the fens but such issues clearly perturb the dramatist, not least because of the grants to favourites that were involved. David Riggs has written that:

> In the final analysis, the playwright acknowledges that the world of Jonsonian comedy, like the urban society it mirrors, is irremediably corrupt. Only the King could restore order to it. Just as James had successfully intervened in the Leicestershire witchcraft trials, he (and he alone) has the power to introduce lasting reforms into Jacobean London.[22]

The Devil is an Ass provided much of the basis for L.C. Knights's at the time innovative reading of Jonson as a critic of early capitalism.[23] Riggs, like Barton, argues for an essentially nostalgic and conservative Jonson in this play who sees the monarch's intervention as a solution to the social disturbance represented by figures such as Merecraft – who is as his name suggests mere craft – a dangerous juncture of greed, conscience-free ambition, fraud and overweening energies, with little personality to balance this out. Yet Merecraft is essentially a failure, certainly so by the play's Prospero-like epilogue; during the course of events he exerts a relatively small degree of control, far less than say Mosca or Face. Those with whose practices we eventually sympathize, Wittipol, Manly and Frances, are shown first in the play and thus to Pug seem the most shocking examples of London's ability to out-devil Hell. This suggests something other than some nostalgic pre-modern, communal social vision on the part of the dramatist: there is instead suggestion of better ways to live in the here and now of 1616: a way that includes empathy for the female condition, respect for communities, and equality before the law and between the sexes.

Riggs goes on to question whether James I would ever have exercised his supposed power to control and contain:

> Merecraft's chief project ... raised the issue of James's responsibility in a very direct way. Although the King had officially repudiated the practice of granting Monopolies, he had recently awarded the right to reclaim the Fens to Sir Robert Carr, a Scot ...

who had danced in *The Golden Age Restored*. Thanks to James's openhandedness, Merecraft's confidence game was Carr's legitimate business venture.[24]

Fitzdottrel's character has been linked to Sir Robert Carr who was himself familially linked to the former Earl of Somerset, also Robert Carr, who was by 1616 in disgrace and imprisoned in the Tower of London, accused of involvement, with his wife, Lady Frances Howard, in the murder of Sir Thomas Overbury. Overbury had been Jonson's friend and the dramatist later told Drummond that he had been accused over the text of *The Devil is an Ass* and that the King had asked him to 'conceal' the satire on the 'Duke of Drowned Land'.[25] Possibly the registered allusion to Sir Robert Carr, and by implication to his troubled namesake, touched James too close to the political and personal bone.

In 1616 the monarch was still promising to restore to Somerset lands and rights confiscated upon his arrest; he had even granted him special permission to wear the garter of a Knight of the Realm whilst in prison.[26] Jonson's own dealings with Somerset (Carr) were typically convoluted – Frances Howard's first wedding to the Earl of Essex had occasioned the controversial and now embarrassing masque *Hymenaei*. Jonson had also written two entertainments for his second marriage in 1613 (*A Challenge at A Tilt, The Irish Masque*), but by 1616 when all three were included in the published *Works* he had meticulously extracted any direct reference to either occasion.[27] More covert references to the whole affair may be embedded in *The Devil is an Ass*, where we see an impotent marriage (the cause of the Essex annulment and a case sanctioned by James himself), various conspiracies and imprisonments, and even accusations of female devilry (bandied around in the scandalous Overbury trial – a famous contemporary ballad satirized Lady Frances – and note the name – as a witch).[28] Overt reference comes at I.ii. when Fitzdottrel attempts in vain, Faustus-like, to conjure the devil:

> Ay, they do now name Bretnor, as before
> They talked of Gresham, and of Doctor Forman,
> Franklin, and Fiske, and Savory – he was in too –
> But there's not one of these that ever could
> Yet show a man the Devil in true sort.
> (I.ii.1–5)

Fitzdottrel names Thomas Bretnor, a maker of almanacs, as an even more recent example of devilry than the various participants in the Overbury trial – Edward Gresham (an almanac-maker also), Simon Forman, an astrologer and quack doctor), James Franklin, the executed apothecary who supplied the poison, Nicholas Fiske (a physician) and Abraham Savory, an actor named by Mrs Turner, also executed, as a sorcerer during cross-examination. Whether Jonson exhibits sympathy for Frances Howard's fate in this play (she was under house arrest in the Blackfriars area at the time of the play's composition and first production) through his empathetic portrait of Frances Fitzdottrel (falsely accused of witchcraft) is a matter for ongoing critical controversy.[29]

Implications of Howard and Somerset (Carr) in this playtext, as well as Sir Robert Carr's monopoly to drain the fens cannot though have gone unperceived, certainly not by the King himself. Fitzdotterel is not Sir Robert Carr, no more than he is the Earl of Essex, nor is Merecraft some direct equation of Sir Robert Carr but the allusion to his involvement in lucrative land drainage, like that of Justice Popham, opens up a whole area of speculation, as much for the twentieth century, as for original audiences.

Jonson had a prescient awareness of the polemic surrounding fen-drainage schemes and not just in terms of Nature's eventual reclamation of this self-fashioned land. In the late 1620s, Charles I would employ Cornelius Vermuyden, a Dutchman, on further projects of this kind, even knighting him at Whitehall in 1629 – the price of which appears to have been to undertake further costly projects. Many villagers began to protest against the dispossession such land policies invariably entailed. Pitched battles ensued. Outsiders were felt to be overturning a perfectly satisfactory agricultural economy, where land was farmed in common and the marshes themselves provided an adequate living for many sedge-cutters, thatchers and so on. Many wetlands were co-operatively managed, thus preserving delicate ecological balances, although it would be naive to present these communities as 'some kind of pastoral socialist Utopia'.[30] Any balance and communality, however, was effectively destroyed by the disembarking adventurers.

The important point to extrapolate from all of this is that fen drainage was to represent a contentious political issue up to and throughout the civil wars. To quote Keith Lindley:

Fenland enclosure had been achieved by a mixture of chicanery, coercion, and persuasion, with royal and conciliar connivance or assistance, and the suppression of local resistance to it followed a similar pattern.... Whatever the level of political consciousness of most commoners, wider constitutional issues were inevitably raised by fenland drainage and enclosure.....[31]

Once again Jonson is registering the tensions of his age. In the 1630s the continuing objections to fen drainage would contribute to the breakdown of Charles I's personal rule.

In Richard Brome's *The Court Beggar* (1639–40), Sir Andrew Mendicant, along with three other projectors, enters onstage in the antimasque that virtually ends the play, 'attir'd all in Patents and with a windmill on his head....'[32] Brome, Jonson's amanuensis, would also author a proto-republican exploration of community in *A Jovial Crew* in 1641, and that this play alludes to Jonson's Buckingham-commissioned 1621 masque, *The Gypsies Metamorphosed* suggests that Jonson was perceived by his contemporaries to be contributing to an ongoing debate about community.

In 1643, another son of Ben, Thomas Randolph, would feature in his printed play *The Muse's Looking Glass* a debate between an engineer named Banausus and a gentleman called Colax:

> BANAUSUS I have a rare device to set Dutch windmills
> Upon New-market Heath and Salisbury Plain,
> To drain the Fens.
> COLAX The Fens Sir are not there.
> BANAUSUS But who knows but they may be?[33]

The East Anglian landscape of windmills and wetlands is here imaginatively transported to a London location. Ben Jonson had achieved exactly this nearly 30 years earlier in a play that is by no means backward-looking, but almost confrontational in its considerations of the present and the future.

8
The Commonwealth of Paper: Print, News and *The Staple of News*

The tangible effects of an emerging print culture in the seventeenth century on the availability of news can and have been dated to the 1620s. That decade witnessed the circulation of *corantos*, newssheets deriving from the Continent and relating the progress of the European wars; it also saw the transition towards domestically printed newsbooks. Such happenings have been seen as liberating and potentially democratizing in their provision of news for a wider audience. David Norbrook has argued that, in the 1620s

> There was a significant expansion in the political public sphere ... an emergent civil society whose means of communication – reports of parliamentary debates, newsletters, satires, and so on – circulated horizontally, cutting across the vertical power structures emanating from the court.[1]

In their political and religious bias, however, these same literary productions in print have been viewed as examples of the susceptibility of news to contentious issues such as 'censorship' and 'propaganda'. Terms such as these require more thoughtful definition in their application to the early modern period. Both are anachronistic invocations, linguistic projections back from later times. Censorship was frequently the result of arbitrary whims or decisions, or of the political 'moment', rather than an established policy or regime. 'Propaganda' in our modern understanding suggests a manipulative state operation: no comparable notion of the 'state' existed in the early seventeenth century. The sense of print as a commodity open to the usual interpretations and fetishizations of commodification is therefore the one I wish to invoke in this chapter.

The Staple of News (1626) is set in and around a Caroline news-office. In a reworking of the 'prodigal son' play which had been popular in the Middle Ages and which had found new life in seventeenth-century urban city comedies by Jonson, Marston, and Middleton alike, Pennyboy Junior is 'tested' by his father Pennyboy Canter. Canter has feigned his own death and entered into his son's company in disguise as a beggar. Just turned 21 at the start of the play, Pennyboy Junior believes himself to have inherited his father's wealth and immediately sets out on a course of conspicuous consumption, beginning with the commissioning of new clothes from the tailor and culminating in his purchase of the Staple of News. Pennyboy Junior also woos one of the Staple's chief financial investors, Pecunia the Infanta of the Mines, with whom his uncle Pennyboy Senior is equally besotted. A complicated triangle results which reaches its peak in Canter's revelation of his true identity and the explosion of the news-office. In related scenes in the play we see the office emissaries (reporters) involved in the production (and construction) of the news, an activity which is consciously parallelled with Pennyboy Senior's cook, Lickfinger's extravagant culinary creations. The entire play as we have seen (see Chapter 4) is framed by the exchanges of an onstage audience of female gossips.

With its innovative plotline, *The Staple of News* was an important play for the 1620s not because it was a pro-republican exposé of monarchical manipulation of print through ownership, censorship and other forms of state control, but because it brought into the public theatre domain the question of exactly what news and print (and printed news) constituted (or could constitute) for society at large.

The very use of the term 'news' in this play to refer to numerous forms of literary production complicates the general critical understanding of Jonson's 'elitist politics', especially with regard to the operations of the stage. Jonas Barish has implied that Jonson established a literary hierarchy in which plays and theatrical ephemera were fairly low on the ladder of importance; he therefore regards the publication of the 1616 Folio as the act of a literary exclusionist.[2] Yet Jonson's understanding of 'news' brings into play news-sheets, pamphlets, ballads, prose, poetry, plays and puppetry, and potentially legitimizes them all. News in this period was available in both manuscript and printed form.[3] Jonson does not prioritize one over the other: what is fascinating about *The Staple of News* is that it does not condemn the expanding print culture of the age (which might be the approach expected of a 'conservative traditionalist Jonson') but instead critiques social resistance to print. In his depiction of the news-staple or office Jonson embraces the form's possibility for both elite and popular cultural practice.

The title of *The Staple of News* also connects Jonson's own generic (and cross-cultural) range – from masques to public theatre plays, from commonplace books to grammars, and from poetry to prose. The play, in its linguistic structures, is an interesting blend of the poetic and the prosaic (the play proper is in verse, the Intermeans in prose) and implicitly engages with the theme of its own intertextuality.

News in this period was both lasting and ephemeral, because it appeared in both book and manuscript form (although I would want to stress that the application of the term 'ephemeral' to manuscripts is in no way intended to devalue their significance in seventeenth-century society: it is, however, to suggest that these categories of literary production were seen as discrete in their politics of production as well as their intrinsic socio-politics during the period). *The Staple of News* represents, I would argue, a conscious intervention in the debate over print and the availability and accessibility of news. The 1620s was a crucial decade for Jonson in careerist terms, not least because it witnessed the transition from Jacobean patronage to the more complicated negotiations he was forced to undergo during the Caroline reign when yet another redefinition of his personal and public politics became necessary. What emerges in its most paradoxical form in *The Staple of News* is Jonson's 'elitist republicanism', or 'republican elitism' (and the two are subtly different). Jonson considers the fate of printed news: its likely audiences and the impact this form as opposed to manuscript circulation has on the reporting of that news and on literature at large. Jonson did not see print as a threat to drama. As Tom Hayes has stressed: 'Print did not replace the theater as the central legitimizing medium in early modern England. It expanded the influence of writing.... The increase in popular literacy worked against monolithic, centralized authority, against the idea that there was one legitimate voice in the text.'[4] Jonson does not satirize the press *per se* but explores the politics of certain responses to it and its commodification. He recognizes republican potential in the press but not in the form of its unlimited freedom. In this way his form of republicanism turns out to be not opposed to censorship but to depend upon new forms and new understandings of that term as well as of community *per se*. Jonson seeks to expand the range of discourses available through the medium of 'news', and in particular printed news, and to regulate them critically.

The triumphant triple repetition of 'News, news, news!' in the opening line of Jonson's 1620 masque, *News from the New World Discovered in the Moon* ushers the Heralds onto the court-stage before King James and announces an interest in the emergent medium of print that would characterize the forthcoming decade, outlast the reigning monarch, and endure well beyond Jonson's own demise in 1637. Additionally present onstage with the Heralds are the diverse literary figures of a Printer, a Factor, and a Chronicler: all producers of this 'news' in some respect, but all possessing startlingly different, indeed completely antithetical, understandings of their art/trade (that oblique signalling some of the inherent paradoxes of the print medium). The Heralds are astounded that the Printer enquires as to the cost-price of their news; such nascent capitalism seems anathema to them. The Printer, on the other hand, appears to harbour no such qualms:

> Indeed I am all for sale, gentlemen, you say true. I am a printer, and a printer of news, and I do hearken after 'em wherever they be, at any rates; I'll give anything for a good copy now, be't true or false, so't be news.
>
> (ll. 14–17)

The element of snobbery and hierarchism in the Heralds' dismissal of the Printer as a 'dull tradesman' does not escape attention; the Factor (a newspaper columnist) is quick to express the egalitarian qualities of print: 'I have friends of all ranks and of all religions' (l. 36). For these 'friends' (a word dangerously interchangeable with the more impersonal 'clients', and the accordingly less friendly relationship of clientage that Jonson explored in such plays as *Volpone* and *Sejanus*), the Factor maintains an 'answering catalogue', and he has ambitious plans to expand his enterprise:

> And I have hope to erect a staple for news ere long, whither all shall be brought and thence again vented under the name of staple-news, and not trusted to your printed conundrums of the serpent in Sussex, or the witches bidding the devil to dinner at Derby – news that, when a man sends them down to the shires

where they are said to be done, were never there to be found.

(ll. 41–7)

Jonson would erect a staple of news for himself before long; in the play of that title he enlarged upon the intellectual consternation expressed in this masque about the growing power and influence of the press and the printed media. Pamphlets and broadsheets had long been in existence and were accessible to the literate sector of the populace, but the 1620s, on the very cusp of which *News From the New World* stands, was a decade that witnessed the arrival of regular newsbook journalism.

The significant cultural shift from the copyist's workshop to that of the printer has been well documented:

> One of the milestones of the Renaissance/early modern age, however we define it, was the invention of printing and a massive, if gradual, shift in the way ideas were being presented and disseminated as the technology became widespread.[5]

In 1620 *corantos* (single sheets of news in folio size) began to appear in London with some regularity, deriving from and reporting upon events occurring on the Continent, in particular the Thirty Years War. The implicit politics of these reports is significant: many news-sheets that were circulating in England originated from the Dutch republic.[6] Increasingly these single-sheet *corantos* yielded their market dominance to the weightier quarto newsbooks that were between 16 and 24 pages in size. In truth, much of the content of the latter was news of the same war that had simply been extrapolated from the Dutch news-sheets and reshaped.

Writing was clearly metamorphosing, both economically and politically, into a new commodity, a fact acknowledged in the capitalistic tones of the Printer in *News from the New World*. The colonialist implications of the masque's title should not be underestimated, even though the New World it speaks of is not that of the Americas but of the moon. Yet the printing trade in its earliest days possessed vast and untrammelled potential. A 'responsible' form of journalism might after all establish a close, if not liberating, communication with 'ordinary people' (the inverted commas signal my awareness of the socio-political difficulties involved in defining that particular target population).[7] Elizabeth Eisenstein has demonstrated how print culture rendered ideas far more widely accessible, discussing the potential democratization represented by the preservative powers of print: 'it secured precious documents not by putting them under lock and key, but by removing them from chests and vaults and duplicating them for all to see ....'[8] Eisenstein's description unwittingly evokes the stage destiny in *The Staple of News* of Pecunia. She is lifted out of virtual captivity in the household of Pennyboy Senior (the names of her ladies-in-waiting – Statute, Band and Mortgage – stressing the financial and emotional constraints involved) and into the space and sphere of possibility that constitutes the Staple news-office.

Democratic arguments of this nature are generally countered by modern critics with the suggestion that censorship enacted its own restraints upon the press; that royal control was exerted over this form, rendering it less than populist, if not quasi-absolutist, in content. Such readings are, however, generally more indicative of our own era in which there exists a sense of the news as being manipulated by a minority in control, be it due to financial or political power. D.F. McKenzie states that the popular press in the early modern period was a reflection of an egalitarian movement, as well as immensely educative in forming a new language for talking about politics,[9] at a time when, as Anthony Parr puts its, 'people were ready to learn the language of that debate'.[10] It has been suggested that illiteracy excluded many from the brave new world of printed culture, but news-sheets were read to those who could not read for themselves and grass-roots movements in the early part of the century certainly looked to print to further their cause.[11]

Blair Worden has reassessed the contribution made by censorship in this period to the freedom, or otherwise, of speech in print. He comments that 'the problem of censorship is vulnerable to distortion', and questions whether the freedom of the press was even under debate in this period.[12] Richard Burt has made a valuable contribution to the currently raging censorship debate, by suggesting a new model that involves not removal and replacement by the censoring body but rather dispersal and displacement. He argues that censorship was a far more collaborative and complicit series of actions than monolithic notions of 'Censorship' allow. Just as no Ur-text can be uncovered in terms of authorial intention, neither does there exist some Ur-pre-censorship text; he argues that the text will always prove castrated, feminized, and therefore disappointing to those who seek such an artefact. Those who seek some original, radical politics are also likely to be disappointed. It is in this complicit and yet also questioning light that I wish to discuss Jonson's approach to the press and print culture.[13]

Undoubtedly the Crown intervened frequently in the operations of the print industry, tending to grant patents, for certain classes of publication, to the monarch's favourites. English printing patents were broad grants and often proved extremely lucrative. The medium of print existed uneasily between the worlds of royal licence and oscillating market forces; this forms part of the anti-masque debate in *News from the New World* and constitutes a central topos of *The Staple of News*.

Like many other seventeenth-century authors, Jonson recognized the new opportunities proffered by the printed book, not least its capacity to reach far wider audiences than manuscripts: its capacity to perform that function of being, to employ Natalie Zemon Davis's term, 'a carrier of social relationships'. Combined material and artistic success was Jonson's objective, as his sharply registered disappointment(s) at the poor reception(s) of his plays indicates. Yet, in acknowledging, and possibly even catering for, the new 'popular' potential of his work, he continued to make ostensibly elitist and exclusive gestures through the medium of those books, displaying the 'neurotic' personality he has been accused of, if not necessarily the pre-established elitism Stanley Fish has credited him with.[14]

D.F. McKenzie regards *The Staple of News* as 'the hardening point of Jonson's isolation', partly because, he argues, though the dramatist was pushing for the political awakening of the '*menu peuple*' he made no allowance whatsoever for the struggle and the difficulty this would entail.[15] In his very gesture of accommodation towards the general public, then, Jonson abstracts himself from the situation in hand:

> Jonson evidences the same virtues and limitations of all whose passionate defence of minority culture is beyond criticism so long as it remains in a condition of high-minded self-abstraction from mass civilization.[16]

Contradictory drives of this nature characterize the writing profession and the volumes it produced in the seventeenth century: 'There was a tension, often quite explicit in these volumes between the intellectual elitism claimed for authorship, and the broader appeal required if authorship were to prosper in the marketplace.'[17]

Frontispieces in particular simultaneously represented inclusive and exclusive gestures. For example, the frontispiece to Jonson's 1616 *Works* cites Horace in Latin; Latin was a language available only to the discriminating and well-educated few.[18] Yet the time-consuming and meticulous preparation of his copy-texts for print would imply that Jonson fostered hopes of attracting a wider readership than the limited Latinized sector of the literate population. The careful creation and fashioning of the Folio certainly constituted a play for respectability on Jonson's behalf within the early modern republic of letters.

The notion of print as a fixing agent, preserving texts and regulating spellings and layout has been explored by Eisenstein and others. In an article on the early modern printer John Wolfe (whose own foreign newsbooks purported to be little more than officially sanctioned propaganda), Joseph Loewenstein has stressed that the age of print witnessed a regulation of English writing: uniform orthography and appearance became pressing concerns.[19] But print is not necessarily a stable medium – Jonson's revisions and amendments to previous quarto copytexts, and his suppression of details no longer relevant or now simply embarrassing, are indicators of the instabilities of texts, printed or otherwise.[20]

Print can also be a destabilizing medium – a medium that can mobilize, change, or protest; it can prove to be a liberating force within society at large. Jonson's marginalia and annotations may suggest acts of containment by a paranoid author but the fact that these emendations themselves shifted and altered suggests a wholly more complex situation. In *The Staple of News* the much-desired Pecunia does not represent a single text – she exists in numerous versions. Men reinterpret and differentiate Pecunia in order to assert some personal claim over her. This can be viewed as a parallel to what Richard Burt has designated 'censorship as "fetishism"'. He has demonstrated the way in which 'Texts circulate as desirable/exchangeable/receivable commodities insofar as they are differentiated from other versions in the same or different media ....'[21] In this reading, each character seeks to liberate Pecunia from one defining reading only to impose on her another version; she is never allowed full entrance into the social field as an uncensored whole – instead each character produces a partial and censored reading which is both dependent upon, and a departure from, that of her previous interpreter.

The early-seventeenth-century act of literary creation was therefore characterized by several factors; one area of impact was the heightened sense of tension between attempts to 'democratize' the art, opening it up to ever-wider audiences and attaining to new readerships, and the increased demands for the safeguarding of intellectual property rights. The latter objective necessarily raises questions of exclusivity and elitism for the critic of this period, and of tyranny amidst the new republican spirit of print.

If the expanding print industry drew attention to the problematized and potentially conflictual area of 'rights' in the realms of politics and literature, it also began to substantially alter author–reader relationships from their pre-existent states, creating, not least, a forum for debate both political and theatrical:

> Broadside ballads had long been a profitable way of exploiting public curiosity about current sensations, but the growth of literacy and awareness of the world at large, especially as England became more involved in Continental politics, created the conditions for a new kind of journalism, one that might demand a more sustained effort from the reader and mediate responsibility between news and its recipients.[22]

Jonson was both struggling to cope with these redefinitions and striving to harness them for his own benefit; possibly this lies behind his efforts to contain and control the more wayward performative energies of his texts in his careful oversight of their journey into print.

Jonson was engaged with the potential of print in both its advantageous and disadvantageous sense. *The Staple of News* is an effort to explore the problems of the medium in literary, political and sociological terms. The play also highlights the tensions at large, locally, nationally and on a European scale. In 1620s England, political and religious spectators were witnessing a period of massive transition and the precarious nature of this situation was exacerbated in 1626 by the accession of a new monarch. This is not to claim that the tensions of the play in any direct way presage or prefigure the complexities of the 1640s conflict or the eventual deposition of the king, but, as previously suggested, the doubts accompanying the new reign are surely embedded in the contemporaneous text of *The Staple of News*. Charles I was the 'new news at court' and Jonson was acutely aware of a shift in his own relations with the Crown.[23] In 1626 it seemed unlikely that he would enjoy the sort of favour he had previously received from James and so the authorial relationship was being redefined in another crucial sense.

In 1624 Jonson had conveniently reshaped the political disaster that constituted Prince Charles's and the Duke of Buckingham's trip to Madrid in pursuit of the hand of the Spanish Infanta in marriage; this abortive effort was now entirely reformed into a celebration of Charles's safe homecoming in the masque *Neptune's Triumph*.[24] Jonson was ostensibly employed as a court propagandist on this occasion with 'ephemeral work to do'[25] in reclaiming popular support for Charles. The commission, however, still derived ultimately from James and it is therefore he who is celebrated in the text as Neptune, King of the Sea – the sea that carried his son safely home from the dangerous Continent.

1624 as an historical moment has attracted much attention, not least because of the exceptionally co-operative parliament that was summoned that year. Wooed by Charles and Buckingham to make war on Spain (a complete reversal of Buckingham's previous reputation as pro-Spanish and crypto-Catholic, a reputation compounded by the secret assignations to Madrid), a predominantly anti-Habsburg Parliament happily voted the subsidies necessary for the preparations for war to begin. This accord had, however, virtually collapsed by the time of Charles's accession a year later and historians have naturally been anxious to examine the reasons why this might have been so.

Thomas Cogswell has recorded the deep national excitement at Charles's safe (and unmarried) return from Spain in 1623, suggesting that fears of Habsburg domination and Catholic invasion were quite genuine at this time.[26] The question begs asking why a propagandistic text such as *Neptune's Triumph*, seemingly so suited to 1623, took a further year to be commissioned at a Court not usually slow to capitalize on such opportunities. The answer lies in James's self-appointment as European peacemaker: he was still hopeful, even in 1623, of averting war with Spain, and even of a Habsburg marital alliance. The question of delay is not evaded by Jonson's masque-text; as ever, more complex in the reading than on its surface. The Poet of *Neptune's Triumph* has had to bide his time before treating the failed Spanish marriage negotiations in masque-form. This constitutes the operation of a form of royal censorship – restricting subject-matter until a considered appropriate time – but the political efficacy of such an action is subtextually questioned by

Jonson since balladeers and gossips have, we learn, had their fill of the theme:

> It was not time
> To mix this music with the vulgar's chime.
> Stay, till th'abortive and extemporal din
> Of balladry was understood a sin,
> Minerva cried; that what tumultuous verse
> Or prose could make or steal, they might rehearse,
> And every songster had sung out his fit;
> That all the country and the city wit
> Of bells and bonfires and good cheer was spent,
> And Neptune's guard had drunk all that they meant;
> That all the tales and stories now were old
> Of the sea-monster Archy, or grown cold;
> The muses then might venture undeterred,
> For they love then to sing when they are heard.
> (ll. 115–28)

Jonson exposes the futility and belatedness of the retrospective rewriting of events he is being employed to produce. Admittedly, the negative treatment here of popular media such as ballads suggests an unduly aggressive attitude on Jonson's part towards the cultural exercises and flexings of society beyond the court, but the description also possesses a sense of the cultural energy of such forms and the inertia of a court that waits so long to comment with a 'celebratory' banquet that events have now grown cold.[27] The vivacity of Nightingale's ballad-singing scene in *Bartholomew Fair* provides a dramatic counterpart to this speech and Jonson is after all biding his own time with the heir to the throne at this stage, negotiating his own future. Hasty pronouncements on the Spanish affair could have proved disastrous.

By 1626 and *The Staple of News* Jonson is less reserved. A supposedly dead father authors his son via a written contract; James I himself, dead a single year, had written *Basilikon Doron* as a text to author his now-dead son Prince Henry.[28] When Henry died, so did many of the hopes for the Stuart reign[29] and he may therefore be regarded as an absent presence in this prodigal son play. Pennyboy Junior woos his own 'Spanish Infanta', the infinitely desirable Princess Aurelia Clara Pecunia (Golden Bright Money) and Jonson no longer seems to be hedging his bets with the new monarch.

The female gossips of *The Staple of News* Intermeans capture the sense of political disillusionment that followed the high hopes of 1624. It is Censure (her nomenclature implying political censorship perhaps) who declares: 'Well, they talk we shall have no more Parliaments (God bless us);' (III. Intermean, 49–50), referring to Charles's dissolution of Parliament in 1625 after bitter dissent by MPs over his request for further subsidies towards the war. By now a number of military failures, and revived doubts about the sheer extent of Buckingham's power at court, had dampened parliamentary spirits.

In Act V Sc.i of *The Staple of News* Thomas announces: 'Our Staple is all to pieces, quite dissolved.' (V.i.39). The news-office in an extreme act of self-combustion (self-censorship?), has blown up:

> Shivered, as in an earthquake! Heard you not
> The crack and ruins? We are all blown up!
> Soon as they heard th'Infanta was got from them,
> Whom they had so devourèd i'their hopes
> To be their patroness and sojourn with 'em
> Our emissaries, Register, Examiner
> Flew into vapour; our grave governor
> Into a subtler air, and is returned
> (As we do hear) grand-captain of the jeerers.
> I and my fellow melted into butter
> And spoiled our ink, and so the Office vanished.
> (V.i.40–50)

The mention of Pecunia as 'th'Infanta' again stirs memories of the Spanish match and the dissolution of parliament.

In truth, Thomas has not melted into butter; this is simply a metaphor for his loss of position and, as such, part of a general pattern of butter puns in the text which play on the name of a famous contemporary printer Nathaniel Butter (who was reportedly not amused). It also implicitly questions the assumed fixity of print, assumed even by the Staple's workforce:

> FITTON   O, sir, it is the printing we oppose.
> CYMBAL We not forbid that any news be made
>   But that't be printed; for when news is printed,
>   It leaves, sir, to be news. While 'tis but written –
>   (I.v.46-9)[30]

Such opinions are cited as further evidence of Jonson's view, suggesting that he was directly opposed to the new print culture, but this is wholly inaccurate.[31] In her article on the masques of the early 1620s Sara Pearl remarks that *News from the New World* is a text that parodies the capitalistic print culture but her argument cannot easily be extended to *The Staple of News*.[32] This is not a play that satirizes printed news, which might logically appear to be its target; rather it attacks certain interpretations and appropriations of the press. Cymbal (his name, resonant of course of noise and the power of news to be heard, may also attest phonetically to the symbolic nature of print) resists putting material into printed form; this is a ridiculous stance for the governor of a news-office to adopt (and note how the supposedly democratic new enterprise has rapidly established its own internal hierarchy). There is no possible way in which the Staple can thus succeed as a financial venture: a news-office that resists the new print culture is doomed to failure.[33] The employees' written contracts barely prove more durable; ink after all can run and dissolve. The description of the office explosion can then be viewed as another variation on the overblown, hyperbolic accounts (such as that of Spinola and his eggs (I.iv)) that have indeed been its staple diet and production; it is an exaggerated account of financial dissolution, a company going as we still say 'into liquidation' after failed attempts to woo investors.[34]

A crucial paradox of print is that although it was the medium expected (certainly by Jonson) to bring new depths of consideration and greater durability to already-circulating manuscripts, it was itself highly dependent upon surface appearance, and matters of immediacy, fashion, and the visual – all those ephemeral elements for which Jonson seemingly berates the stage in *The Staple of News*. Surfaces are widely prevalent in the debates and dialogues of this play: questions of fashion, trends, and ephemera proliferate, and thus the most pressing connection between the four gossips of the Intermeans and the onstage action becomes plain.

The gossips are, according to the Prologue, as much attracted by the costumes and hairstyles of the acting company as by the play or the performances; the surface aspects of the production draw their attention:

O, Curiosity! You come to see who wears the new suit today, whose clothes are best penned (whatever the part be), which actor has the best leg and foot, what king plays without cuffs and

> his queen without gloves, who rides post in stockings and dances in boots? (Prologue, ll. 40-4)

The phrase 'whose clothes are best penned' is another instance of how the discourse of writing and print pervaded that of fashion and performance.[35] The reference to the king and his queen would have carried a precise register for contemporary audiences, since Queen Anne had notoriously performed without gloves, and blacked-up, for the *Masque of Blackness* which she commissioned from Jonson himself: *The Staple of News* is not afraid to write into its own performance an often ambivalent account of the Jacobean court penchant for the masque-form.

The opening section of *The Staple of News* draws much of its performative energy from themes of fashion and surface. Pennyboy Junior stands on the brink of manhood; when the play proper commences, the clock is about to strike and beckon in his twenty-first birthday. His period of wardship is drawing to a close.[36] His first act as an adult is one of expenditure – he 'writes man' by commissioning an entirely new wardrobe. The tailor who eventually arrives bears the significant title of 'Fashioner'; the *dramatis personae* describes him as 'the tailor of the times'. He caters to the self-fashioning demands of Renaissance men and women as much as the news-staple itself.

The speed with which the discourses of print and fashion began to merge in this period was astonishing: if clothes sat well they were said to be 'in print'. Print was encouraging the identification of spheres via their attendant jargons, that surface element of linguistics which dominates *The Staple of News*. This is a play much concerned with the varying ramifications of language, be it in print or conversation. Richard Levin has demonstrated the link between the Staple itself, the society of jeerers (many of whom also work as emissaries or reporters at the press), and the projected Canters' college of Act IV.[37] The press, the planned College, and the jeerers are all concerned with increasingly superficial and exaggerated forms of language. The emissaries may make a living from spurious news items but the jeerers exist merely to throw people's words back at them. Though this is rather different from the 'nonsense' competition of the game of vapours in *Bartholomew Fair* and the word-games of *Cynthia's Revels*, there is nevertheless an important link between all three forms of jargon or language and the way in which the diversity of languages function in the Jonsonian text.

Language carries the potential of unifying but also of disunifying and Jonson appears fascinated by the factions of language that occur in any number of different and disparate communities. Fittingly enough, the redundant management of the Staple subsequently take over the jeerers: so averse to the construance of positive meanings are Cymbal and Fitton that they have attempted to prevent anything from making it into print, scorning the public for the trust they place in such a surface form.

The culinary trade has its specific discourse which continues to inspire printed matter. What is particularly remarkable about Lickfinger, Pennyboy Senior's cook in *The Staple of News*, is that his reading is far from confined to a specialized area such as recipe books. Unlike the superficial Pennyboy Junior, Lickfinger can truly claim to be a man of arts and arms (albeit that his weaponry is of the kitchen utensil variety); he is well read in a wide range of subjects, from military manuals to books recording Vitruvian architectural dimensions. He can appropriate the jargon (and the 'news') of each domain to suit his own discursive purposes:

> A master cook! Why, he's the man o'men
> For a professor. He designs, he draws,
> He paints, he carves, he builds, he fortifies,
> Makes citadels of curious fowl and fish;
> Some he dry-ditches, some moats round with broths, ...
> He is an architect, an engineer,
> A soldier, a physician, a philosopher,
> A general mathematician,
>
> (IV.ii.19–23, 35–7)[38]

Lickfinger is clearly akin here to a masque-maker, and once again Jonson has embarked upon a popularization of that elite form which, as well as being occasional and ephemeral, was dependent upon surfaces and spectacle for its full effect.

Neptune's Triumph commenced with a debate between a poet and a master-cook on the validity of their respective trades. The Cook puns on their shared site of operation, 'Sir, this is my room and region too, the Banqueting House!' (l. 13); both masques and huge feasts were enjoyed and 'staged' in the Banqueting House at Whitehall (in an ultimate act of fusion, Inigo Jones would design not just sets for masques there but the building itself). Descriptions of Lickfinger's meals are certainly proof that the food was staged as carefully on big occasions as any play.³⁹ The Poet bemoans the seasonal nature of his employment as writer of the Christmas masque: 'The most unprofitable of his servants, I, sir, the poet. A kind of a Christmas ingine, one that is used at least once a year for a trifling instrument of wit, or so.' (ll. 19–21). Jonson's own disgruntlement at his under-use as court-poet may be registered here, but the Cook dismisses such self-piteous whimperings, 'Then you can be no good poet, for a good poet differs nothing at all from a master-cook. Either's art is the wisdom of the mind' (ll. 24–6). Much of this is an in-joke served up for the pleasure of the masque's (in the end hypothetical) Twelfth Night Court audience, no doubt about to enjoy or having enjoyed a sumptuous banquet. The Cook has pleased their palates and now the Poet hopes to achieve the same, although the near impossibility of satisfying expectations now faces him, 'That were a heavy and hard task, to satisfy Expectation, who is so severe an exactress of duties, ever a tyrannous mistress, and most times a pressing enemy' (ll. 33–5).

Lickfinger proffers a version of his aesthetic which is almost identical to Madrigal's, the sub-poet of *The Staple of News*. His extravagant culinary creations can be perceived as an alimentary equivalent to the court masque, served up as it were for royal delectation; as Captain Shunfield so vividly describes:

> Gi' him allowance,
> And that but moderate, he will make a Siren
> Sing i'the kettle, send in an Arion,
> In a brave broth and of a wat'ry green
> Just the sea colour, mounted on the back
> Of a grown conger, but in such a posture
> As all the world would take him for a dolphin.
> (III.iii.34–40)⁴⁰

The watery pageants that greeted Elizabeth I at Kenilworth Castle and other country estates during her summer progresses are recalled here;⁴¹ the links with royal shows, pageants, and processions are clear and this connection would have been intended for 'public consumption' in the seventeenth century. In this central scene and in the play as a whole the masque genre is utilized and commodified in a public theatre context, allowing for the attendant redefinitions of space, purpose and target population – a democratization of an elitist form comparable to the workings of the press.

As in Jonson's generic alignments, the masque is made 'news' and the prodigality surrounding its spectacles potentially exposed.

A lack of interest in the harsh fiscal consequences of his behaviour marks out the conspicuous consumption of the prodigal son figure, but to proffer this as a sole reading of *The Staple of News*'s protagonist is inadequate. Pennyboy Junior demonstrates occasional depth of understanding, not least of the central topos of the press.[42] Whilst he seems to pour money into the Staple with little regard, purchasing positions at will for his friends, he is also manifestly sympathetic towards the consuming public (perhaps due to empathy with their position), unlike the jeering Fitton who wishes to deny them their printed stories:

> Why, methinks, sir, if the honest common people
> Will be abused, why should not they ha'their pleasure
> In the believing lies are made for them,
> As you i'th'Office, making them yourselves?
> (I.v.42–5)[43]

John Milton's *Areopagitica* would not sound so different a few decades later:

> Nor is it to the common people less than a reproach; for if we be so jealous over them, as that we dare not trust them with an English pamphlet, what do we but censure them for a giddy, vicious, and ungrounded people; in such a sick and weak estate of faith and discretion, as to be able to take nothing down but through the pipe of a licenser ... .[44]

Milton's own text on the freedom of the press is undergoing critical revision at present. Many argue that it is a response to an increasingly capitalistic system, a demand for individual liberties, but critics such as Burt and Norbrook argue that Milton, like Jonson, was not anti-censorship *per se* but rather demanding new forms of it. Norbrook in particular sees it as a defensive text, a comment on the ideological struggles occurring in contemporary Europe, and says that we should view it against the background of Renaissance republicanism rather than later liberalism.[45] For a re-reading of Milton's pamphlet, he argues that we need to connect the development of Parliament, political theory, literary history and a study of the mass media. This is exactly what I argue is necessary for a re-evaluation of *The Staple of News*; it needs to be seen as a response to the political crises of its own time and as an intervention in the debate over press and censorship, rather than as either a purely supportive or oppositional text.

Pennyboy Junior's debate with Fitton and Cymbal over the press prefigures modernist dilemmas about the fixity of form. For Fitton and Cymbal, the written as opposed to the printed retains a sense of being corruptible (that is, possible to corrupt in the same way as their jeering corrupts language and conversation) yet, in the text, printing is regularly associated with waxen or melting metaphors and this would seem to deny their sense of rigidity. For them, however, printing accords a sense of fact and permanence that inclines people to believe what they read, whatever they read. As Pennyboy Junior recounts:

> See divers men's opinions! Unto some,
> The very printing of them makes them news,
> That ha' not the heart to believe anything
> But what they see in print.
> (I.v.51-4)[46]

Print as a controlling force only ever constitutes a superficial understanding of the form. For all the potential democratization and liberation of the print, however, the Staple office is by and large scornful of their target population:

> REGISTER   'Tis the house of fame, sir,
> Where both the curious and the negligent,
> The scrupulous and careless, wild and staid,
> The idle and laborious; all do meet
> To taste the *cornucopiae* of her rumours,
> Which she, the mother of sport, pleaseth to scatter
> Among the vulgar. Baits, sir, for the people!
> And they will bite like fishes.
> (III.ii.115–22)

As if to prove the Register's point, at this moment a variety of customers arrive. The first couple are Anabaptists, the third is Lickfinger himself seeking some pamphlets to circulate at his forthcoming banquet. Court news is his initial hope: 'To strew out the long meal withal,' (III.ii.183) but he is happy to settle for news of the stage, of new plays, and the fate of acting companies.

The implicit interconnection of all these worlds is significant for Jonson. The recent censorship of Thomas Middleton's *A Game at Chess* (1624) is alluded to, suppressed as it was following Count Gondomar's outrage at its anti-Spanish content and propagandistic effects during the unprecedented success of its initial nine-day run:[47]

> LICKFINGER   What news of Gondomar?
> THOMAS [*Reading another roll*]   A second fistula,
>   Or an excoriation at the least,
>   For putting the poor English play was writ of him
>   To such a sordid use, as is said he did,
>   Of cleansing his posteriors.
> LICKFINGER   Justice! Justice!
> THOMAS   Since when he lives condemned to his chair at
>   Brussels,
>   And there sits filing certain politic hinges
>   To hang the States on h'has heaved off the hooks.
>   (III.ii.207–14)

The reference is not only to the special chair which Gondomar had to accommodate his infamous fistula, and which was notoriously used in actual English stage performances of *A Game at Chess*, but also to Spanish offensives in the States General of the United Provinces, that is to say, the Protestant Low Countries. The importance of that situation to Jonson's life and art was suggested in the introduction to this book, but it is worth recalling that many 1620s *corantos* were of Dutch origin: that republican context for print culture is highly significant.

Richard Burt regards this episode of *The Staple of News* as an 'excoriation' of Middleton but it would seem to me that the tone of the episode is sympathetic towards the 'poor' suppressed play and rather more anti-Gondomar in its focus.[48] The attack on Spanish aggressive policy in the United Provinces (that poignant image of states hung on 'politic hinges' for which Gondomar himself files the hooks) seems to be at the heart of the matter rather than a critical censuring, or censoring, of Middleton. This might suggest an anti-Spanish stance for the play which would seem supportive of Caroline policy towards Spain, and critical of parliament's failure to provide funding for military preparations for war in 1625, but I would argue instead that it defends the potential republicanism involved in the allowing of critical, censoring texts, such as *A Game at Chess* and, by implication, *The Staple of News*, to be performed in the public sphere.

The political and religious sympathies of *The Staple of News* are typically vague and insubstantial. Ostensibly it manufactures gossip (a male gossiping counterpart to the female audience of the Intermeans) and tabletalk and the journalists merely adapt the stance of stories to suit their intended recipients. The Anabaptists, for example, receive Protestant polemic in the pamphlets they purchase. Jonson's own oscillations between Protestantism and Catholicism are perhaps also embedded in the Staple's fluidity on religious issues according to who is paying for the pamphlet. He is expertly capturing the uncertainties and instabilities of the early days of the print – its democratic potential is present but also its vulnerability to corruption, not least of the fiscal variety.

In terms of its historicity *The Staple of News* is a remarkable dramatic document. In an interesting example of textual instabilities, the printed text of *The Staple of News* prepared at least two years after the first performance, and possibly as late as 1631, added to the ending of the play. These interpolations reflect on the theme of civil liberties, even more prescient in 1629 after the King's dissolution of Parliament and the instigation of the 'Personal Rule'. Devra Kifer has suggested that the additional section represents an attempt by Jonson to protect himself against charges of slandering the former Lord Chief Justice, Sir Edward Coke in the character of Pennyboy Senior. Coke had been in disgrace in 1626 the year of the play's first performance; he had effectively been banished to his county to perform the local duties of sheriff. By 1628, however, he had regained his parliamentary position. He was one of the Petition of Right's main presenters and was opposed to the imprisonment of any subject without due process of the law, yet this would seem to be the import of Pennyboy Senior's statements at V.vi (ll. 42–7). Lickfinger questions his abuse of the 'liberty of the subjects' (V.vi.48) and Kifer suggests that by making Lickfinger author of these views Jonson covered his own back against charges of libel, taking advantage of a possible pun on Coke and 'Cook' (the favoured pronunciation of his name).[49] What is clear, however, is that in this play Jonson, in addition to capturing the emergent medium of print and providing considerations of the new monarch, attends to complex questions of democracy, constitutional change, and social, civic, and intellectual property rights. Like the news-sheets that provide its subject-matter, this play, with a heightened sense of its politicized discourse, offers 'news' of its own time and manner of production.

9
Alternative Societies: *The New Inn* and the Late Plays

The traditionalist view of Ben Jonson has been that of a theatrical absolutist, of someone who struggled with the inherent heterogeneity of theatre audiences and to control the meanings of his texts. Those meanings have themselves frequently been read as absolutist in their sympathies.[1] Jonson's 'late' plays have, however, a particular investment in questions of community, from the fractious dinner-party guests at Lady Loadstone's house in *The Magnetic Lady* (1632) to the Sherwood Forest groupings of the unfinished *The Sad Shepherd* (1637).[2] *The New Inn* (1629) offers a number of theatrical alternatives as well as a vision of an alternative society amidst its alehouse gathering.

The New Inn is essentially about a group of unlikely individuals gathered together for a day under the roof of 'The Light Heart' inn. Presided over by the jovial host Goodstock, we see various characters fall in and out of love in the course of that day. Lord Lovel, a melancholic ex-soldier, confesses his love for Lady Frances Frampul to whose suitor, Beaufort, he had promised to act as a father. Beaufort, however, falls in love with Laetitia, Goodstock's adopted son Frank in disguise. Such are the complexities of the family and quasi-familial relationships of this play that 'Frank' turns out really to be Laetitia and Frances's long-lost sister into the bargain. Goodstock is their true father, in reality Lord Frampul who had left his family and lived a life with gypsies and puppet-masters in the intervening years. Frank's attendant Irish nurse is Frampul's wife and the sisters' mother. Act V of the play witnesses a remarkable, and at times somewhat laughable, family reunion. Beaufort has married Laetitia, Lovel is reunited with Frances, and Prudence, Frances's intelligent and vivacious chambermaid who, in her role as queen for the day in the inn, has presided over these various couplings and reunions finds a partner of her own in Lord Latimer. There has been much debate as to the merit or otherwise of

Jonson's 'happy ending' but of interest to me here is instead his questioning of blood ties and arranged marriages and his stress on merit and the earning of relationships as well as the particular context and community in which he chooses to explore these themes.[3]

'The Light Heart' is the 'new inn' of the play's title and the setting for the entire five acts of the play. It is an interior domestic space as Rebecca Ann Bach has stressed; but it also an 'othered' place, not the 'home' of any characters present (not even of Goodstock since the Frampul country estate is a world elsewhere).[4] What we have here is another gathering place, akin to the fair of *Bartholomew Fair* or Lovewit's house in *The Alchemist* and of course akin in its nature to a theatre. As the work of social historians of this period has detailed, inns were commonly places of entertainment – used for dicing, dancing, skittles and 'sports';[5] the latter term describes the day's events in Jonson's dramatic creation: 'the day's sports devised i'the inn' (I.vi.44).

The Argument to *The New Inn* (another textual marker of Jonson's anxiety to produce 'right' readings of his texts) describes how Prudence is elected 'Governess of the Sports' for the day's shenanigans in 'The Light Heart': she is a mock-sovereign in true carnivalesque tradition. From the outset, her name denotes that she possesses one of the essential qualities for good government, if not the blood and breeding that usually determine such a position. This is perhaps further evidence of Jonson's ideological support of a meritocracy as opposed to a hierarchy determined merely by birth, scarcely the stance of a radical but certainly one demanding of constitutional change at this time.[6]

If, as Mikhail Bakhtin suggests, the marketplace was one of the prime *loci* of the carnivalesque,[7] then inns and alehouses became in the early modern period alternative marketplaces – there goods were frequently sold, or prices negotiated before the buyers and sellers reached market. Inns could even provide an alternative barter economy whereby victuals could be received or credit given instead of a straightforward financial transaction. The inn was a potential rival to the parish church in a time of sociological transition.[8] The inn also signified a marketplace of sorts in its conglomeration of guests of different rank, background, and gender: akin indeed to the heterogeneous gathering at Bartholomew Fair.

Of great significance when considering the role of 'community' in Jonson's plays is the political period in which any single drama was written. *The New Inn* has often been labelled a 'late romance' by critics as a convenient excuse for ignoring its compositional context – that is to say, not merely the time of the Caroline masque and of neo-platonism at court,[9] although these too feature in the make-up of this play, but more specifically of 1628–29. The submission to the King by Parliament of the Petition of Right had taken place in 1628, and in 1629 Charles I, out of frustration with these attempts to curb his royal prerogative, would dissolve Parliament, not to summon another until some eleven years later by which time Ben Jonson would be dead and England would be taking its first hesitant steps towards civil war. In an article on 'Late Jonson' Martin Butler has mapped out the immediate context of this play:

> The political interest of *The New Inn* derives from its composition immediately prior to the recall of the last of Charles's early Parliaments, in March 1629 ... the play may be read as partly a response to the expectations of a moment in which rapprochement or accommodation, rather than confrontation, might at last have been achieved between the court and the court's critics – expectations brought about, needless to say, by the assassination of Buckingham six months earlier. With Buckingham removed, the possibilities of a new relationship between King and Parliament became suddenly available ....[10]

That particular political context will be seen to be crucial to a full understanding of this play, as will the topographical siting of its events.

Whereas the *loci* of Jonson's Jacobean plays have been the subject of intense critical scrutiny, the romance labelling of *The New Inn* seems to have led to an omission in critical discussions of adequate consideration of the drama's inn-house setting. 'The Light Heart' is in Barnet, nowadays a suburb of North London, but in Jonson's time rather further removed from the city's edge, an important staging-point on the old post road. Watson suggests that 'the location of the inn ... may reflect the location of the play halfway between the satiric world of city-comedy and the romantic world of pastoral'.[11] The exact topography is, as always in Jonson, significant: the later plays interest themselves in these rural communities barely within sight of Westminster, and yet frequently exploited by it – witness Tottenham Court and Finsbury Park in *A Tale of a Tub*.

The aristocratic participants in the day's sports (disguised or otherwise) are not attending some large private-house gathering: 'The Light Heart' is no Penshurst. They are in a public place, mingling with other levels and sectors of society, and not necessarily always on their own terms.

Inns, alehouses and taverns (and these are distinctions to which I wish to return) witnessed massive expansion during the Tudor and Stuart reigns. Admirable work by social historians such as Peter Clark and Keith Wrightson has demonstrated the importance of public drinking houses in social, financial and political terms and such work has much to offer any reading of *The New Inn*.[12] Alehouses tended to represent the lower end of the drinking-house spectrum and had various synonyms in the Stuart period – tippling houses, boozing kens, tup houses. Taverns sold wine to the more prosperous but could not offer lodgings. By comparison, inns tended to be large, often fashionable establishments offering wine, ale and beer, together with food and lodging (of an elaborate kind) to well-heeled travellers and since their façades tended to dominate the main street of a given community they were important cultural centres. Clark recounts that some establishments, such as the New Inn at Gloucester, followed a courtyard plan, with four ranges, two or more storeys high, surrounding a central yard: these were often employed for a theatrical purpose. Impressive inn-signs, furnished in wood or elaborate wrought iron, overarched the road, to draw in customers, just like those of the South Bank theatres.[13] In the 1570s some inns were able to lodge as many as two to three hundred people, equivalent to a theatre audience.

Drawn into the interior of 'The Light Heart' is a variable 'audience' or community – varied in terms of rank, sex and background; the setting provides a typically Jonsonian cross-section of society. As with the fair in *Bartholomew Fair*, both guests and those whose livelihood depends upon the inn are present: no one more so than Fly, whom the Host claims to have received as part of the 'household stuff' when given the inventory of the place:

> I had him, when I came to take the Inn here,
> Assigned me over, in the inventory
> As an old implement, a piece of household stuff,
> And so he doth remain.
> (II.iv.16–19)

Goodstock later contradicts this tale by implying that Fly was one of the band of gypsies with whom he previously took up and travelled, but the story nevertheless indicates Fly's dependence upon the inn. He is, as his name suggests, and like his forebear Mosca, a parasite, but one living less directly off his master than off the establishment he owns.

The staffing of such establishments was important: 'Inns usually had a bevy of maids, tapsters, chamberlains, and ostlers to serve the multitude of guests.'[14] A glimpse at Jonson's *dramatis personae* for this play reveals just that: we have Jordan the chamberlain, aptly named after the word for a chamberpot (no doubt one of his primary responsibilities), Jug the tapster, and Peck the ostler. According to Clark, a number of these servants were often hired orphans, particularly in lower-class establishments (the same is true of many boy actors in the London boys' companies) and we witness the same phenomenon in the Host's adoption of the 'boy Frank' and 'his' attendant nurse.

The Host of *The New Inn*, though in a job of service, still discourses in lordly terms, telling the melancholic Lovel:

> It is against my freehold, my inheritance,
> My Magna Charta, *cor laetificat*,
> To drink such balderdash, or bonny-clabber!
> (I.ii.23–5)

Lovel is surprised that someone as articulate as Goodstock should elect to pursue such a lowly profession:

> methinks a man
> Of your sagacity and clear nostril, should
> Have made another choice, than of a place
> So sordid as the keeping of an inn:
> (I.iii.109–12)

In expressing such a pronounced opinion, Lovel is voicing a common theory of the age that only the lowest sectors of society – morally and financially – ran alehouses and taverns, thus rendering them breeding grounds for thieves and canting crews, as well as general drunkenness and disorder. It does appear from historical records that a majority of alehouse owners were poor – often forced to take up victualling for want of any other trade – but this did not necessarily hold true across the spectrum: inn-house keepers did become important if not elite members of the community.[15]

Like the theatres, the drinking-houses of the early modern period were railed against in pamphlet publications as sites of drunkenness and general moral disorder, and as purveyors of paganism in their festivals and entertainments. All this invective had a strong political dimension, particularly following the publication in 1617 of King James I's *Book of Sports*; James recognized the political value of sports and entertainments as a means of releasing and controlling public energies.[16] There certainly appears to be a political motive to Goodstock's mirth in *The New Inn*; he defends against social prejudice those who are forced by circumstance to pursue such lifestyles, instructing Lovel that not all are as blessed and fortunate as he.

In the course of their dialogue, Lovel learns from the Host's moral instruction (undoubtedly a Jonsonian theatrical ideal) to have a lighter heart. In the second courtroom assembly of the play he debates the meaning of *virtù*, an ongoing debate in Jonson's drama; his speech is largely culled from Seneca but nevertheless in its humanitarian, pacifist, and egalitarian ethos, something of Ben Jonson may also be heard:

> The things true valour is exercised about
> Are poverty, restraint, captivity,
> Banishment, loss of children, long disease:
> The least is death.
> (IV.iv.106–9)

Like Lovel, Jonson learned not to be angry with the ostlers, the tapsters, and the under-officers, and to celebrate their diversity. He also learned not to be angry with those above him in rank and responsibility. He stared poverty and disease in the face in the final few years of his life; he had lost his wife and children, was effectively banished the court, and, restrained by a stroke, was virtually bed-ridden at the end. He seems almost to have been preparing for such eventualities when he wrote these magniloquent lines for Lovel in 1629:

> I am kept out a masque, sometime thrust out,
> Made wait a day, two, three, for a great word,

> Which, when it comes forth, is all frown and forehead!
> What laughter should this breed, rather than anger,
> Out of the tumult of so many errors,
> To feel, with contemplation, mine own quiet?
> If a great person do me an affront
> A giant of the time, sure, I will bear it
> Or out of patience, or necessity!
>
> (IV.iv.184–92)[17]

Jonson was able to look to a time when his works would be 'out of the time'; at the beginning of *The New Inn* Lovel believes, albeit somewhat nostalgically, in the chivalric code of honour and a correlative feudal system:

> Call you that desperate, which by a line
> Of institution from our ancestors
> Hath been derived down to us, and received
> In a succession, for the noblest way
> Of breeding up our youth, in letters, arms,
> Fair mien, discourses, civil exercise,
> And all the blazon of a gentleman?
> Where can he learn to vault, to ride, to fence,
> To move his body gracefuller? To speak
> His language purer? Or to tune his mind
> Or manners more to the harmony of nature
> Than in these nurseries of nobility?
>
> (I.iii.40–51)

Many critics regard this as the central political argument of the play but to do so ignores its early positioning, the changes undergone by Lovel, and the Host's answering scepticism:[18]

> Ay, that was when the nursery's self was noble,
> And only virtue made it, not the market,
> That titles were not vented at the drum,
> Or common outcry;
>
> (I.iii.52–5)

Goodstock is here attacking the Sale of Titles, which was one of the infamous emergency or 'extraordinary' measures taken by the bankrupt Stuart Treasury, and which led to the creation of 'mushroom knights' who sprang up overnight by dint of their financial buying power; in doing so Goodstock is also counselling Lovel in the need to respond to the actualities of the present instead of yearning for some false arcadia of the past. Similar concerns drive the plot of *The Devil is an Ass*, as the adventurer Merecraft is thwarted by the honest friendships of the like of Wittipol, Manly and Frances Fitzdottrel.

If the noble academies have become so corrupt, Goodstock suggests that it is entirely plausible that an alehouse or inn might be a site of better qualities: Pru is surely confirmation of this. 'The Light Heart' functions as a quasi-pastoral setting; it is not London and yet not quite the country either, but stands instead on the margins of each. The alternative community it offers also represents a subtle critique of the Court and its environs (an operation we might like to see as analogous to the role of the public and private theatres at this time).

In considering Lovel's chivalric code critics appear persistently blind to his overly idealistic and frankly snobbish views which are so obviously qualified throughout by the Host's statements and thus nurtured into offering a more expansive and tolerant outlook. One of the educative processes of 'The Light Heart' is to instruct Lovel in the value of community, of interhierarchical community, something he is clearly unappreciative of at the outset of the play:

> An host to find me! Who is, commonly
> The log, a little o'this side the sign-post!
> Or at the best some round-grown thing, a jug
> Faced with a beard, that fills out to the guests,
> And takes in fro' the fragments o'their jests!
> (I.iv.11–15)

In comparing the bearded and portly Host to a jug Lovel is making a pun on the inn's serving containers but he also invokes a comparison between Goodstock and Jonson. The dramatist consistently fashioned himself as a container in his own poems,[19] and by this stage of his career he was also a jovial and tolerant host with the same interhierarchical perspective and experience. The metaphor seems to identify Jonson more with the Host's anti-nostalgic discourse than Lovel's initial extremism.

Lovel's initial absolutist discourse is in truth closer to that of the ridiculous Colonel Glorious Tipto, a descendant of *Every Man In His*

Humour's braggadocio soldier Bobadill(a), and one of the more regular customers at 'The Light Heart'. Tipto talks of the inn as a city-state republic, but more specifically as Sparta. Simon Hornblower has outlined the political paradox represented by the Spartan constitution:

> The history of European democracy begins arguably not in Athens but in Sparta. This is a paradox because Sparta has usually been seen as the opposite of the 'Open Society' which Periclean Athens is taken, by a simplification, to represent. But youthful Sparta was different from the totalitarian monster she grew up to be. A constitutional document, whose date and interpretation are one of the fiercest battlegrounds of ancient Greek history, stipulates that a Spartan popular assembly should meet at regular intervals ....[20]

Tipto might not see the paradox, but Jonson would have known that the 'republic' of Sparta (also a major focus of Machiavelli's *Discourses*) had two kings, and the colonel certainly envisages himself as the oligarch of his particular city-state,[21] for he assumes command of the inn's 'citizen militia' – that primary requisite of the successful republic according to the *Discourses*. Tipto is akin in this to the monomaniac Sir Epicure Mammon in *The Alchemist*, who also dreamed of an alternative society which he could rule. The inn-house environment, let alone the drink, contributes to Tipto's delusions of grandeur: 'the alehouse was perceived as the command-post of men who sought to turn the traditional world upside-down and create their own alternative society'.[22]

The theme, albeit comic, of a citizen militia was, as it had been in *The Devil is an Ass* in 1616, a pointed contemporary reference; since Charles I's accession to the throne in 1625 the country had witnessed an immediate stepping-up in the recruitment and training of local militia, the militia tradition having lapsed during James's reign. Tipto, who is to be Colonel of this particular motley crew, is another glorious example of consumption in the Mammonian vein. His projects soon far exceed their locality. Tipto half-jokingly names Fly as 'Lipsius Fly', thus comparing him to the Dutch political and military author Justus Lipsius whose influence on Jonson has been well-documented,[23] imagining him to be too good for 'The Light Heart' (although, as we have seen, Fly is dependent upon the inn for survival. Contemporary anxieties that the alehouse, inn or tavern might constitute a hotbed of political and republican sedition were equally exaggerated:

> There was no master-plan for a new levelling republic commanded from the alehouse. Rather the tippling-house's growing importance as a social and commercial centre was primarily a development that occurred in response to the major economic, social and other changes affecting society in the century or more before the English Civil War. The alehouse stood less in the van than in the baggage train of an alternative society.[24]

Jonson seems to be gently mocking such political anxieties in the Tipto/militia scenes but he is also registering the increasing use of the inn as a political as well as social meeting-place, and as a means of levying troops. Despite his comment that there was no master-plan for a republic born in alehouses, Peter Clark acknowledges that inns and taverns were the favoured assembly-points of both royalists and parliamentarians in the 1640s. Governmental activities also took place there – local meetings which were themselves a source of tension due to their often oppositional stance towards the policies of central government:

> Most important county business was transacted at inns up to the late eighteenth century, including meetings of quarter and petty sessions, committees to levy taxes and troops, enclosure and bankruptcy commissions, canal companies and turnpike trusts.[25]

The seventeenth century had been party to a storm of invective against drinking establishments, and early Stuart policies aimed at regulating and controlling them can at best be described as fluctuating. One reason for this is that patents, licences and drinking taxes for inns were a lucrative source of revenue (then as now), and the Treasury was, as we have seen, already hard-pressed. The corrupting effects of this reached their zenith in 1617 with the sale of the monopoly on the granting of inn licences throughout England to three men, Giles Bridge of Hereford, James Thurborne of Middlesex and Sir Giles Mompesson.

Mompesson is the most renowned of the three. The licensing procedure was supposedly an attempt to limit the number of illegally controlled inns and yet he steadfastly abused the system by selling to all and sundry: 'The Mompesson patent abdicated the responsibilities of executive government in favour of satisfying patronage demands at court.'[26] His indictment was one of the main grievances of the monopolies-focused 1621 parliament. The character of Sir Giles Overreach in Massinger's *A New Way to Pay Old Debts* (1625, published 1633) is believed to be partially based on Mompesson.[27] Interestingly enough, *The New Inn* exhibits a strong awareness of the Massinger precedent not only in the setting (in *A New Way to Pay Old Debts* the opening situation is a tavern run by the aptly-named Tapwell and his wife, although this is a distinctly more disreputable establishment than 'The Light Heart') but also in the naming of the character Lovel (Massinger's presiding lord is called Lovell).

James I and Charles I both frequently sacrificed governmental responsibility over drinking-houses in the face of more immediate financial needs, enforcing and ignoring regulations (not least on monopolies) as it suited them. Such political vacillation could be seen as a contributing factor in the eventual dissolution of the much anticipated 1629 session of parliament, amidst an atmosphere of political questions and grievances.

In 1610 James I had declared in a speech to the Lower House that he sought to create at that session a 'parliament of love'.[28] In theatrical terms it is self-evident that the Court or Parliament of Love scenes provide the central motif of *The New Inn*. Much useful critical work has been done on the sources and origins of this motif, especially so by Michael Hattaway in his Revels edition of the play; he demonstrates the way in which Jonson draws on a triple strand of influence. There is a medieval strand, that is to say, the medieval courts or parliaments of love, such as in Chaucer's *The Parliament of Fowls*; there are the Renaissance 'banquets' or symposia; and, in so far as the parliament of 'The Light Heart' is presided over by a chambermaid, a servant of the household or group gathered there, there is the carnival tradition of electing a Lord of Misrule for the day.

That Jonson elects as his figure of misrule a woman, and a working-class one at that, is significant as part of a wider expansion of roles for women in his later drama, or at least of female roles for boy actors. *The New Inn* alone has five important and articulate female characters. The venison for the Sherwood Forest feast in *The Sad Shepherd* is killed not, as might be expected, by Robin Hood but by Marian:

ROBIN	Had you good sport i'your chase to day?
JOHN	O prime!
MARIAN	A lusty Stag!
ROBIN	And hunted you at force?
MARIAN	In a full cry!
JOHN	And never hunted change!
ROBIN	You had staunch Hounds then?
MARIAN	Old and sure, I love

No young rash dogs, no more than changing friends.
(I.vi.21–5)

Not only is Marian a strong and articulate character whose cloning by the witch Maudlin (another emblem of female agency in the text) forms a large section of the extant scenes, but her romantic relationship with Robin is clearly a 'mature', 'settled' and affectionate one.[29] The Robin–Marian pairing has a possible precursor in the shape of Lovel and Lady Frances; the lovers, like the courtroom situation of their love, are an innovative reworking of an old theme.

In recounting the long literary history of the motif of a parliament or court of love,[30] Hattaway observes:

> as a parliament it was an assembly in which noble men and women assembled to hear 'questions' of love, definitions or praises of love, or to discuss matters of etiquette; as a court it served to resolve differences.[31]

This functions well as a working definition of the Court of Love in *The New Inn* but its suggestion of the movement towards resolution through debate has led Butler to regard this as proof once again of the play's, and Jonson's, unquestioning endorsement of the Caroline court and its policies, in this case in 1629. To me the play does not seem so clear-cut in any direction as to allow for discussion of 'endorsement'; it would be false to describe the play as an explicit critique of monarchy but nevertheless, as in *A Tale of a Tub*, the plot's romantic resolution should not blind us to potentially more subversive ideas contained elsewhere in the text. There is a radical subtext to the dialogue and debates of the courtroom scenes and it is one of which Jonson was fully aware. That the main event of the play should be a mock-parliament when, as Butler himself has shown, that very play was licensed only ten days before the new parliament assembled in 1629 is a coincidence that cannot be regarded as dramatically tangential; it charges the political vocabulary of the relevant scenes, not with nostalgia but with topical importance.

What has been recognized as topical in the play is its employment of neo-platonist themes and ideas. The academic debate or symposium, which is also an important source for Jonson's play, has as its classical archetype Plato's dialogue on love, the *Symposium*. This text had a huge influence on early modern literature from Sidney and Spenser through to George Herbert's *The Temple* in 1633. Jonson is no exception: a number of Lovel's lengthy discourses on love are directly transcribed from Plato. In addition, some of the love debates in *The New Inn* resemble Book IV of Castiglione's *Il Cortegiano*. If Lovel articulates conventional neo-platonic doctrine as espoused in Castiglione by Cardinal Bembo, then Lord Beaufort is the voice of the Ovidian sensualist. In accordance with Jonson's complex relationship with Ovid, Beaufort's views are not entirely discounted within the play; his reflections reveal the impracticalities of a doctrine that counsels that love can and should survive without descending to the fleshly. This debate often featured in the poetry of John Donne and Jonson himself had dealt with it as early as 1601 in *Poetaster*.

Queen Henrietta Maria is the person most often attributed with bringing the cult of neo-platonism to England, thus rendering the English monarchy a wholly more Eurocentric affair than it had been under the parochial James I.[32] It is now a literary commonplace that the Caroline masques reflect these new Eurocentric tastes and interests. In contrast to his Jacobean commissions Jonson was largely excluded from these Caroline masques composing his last, *Love's Triumph through Callipolis*, where he did indeed celebrate the myths of Plato, in 1631. This exclusion also appears to have increased with the years, as the Caroline court established its identity, and Henrietta Maria became a more powerful force both at court and upon her husband. Jonson's personality now seemed 'out of the time' in an era of more refined and elitist court drama.[33] Exclusivity is precisely not the case with the inn-house gathering of 'The Light Heart' or the public theatre play *The New Inn*. Though they have their own politics, neo-platonic strains in the text have been concentrated upon to the detriment of more parliamentary strains.

Hattaway acknowledges in passing the political sphere of reference in the play's language:

Jonson's assembly is both a court of justice to which Lovel brings a Bill of Complaint for the disrespect he has 'conceived if not received' (II.vi.143) from Lady [Frances] Frampul, and a parliament in which he propounds *quaestiones* of love and valour.[34]

Butler carries this a stage further, acknowledging that whilst this assembly is strictly speaking a court of love and not a parliament, Pru is nevertheless a mock-sovereign and she and the other characters 'have a way of creating situations or using language which resonate with the political discourse of 1628–9'.[35]

For those parliamentarians who used republican parlance if not necessarily republicanism in its overt sense in their challenging of the unlimited exercise of the royal prerogative in the period, Magna Carta was a crucial touchstone document. Goodstock, the Host, invokes Magna Carta in his opening debate with Lovel. On the surface this might be taken as the Host revealing his true aristocratic background by speaking in the language of monarchy and government, for Magna Carta was a non-authoritarian, not a non-aristocratic, document; indeed, defining aristocratic rights was one of its contemporary manoeuvres. Magna Carta was, though, a significant document in the history of monarchy since it sought to curb and constrain the powers and prerogative of King John:

> Seventeenth-century Parliamentarians who quoted Magna Carta were perhaps nearer the mark than they have sometimes been recognized to be. The crisis which produced Magna Carta was an unpopular and unsuccessful foreign war, and no less than two-thirds of Magna Carta's clauses prohibited various methods by which the king had been raising money. Many more crises occurred before the principle was firmly established that the king needed the consent of the political community for extraordinary taxation, and even more before it was clear that Parliament was the proper body to express that consent.[36]

Similar grievances over extraordinary taxation would gain ground amongst parliamentarian support groups during the period of personal rule, reaching something of a culmination in 1640 with the abolition of the universally despised Ship Money.[37] Yet what the Host's use of terminology indicates is that discussions centring on the King's accountability to the political community, an idea enshrined in Magna Carta, were current in the late 1620s and, in particular, both prior and subsequent to the issuing of the Petition of Right in 1628.

Jonson would use the term 'Magna Carta' in another intriguing instance in *The Magnetic Lady* (1632). Damplay, a Chorus member of sorts, insists upon his *'Magna Charta* of reprehension' (III. Chorus, ll. 24–5), citing his ancient precedent for this, just as parliamentarians would cite the ancient constitution in defence of their manoeuvres against the monarchy in the 1640s. Damplay is an interesting figure in this respect: his nomenclature might suggest that Jonson requests spectators and readers to dismiss him as a character, since he damns the very medium in which they all believe. In his turn, Damplay charges Jonson with a kind of authorial tyranny:

> Why, *Boy*? This were a strange Empire, or rather a Tyranny, you would entitle your Poet to, over Gentlemen, that they should come to hear, and see *Plays*, and say nothing for their money.
> (II. Chorus, 53-6)

When *The Magnetic Lady* is accorded rare critical attention, the ubiquitous point appears to be that Compass and Ironside, those 'honest, and adopted' brothers of the text (II.vi.145), represent contradictory sides of Jonson's own nature: the urbane epigrammatist and the brawling soldier who boasted of killing men in the Netherlands whilst a soldier there. More intriguing, however, are the contradictions contained within the single figure of Captain Rudibras Ironside – his very name a heterogeneous yoking of fictional Spenserian knight and real infantry member; therein lies a truly Jonsonian dilemma. Ironside's surname would later come to be suggestive of the Parliamentarian forces and in particular the New Model Army – the nickname derived from the appearance of their armour; yet Ironside wears the feather in his cap more typically suggestive of a cavalier or royalist soldier. The distinctions were not fully formulated in 1632 but the point is rather that Ironside is an uncomfortable and often confused accommodation of the battlefield and puritan austerity alongside an almost aristocratic urbanity (the latter figured in his eventual marriage to Lady Loadstone, the magnetic lady of the title). At times one sphere invades the other, as when he threatens the dinner guests at Loadstone's alluring house. In this simple construction Jonson is figuring many of the tensions, social, religious and political, of the early 1630s, as Puritan notions did theoretical battle in social circles with the decadence and extravagance of an increasingly distanced and detached court. The billeting of soldiers on often unwilling households, many of whom had refused to pay the so-called benevolence, or 'Forced Loan' of 1626, was a major grievance of the 1628–29 sessions of parliament and this may not only have influenced Jonson's portrayal of the ultimately expelled Colonel Tipto in *The New Inn* but also have been recalled by him when creating Ironside in the early 1630s.[38]

In the Induction to *The Magnetic Lady* Probee declares: 'We are sent unto you, indeed, from the people' (Induction, l. 27). The Boy hopes that they have come to discuss the 'state of the Stage' (Induction, l. 23); the pun is surely a double one, referring both to the state in which they find the theatre and the theatrical medium, and the theatre itself as a symbol for state affairs. Significantly enough, the Boy goes on to ask them 'which side of the people' they represent and Probee and Damplay assure him that they come from its upper echelons, that is to say that they are gentlemen. This republic of the audience is then a highly oligarchical affair but nevertheless one that aspires to represent the people, if not the 'faeces or grounds [groundlings]' exactly. The House of Commons maintained similar aspirations and it is to that particular stage that we now return.

When the Host of *The New Inn* complains about his *'magna charta'* in the inn not being upheld by Lovel, he is articulating not simply the straightforward language of inheritance and right but also that of parliamentary complaint. Lovel is somewhat peevish in reply, although he denies that he aims to offend in any way against the Host's civil liberties:

> Not to defraud you of your rights, or trench
> Upo' your privileges or great charter,
> (For those are every host'ler's language now)
> Say you were born beneath those smiling stars
> Have made you lord and owner of the Heart,
> Of the Light Heart in Barnet; suffer us
> Who are more saturnine, t'enjoy the shade
> Of your round roof yet.
>   (I.ii.34–41)

Lovel again subtly compares the inn to a theatre with mention of its round roof, an important architectural feature of the Globe, attention to which is drawn in *Hamlet* (interestingly, another play concerned with themes of melancholy). He apparently resents the fact that the language of official complaint is now spoken by those of all ranks, even inn ostlers (the ostler of this inn, Peck, is part of the aforementioned citizen militia established by Tipto); this is again a mark of his class-ridden consciousness. In saying this Lovel is unaware that Goodstock is indeed a lord and not simply of 'The Light Heart'.

In *The New Inn*, interestingly enough, it is the self-appointed leader of the 'militia', Glorious Tipto, who also voices the language of royal prerogative and right. Jonson's gypsies in his masque, *The Gypsies Metamorphosed*, describe their community both in terms of a civil militia and as governed by a 'Magna Carta' (ll. 229–42). That masque has been read alternately as supportive and subversive of monarchy. The gypsies' community provides an alternative realm in which to examine questions of rights and liberties as in Richard Brome's *A Jovial Crew*.

Tipto apparently assumes that as a knight or aristocrat, however debauched, he will be the 'favourite' of Queen Pru (the role Buckingham held in relation to Charles); he therefore nominates Fly for an important position in her court. When she denies him this he demands his 'petition of right': he is of course completely forgetting his duties to Lady Frances and underestimating Pru's new-found authority. She quickly instructs the over-attentive Beaufort in her hands-off approach to monarchy (despite the Host's mocking interjections):

PRUDENCE	Sweet my lord, hand off;
	It is not now as when plain Prudence lived,
	And reached her ladyship –
HOST	The chamber-pot.
PRUDENCE	The looking-glass, mine host, lose your house metaphor!
	You have a negligent memory, indeed;
	Speak the host's language!

(II.vi.3–8)

It is the Host who insists on presenting 'his' Fly to the 'Queen'; Tipto is furious that he thus seeks to share in his glories:

> Host'lers to usurp
> Upon my Sparta or province, as they say?
> No broom but mine? ...
>   I ask my rights and privileges;
> And though for form I please to call't a suit,
> I have not been accustomed to repulse.
>   (II.vi.43–5, 48–50)

Just as this is a 'New Inn' so this is a new society where Tipto must grow accustomed to repulses of this nature, unless he be prepared to change and listen to the opinion of the court. Surely an implicit warning is present here, a warning issued to a monarch about to resume a parliament anxious to express its complaints and grievances and to be heard (the Petition of Right having been presented in the parliamentary session of the previous year, 1628). Tragically, Charles chose not to heed such counsel, silencing parliament for eleven years in an act of pomposity comparable to Tipto's indignance here: Prudence is by contrast, as her name suggests, a conciliatory sovereign.

This is not to suggest that *The New Inn* is somehow Jonson's Magna Carta, his direct instruction to the king as to how he should conduct himself in the new parliament; it is, however, engaging with the thoughts and hopes of the time. In that respect, *The New Inn* is an eminently optimistic text, counselling Charles and the country in the potential and possibility of the new assembly and a limited monarchy, in the same way perhaps that *Sejanus* had in 1603 sought to make creative suggestions to the incoming monarch, James VI of Scotland, as to how he might govern the new realm of England. 1629 was not a time when the road to civil war was even visible on the horizon but it was an age in which people sought to redefine the monarch's relationship with his subjects, contractual or otherwise, via ancient precedents such as Magna Carta. Despite the recent rejection of such readings by revisionist historians, I would argue that this was the reasoning behind parliament's refusal to grant Charles the customary revenue from tonnage and poundage for life, but rather only annually: in order to stress that new laws and taxation were to be dependent in the future upon parliamentary consent, and by extension the approval of the entire political community.[39]

When Prudence first enters in her queenly attire, the Host remarks: 'First minute of her reign! What will she do/Forty year hence, God bless her!' (II.vi.10–11); this does recall Elizabeth I who ruled for 47 years. But the play and the Host essentially look backward in the act of looking forwards: like those invocations of Magna Carta, they indulge in a very politicized form of nostalgia, still at this stage with a large degree of hope. Perhaps this sense of optimism is why Jonson's later plays are felt by critics such as Barton and Butler to be so supportive of the monarchy: because they are not outright condemnations. Yet hostility towards arbitrary rule and the continued employment of republican parlance is prevalent in these later texts. The late 1620s and even the early 1630s were a time that felt capable of change and adaptation, but they were also a time that felt in need of change, possibly constitutional, certainly in terms of reverence for the ancient constitution and the rights of the subject as expressed therein. To regard Jonson's plays of that era as mere iterations of the dominant ideologies is a reductive reading. As Margot Heinemann has stated, in a prerevolutionary period such as this there is no single dominant ideology: 'that is one reason why it is a prerevolutionary situation'.[40]

The New Inn engages with residual, dominant and emergent philosophies within the confines of its playtext. This is best exemplified, as ever, by direct quotation; when Lady Frances questions Pru's order that she should kiss Lovel, Pru stresses that Frances herself invested the power in her chambermaid to command thus:

> PRUDENCE   The royal assent is past, and cannot alter.
> LADY FRANCES   You'll turn a tyrant.
> PRUDENCE   Be not you a rebel,
>   It is a name alike odious.
> LADY FRANCES   You'll hear me?
> PRUDENCE   No, not o'this argument.
>   Would you make laws, and be the first that
>   break 'em?
>   The example is pernicious in a subject,
>   And of your quality, most.
>   (II.vi.125–31)

This recognizes, naturally enough, the final say of the monarch but also stresses the importance of oaths and promises; Charles I in his dealings with parliament was answerable to a number of such promises, not least in respect to those laws and extraordinary measures that required parliamentary assent. Pru may emphasize royal prerogative but she also concedes its accountability on certain conditional matters. In this instance she is responding to the exact duties prescribed by the same Lady Frances who now seeks to redefine them at will:

PRUDENCE	Sovereigns use not To ask their subjects' suffrage where 'tis due, But where conditional.
HOST	A royal sovereign!
LATIMER	And a rare stateswoman. I admire her bearing In her new regiment.
	(II.vi.249–53)

The hope in 1629 must have been that Charles I would also bear himself well in his new regiment. This did not prove to be the case; the parliament that had raised such high hopes of rapprochement and reconciliation ended in prorogation and dissolution, like the dinner party at Lady Loadstone's in *The Magnetic Lady*, which was only ever just held in check. In the Court of Love in *The New Inn* which ends, for Lovel, like a play ending, amidst a genuine feeling of loss and despair, the soon-to-be dissolved parliament of 1629 was uncannily prefigured just days before it opened.

10
Local Government and Personal Rule in *A Tale of a Tub*

I QUESTIONING NOSTALGIA

The prologue to *A Tale of a Tub* (*c*.1633) takes pains to stress that the playtext does *not* engage with state affairs:

> No state affairs, nor any politic club,
>   Pretend we in our Tale, here, of a Tub,
> But acts of clowns and constables today
>   Stuff out the scenes of our ridiculous play.
>   (Prologue, ll. 1–4)

But the question must surely be posed whether by emphasizing the absence of allusions of a contemporary, politicized nature, the text does not draw attention to their presence, subversively suggesting the potential for just such topicality on and about 'state affairs'.[1] Martin Butler argues, in a related vein, that the drama's happy and harmonious ending transcends the social tensions otherwise registered in any given performance, thus consolidating rather than subverting Caroline rule in the 1630s.[2] For me, though, the play's close merely constitutes a theatrical veneer, a 'happy ending' that barely conceals the political and social problems revealed elsewhere in the text.

Similarly double-edged is the Prologue's confident declaration that: 'We bring you now, to show what different things/The cotes of clowns are from the courts of kings.' (Prologue, ll. 11–12). This assertion has the potential to suggest either its exact antithesis – that the 'cotes' and the 'courts' are in as much proximity as their all too possible aural slippage might imply – or conversely that there is a vast difference between these two entities, thus indicating how far removed from the reality of provincial life the monarch's experiment with so-called 'personal rule' in the 1630s truly was.

Renewed political and historical attention has recently been paid to the 1630s, known by historical interpreters as the period of 'Personal Rule', the 'King's Peace', or the 'Eleven Year Tyranny' (depending upon the political viewpoint of the interpreter). In 1629, Charles I had dissolved Parliament, with a show of elation according to the dispatches of the contemporary Venetian ambassador; he did not summon another until 1640.[3] This is the context for Jonson's composition of *A Tale of a Tub*, which is now generally accepted as his last complete extant play.[4] Barton views the play as a nostalgic retrospective on the veritable 'Golden Age' of Elizabeth I and certainly nostalgia has a role to play in *A Tale of a Tub*; a large proportion of the characters persistently dwell on or in the past, reflecting, for example, upon the origins of their names in the 'Scene Interloping',[5] but nostalgia can take a number of often conflicting roles.[6]

Martin Butler has suggested that antiquarianism is mocked in Jonson's Caroline plays, via such characters as the Irish Nurse (in truth Lady Frampul in disguise) in *The New Inn* whose father is said to have been a Welsh herald.[7] There is also a herald of humorous import in *The Staple of News*, although Pennyboy Canter's reflections on the subject are significant:

> ... do not I love a herald
> Who is the pure preserver of descents,
> The keeper fair of all nobility,
> Without which all would run into confusion.
> (IV.iv.151–4)

For Jonson, however, antiquarianism was of great importance, not least due to Camden's influence, but also because it had contemporary political resonance.[8]

The etymology of the word 'radical' is telling here – it derives from the Latin for 'roots': going back to one's roots was then a politically radical move. In relation to this it is intriguing that 'interloping' in the 'Scene Interloping' carries the sense of being 'unauthorized'.[9] In the 1630s theories of the 'ancient constitution' and 'natural law' were to gain increasing significance; many of Jonson's close friends, not least the antiquarian John Selden, who were spokespersons for these 'rooted' or 'authorized' theories, would subsequently find themselves ranged on the parliamentary side in the civil wars.[10]

There is a deep interest in local history in this playtext: both the making and the recording of it. Coats of arms are frequently discussed (perhaps purchased titles do indeed bring the 'cotes' of clowns perilously near the hallowed confines of the court) and, like a quasi-monarch, Toby Turf, the Head Constable, has a personal scribe or chronicler in D'ogenes Scriben.[11] Squire Tub commissions his 'Motion' in the final act in the manner of a monarch commissioning a masque but also as a means of recording for posterity events within his family – it is after all crucial to him that members of his household be recognized for who they really are in the midst of the performance. This constitutes a refusal of the willing suspension of disbelief, a refusal that for Butler characterizes the masque form.[12]

So there is a backward-looking element to this play's community, and its Tudor setting. There is a degree of nostalgic reasoning behind the plot structure, since the proposed, if somewhat deferred, and eventually transferred, marriage of Audrey Turf and John Clay on this raw St Valentine's Day is taking place for the very reason that Clay was her Valentine's Eve lottery selection (Chanon Hugh observes: 'I smile to think how like a lottery/ These Weddings are.' (I.i.97–8)). This repeats the pattern of her own parents' coming together:

> Mistress Audrey Turf
> Last night did draw him for her valentine;
> Which chance, it hath so taken her father and mother
> (Because themselves drew so, on Valentine's Eve
> Was thirty year) as they will have her married
> Today by any means.
> (I.i.45–50)[13]

Such retrospective justification as is carried out by the Turfs for marrying off their daughter takes little genuine account of Audrey's opinions. Toby may criticize John Clay's tardiness, and refuse to have music or female attendants at the ceremony, yet he plays havoc with the arrangements himself when pressures of work crop up; as some of his colleagues reflect:

TO-PAN A right good man! When he knows right, he loves it.

SCRIBEN   And he will know't and show't too by his place
          Of being High Constable, if nowhere else.
                                              (II.i.60–2)

For a contemporary audience, the date looked back to by the Turfs on their Valentine anniversary (that is, in 1633), is another anniversary, national rather than local, since thirty years before the play's performance had been 1603, the year of the Jacobean accession to the English throne. James I had been dead for eight years by the time of this play's composition and Jonson found himself no longer in the privileged position of quasi-court laureate. In many respects he found himself exiled in the 1630s along with James's controversial Scottish jester Archibald Armstrong (about whom Jonson had written on a number of occasions – most obviously as the 'Sea Monster Archy' in the cancelled 1624 masque *Neptune's Triumph*). Like Armstrong, Jonson represented a Jacobean anachronism in the new Eurocentric and aestheticized English court. The pain of this exile is all too clearly spelt out in the plaintive request to Charles and his Queen, Henrietta Maria, for attention and funds in the Epilogue to *The New Inn*:

> Whene'er the carcass dies, this art will live.
> And had he lived the care of King and Queen,
> His art in something more yet had been seen.
>   (Epilogue, ll. 20–3)

Nostalgia alone in such depleted circumstances was surely an inadequate response: Jonson had to carve a niche for himself in this new society and therefore was forced, of necessity, to respond to current political issues. My stress on the contemporary topicality and agitations of the late plays need not preclude concurrent nostalgic impulses. Jonson uses the past in an effort to construct a futuristic politics (this was not an uncommon strategy: it motivated Leveller invocation of the Norman Yoke).

There has been much critical speculation as to the exact date and setting of *A Tale of a Tub*. Certainly Toby Turf describes himself on a few occasions as a 'Queen's man', and Edward VI is referred to as 'our late liege, and sovereign lord' (I.v.33), but there are also a wealth of potential references to post-Elizabethan actualities, under both James I and Charles I. The ambiguity is, I suspect, a quite deliberate Jonsonian strategy – the vagaries of application draw attention back to the present, and therefore pressing, analogies. Like the suppressed truth of the play's prologue over the reference to 'state affairs', the past of the play is almost proof of its dealings with the present.

II INTERHIERARCHICAL FIGURES

A Tale of a Tub is a direct product of the anxieties and discontents of the subjects of Charles I. Indeed, Martin Butler has traced how the play depicts and explores the 'conflict between the centre and the localities, the demands of office and the demands of neighbourliness'.[14]

The Tudor and Stuart periods had witnessed the expansion and extension of parish officials' responsibilities and there was a growing tendency, exacerbated by the period of personal rule in the 1630s, for central authorities to place increasing demands, administrative and otherwise, on local government. Local officials were made accountable to the Crown for such wide-ranging responsibilities as law enforcement, watch and ward, hue and cry, control of vagrancy, road repairs and bridge maintenance, and general social legislation, including the collection of taxes. *The Staple of News* makes passing reference to the 'busy justices' (I.v.37).

The paradox inherent in 'personal rule' is self-evident. In actuality, it was local officialdom which bore the brunt of collecting and enforcing the unpopular extraordinary taxation levied by the Crown during this period (without having sought any form of parliamentary consent or approval, which was the expected line), such as the Forced Loan from 1627 onwards and the infamous Ship Money after 1635.[15] Another paradox may be noted in that the latter tax dealt with the funding of military preparations, something of an irony in a supposed time of 'peace'.

As the historian Valerie Pearl has written:

> We are now aware that from the early sixteenth century the development of government commissions and of special and petty sessions enabled J.P.s to carry far greater burdens of administration created by an expanding range of social legislation, even if that legislation was not always translated into local action.[16]

In an article on county government in Caroline England, L.M. Hill has observed that 'The powers of central government in seventeenth-century England were hollow without the active cooperation of the army of local authorities upon whom enforcement depended',[17] continuing, interestingly enough for *A Tale of a Tub*, by discussing the *'dramatis personae'* of county officials.

In *A Tale of a Tub* we have both a Justice of the Peace (Preamble) and a High Constable (Toby Turf), upon whom the pressures of responsibility fall, with considerable weight in the case of the latter, haring around the provinces on the outskirts of London on the day of his daughter's wedding in pursuit of fictional 'robbers'. Some might argue that Toby creates these difficulties for himself, although perhaps a more accurate rendering of the play's operations is to see how a distinct section of the village community – the parish gentry, such as Squire Tub, Justice Preamble, and Chanon Hugh – acts to prevent and pervert the wedding day.[18]

Nevertheless, the High Constable has a high self-opinion: Toby compares himself to Caesar in a gross exaggeration of office (although it is interesting to think of how Jonson's own dramatic renderings of Caesars – Augustus in *Poetaster* and Tiberius in *Sejanus* – themselves act as absolutists in non-absolutist situations). Toby manages imaginatively to translate the role of Roman Consul (held by all of the Caesars named above) into that of an early modern High Constable, with a little assistance from his chronicler:

SCRIBEN   I can tell you
            A thousand of great Pompey, Caesar, Trajan,
            All the High Constables there.
TURF   That was their place:
            They were no more.
SCRIBEN   Dictator and High Constable
            Were both the same.
MEDLAY   High Constable was more, though!
            He laid Dick Tator by the Heels.
                                              (III.vi.17–22)

As Pearl continues, 'As the temporal power of the Church declined, the activities of the secular courts and lay magistrates expanded, particularly in towns, magistrates grew more sensitive to public opinion ...'.[19] Toby Turf, of course, proves painfully sensitive (or susceptible) to public opinion – which he comes to learn is a less than homogenized entity – changing his mind innumerable times over the suitability of John Clay as a bridegroom for his daughter (having little if any recourse to her view in this matter), vacillating and procrastinating as each new rumour or spurious proof is proffered by the play's community. On one occasion he even attempts to resign and then immediately reassumes his post of High Constable. In one sense Toby's flexibility could be viewed as a positive response to the populace but it also renders the authoritarian position of the High Constable dangerously malleable, and disorder duly ensues.

Butler also focuses on the social dilemma that exists for Toby since he is an 'interhierarchical figure', under special strain because of his conflicted answerability to both Crown and people.[20] Possibly we can read Jonson himself as just such an 'interhierarchical figure', with his middle-class, artisanal background and contrasting court position (during the Jacobean period at least), since in his role as a dramatist he often clashed with authority. Jonson's personal dilemmas might account for the depth of understanding of Toby's position that is evidenced by the play. Toby embodies early modern, and quintessentially 1630s, fragmentation, symbolizing the coexistence of two opposed concepts of order in the provinces at this time. This is the same clash of the official and unofficial sources of both culture and authority that lies at the heart of *Bartholomew Fair*. There, Justice Overdo and his attendant clerks and constables find themselves struggling against the tide of local, public and customary activity at the fair itself.

Ian Donaldson has referred to the image of 'Justice in the Stocks' as central to the 'upside-down world' of comedy and carnival;[21] *Bartholomew Fair* evidently fits this description, with Justice Overdo, disguised in motley, and subjected to various indignities, not least being literally placed in the stocks. In IV.iv., the watch enters the fairground and the stage-scene, puffed up with the pride of their responsibility in a manner suggestive of Toby himself: 'Why, we be his Majesty's Watch, sir' (*Bartholomew Fair*, IV.iv.193).[22] The drunken and disorderly Bristle, Haggis, and Whit are scarcely admirable members of Jacobean society; in this aspect Jonson is continuing a lengthy dramatic tradition of the trope of the drunken or stupid Watch, stemming partly from John Lyly's *Endymion* and famously pursued in the misunderstandings of Dogberry and company in *Much Ado About Nothing*. Joan Kent has discussed the way in which this particular stage tradition contributed to a general and unwarranted reputation for constables as being either stupid or bad at their jobs.[23]

In *A Tale of a Tub*, High Constable Turf is not the sole authority or administrator; in fact the play offers a very detailed depiction of the administrative mechanisms of an early modern village. Toby is undoubtedly its epicentre, but we also have a number of other clearly defined positions and offices of responsibility. As Chanon Hugh outlines when he informs Squire Tub of the proposed Valentine's Day matrimonials (and note how everyone is defined by social status and standing):

> Your mistress,
> Is to be made away from you, this morning,
> Saint Valentine's Day: there are a knot of clowns,
> The Council of Finsbury, so they are ystyled,
> Met at her father's. All the wise o'th'hundred:
> Old Rasi Clench of Hampstead, petty constable;
> In-and-In Medlay, cooper of Islington,
> And headborough; with loud To-Pan the tinker,
> Or metal-man of Belsize, the thirdborough;
> And D'ogenes Scriben, the great writer of Chalcot.
> (I.i.30–9)

This, then, is the 'petty hierarchy' of the play.

III AN EARLY MODERN VILLAGE COMMUNITY

In authority, the Justice of the Peace (Preamble) stands at the head of the social pyramid of this play. In literary terms, the Preamble forms the prologue to the text: it frames and surrounds the localized text. We can see Preamble's social presence in similar terms, and that Jonson draws attention to preambles in this way confirms the importance of this play's prologue. A preamble also possessed all the philosophical teasingness of the notion of a 'preface'. Preambles, coming first, require something to precede. Justice Preamble is constantly seeking opposing points or persons with whom to compete in the play and Jonson himself used the preface form in a similar fashion in his career – I am thinking in particular of the ongoing debate on the masque form and the question of revelry between him and Samuel Daniel.

The office of JP was appointed by the Crown, or more specifically the Privy Council. The Lord Chancellor nominated JPs and it was regarded as a great honour to be offered the role. Kevin Sharpe reveals that in the 1630s in particular the role of JP was invariably taken up by disenfranchised members of Parliament after that institution was dissolved in 1629.[24] Their grievances were now carried back into the community which had previously elected them as their representative officials.[25] This would indicate some likelihood of their popularity and standing in the communities concerned and may also suggest a degree of independence from the Crown in the 1630s. Preamble's popularity may be questionable but he undoubtedly exhibits independence of action. The two highest points in the community, the local Squire and the Justice, are also the two people who devise and perpetrate all the stratagems – those intended to pervert the wedding festivities and, seemingly, the course of justice.[26]

For all his parodic intention, Jonson is typically exact in his research into the political offices he invokes in the course of the play. Each JP had a Clerk of the Peace; in *Every Man In His Humour (Folio)* Justice Clement's is Roger Formal who is tricked by the ingenious Brainworm into both intellectual and actual nakedness since he is so over-eager to hear Brainworm's concocted tales of military exploits (a mirror, of course, of Matthew and Stephen's fascination with the equally false soldier Bobadill in the play). The formality of the clerk's office is thus easily exposed as a surface matter vulnerable to manipulation. In *A Tale of a Tub* Preamble's clerk is the equally vulnerable Miles Metaphor. His is another textually referential name; unfortunately, like the fluid rhetorical figure of metaphor, Miles is not clearly defined. He is redetermined by successive interlocutors, reappropriated to their purpose(s). Employed in the plot of one character, Miles readily confesses it to the next and so becomes a participant in their schemes. It is Miles who is dressed up as a 'pursuivant', a Messenger of the Crown (the Privy Council to be exact): aptly enough he borrows a friend's costume to do so, one act of redefinition in the wake of another. He is thus able to feign the arrest of Squire Tub on Preamble's behalf in order to thwart Tub's pursuit of Audrey.

Preamble's evident abuse of his position, in sanctioning a fake warrant, exposes the ripeness of local events for confusions of this nature. Keith Wrightson has written about how JPs tended to delegate responsibilities downwards to the locally derived, if commission-appointed, High Constables, passing the buck to figures such as Toby Turf, who then found themselves 'Mediating between the national legislative ideal and ambivalent local realities ... [Upon them] was devolved the essential task of balancing out the needs and requirements of both provincial society and the royal government.'[27] Just such a figure is Toby Turf who faces the complicated task of extracting dissenters (such as Clay is presumed to be) whilst remaining loyal to the local populace (including his own daughter): 'What really mattered was the maintenance of specific, local, personal relationships, not conformity to impersonal law.'[28] A very different kind of personal rule is being invoked through Turf's character. If the JP was the mouthpiece of impersonal 'personal rule' then local officials were crucial in the running and management of the parish, the manor, and the 'hundred'.

The hundred did not comprise any uniform territory but varied from region to region and was the responsibility of the High Constable named by the related Commission of the Peace: 'The high constable,' says Hill, 'was the direct link between the JPs and the people of the hundred.'[29] A high constable such as Toby Turf had three unique duties: local police authority, maintaining the watch, keeping out vagrants and so on; local works such as buildings, bridges and repairs; and enforcing the annual wage scheme.

Petty constables, such as Rasi Clench, were elected by fellow householders, that is to say, from local ranks. The post was tenable for a year. Petty constables who refused to serve could actually be prosecuted; many did refuse in the wake of the Ship Money débâcle, but in the early 1630s it was still a relatively respected position: 'the petty constable was the general purpose official in charge of all detection and presentment of crime in the manor, while he was also responsible for punishing the wide range of petty offences which cluttered daily life...'.[30] They were also responsible for raising hue and cry, as happens in *A Tale of a Tub* after the accusations of robbery are made against John Clay, leading to farcical events in the barn and elsewhere (sighting of the devil and all). Petty constables were the ultimate tax collectors although this was a situation beset with problems. Many of those who were elected for office locally were illiterate, or at least only partially literate (Dogberry in *Much Ado About Nothing* and Elbow in *Measure for Measure*, for example) and yet the often poor petty constable was held financially liable to pay fines for failure to make the relevant arrests, even to pay compensation to the victims of crime in some instances. Other positions in the hundred included the

Headborough (In-and-In Medlay, Cooper of Islington) and Thirdborough (To-Pan, the Belsize tinker). In addition to Jonson's meticulous delineation of each person's office we have, to use Michael McCanles's term, the 'Jonsonian discrimination'[31] of their relative geographic locations and localities.

Local politics were crucial to the development of early modern sensibilities, surely especially so in a period when Parliament was virtually defunct, after the stormy sessions of 1628–9, when the Petition of Right had been repeatedly introduced, much to the chagrin of Charles I. Local authorities in this situation provided the only feasible arena for debate: 'By the early seventeenth century Quarter Sessions had increasingly assumed the role of county forum where views could be expressed not only by members of the gentry, but also by men outside of their ranks: some of these lesser families would rise to office after 1642.'[32]

IV LOCAL EXPLOITATION

Tensions between centre and locality are not marginalized in *A Tale of a Tub*. The Totten Court setting (its name surely implying an alternative to the official Court?) stands in uncomfortable proximity to London. Provincial unrest would not take long to reach the enclaves of Westminster in the 1640s; and the tensions of the localities would prove crucial during the political unrest of the following decade. Keith Wrightson has compared the operations of local government in two distinct areas: in a simplified version of that study South Lancashire emerges as conservative and geographically removed from Westminster and therefore from oppositional parliamentary activities and Essex as radical in stance and close to Westminster.[33] The latter, rapidly influenced by events at the London parliaments, is particularly relevant for the Finsbury Park locality of this play. The radicalism of Essex recurs frequently in the parliamentary submissions examined by Sharpe in his work on this period and that emphasizes the importance of these near-London communities and the often autonomous stance they adopted on political issues. In the light of all this it seems critically somewhat blithe to regard the social unrest and political tensions of this play as 'theatrically transcended', evacuating them in the process of any real portent.

It could be argued in response to these observations that as a literary historian I am guilty of projecting backwards from the events of the Civil War(s), or even from the late 1630s, to a period of relative peace and social stability. Sharpe is at pains to stress the success of many of Charles's extraordinary measures before 1635. Ship Money, for example, was collected in vast percentages before 1637, but in the summer of 1626 the Privy Council had issued a demand for Ship Money from the coastal towns of England: so neither was Ship Money new to the 1630s, nor was it without precedent; the Elizabethan fleet that had taken Cadiz had been financed by just such a levy. In 1626 there was admittedly little opposition to the tax; it was duly paid since the towns concerned felt vulnerable to attack. However, when in February 1628 the writs were extended from the ports to the entire realm, disquiet began to be voiced. The Deputy Lieutenants of Essex questioned the legality of the warrants and a number of other counties followed their oppositional suit, refusing to pay. Charles I was forced to withdraw the letters of extension within days of their original issue: this all casts a rather different light on Sharpe's occasionally idealistic readings of the early 1630s. By 1633 and *A Tale of a Tub*, as Richard Cust has indicated in his accounts of the 1620s, there was already a record in England of localized opposition, and it is in this context that we need to re-evaluate Jonson's play.[34] Jonson is to a certain extent exploring the fear of 'popularity' which Ann Hughes has associated with Charles I.[35]

The ending of the play appears to be, if not theatrically, then politically at least, a failed consolatory movement. Butler views the play as 'profoundly serviceable to the political needs of the Caroline Court in 1633', but I see the obverse of this in operation.[36] Not that the play in any sense constitutes a blatant attack on Cavalier personal rule in the 1630s, but it does represent an astute registration of the political tensions which that singular form of government was engendering. London is crucial to the play in the sense that audience expectations of that communal and urban setting in Jonson's work are uncharacteristically thwarted. This play's locality is even more expressedly 'not London' than the Barnet stage-coach stop of *The New Inn*.

People's localized responsibilities are central to the play: what trades they perform – and the trades their patriarchal predecessors performed – prove vital to a communal (republican?) comprehension of their 'characters', as all the excruciating puns on John Clay's profession of tile-maker indicate:

SQUIRE TUB   And what must he do?
HUGH   Cover her, they say:
              And keep her warm, sir.   (I.i.44–5)

The Tub family has vested financial interests in saltpetre, a locally-mined mineral, predominantly found in pigeon and dove droppings. This can be seen as exemplary of a bioregional emphasis in the play, but subversive undertones attach themselves to the family inheritance.[37] At the very start of the play, Chanon Hugh reflects on Squire Tripoly Tub:

> Sir Peter Tub was his father, a saltpetre-man;
> Who left his mother, Lady Tub of Totten
> Court, here, to revel, and keep open house in.
>   (I.i.13–15)

This may seem an innocent enough quotation, allowing for a typical Jonsonian pun on the deceased master's name – Sir Peter Tub, owner of the saltpetre-works – but contemporary audiences would have been well aware that potassium nitrate, the much sought-after mineral (the Parliamentary-established Commission for its retrieval was one of the few institutions not dissolved in 1629), was employed in the manufacture of gunpowder and that it was transported about the country in 'saltpetre tubs'.

Audiences would also have been alert to the fact that in 1633 saltpetre, like Ship Money, was a contentious issue, crucial as they both were to Charles I's war efforts against the Scots. Sharpe returns frequently to the bitterly contested theme of saltpetre in his account of the 1630s. There were constant efforts throughout the decade to secure adequate stocks of gunpowder and houses where saltpetre was believed to exist were often searched at will (barns and dovecotes were its common sites). Such searches were essentially invasive, and often destructive, and the 'saltpetre men' who executed these warrants became understandably unpopular in the localities. Essex was once again, at county level, at the forefront of protests.

The subtext of Tub family wealth is then the exploitation of the localities. Lady Tub has rescued Pol-Martin from the fate of a lifetime's labouring in the saltpetre works and her own face reflects the ravages of the saltpetre searches:

> She's such a vessel of faeces: all dried earth!
> *Terra damnata*, not a drop of salt,
> Or petre in her! All her nitre is gone.
> (I.v.68–70)

Here is a different kind of frigidity or sterility from Audrey's: the very licence allowed Lady Tub has exhausted her stocks. She is akin indeed to the houses her family has ransacked for their contents: the final confirmation of this will be when Pol-Martin ravages her wardrobe to clothe his new bride. The aristocracy in this play, like the magistracy, is subtly questioned, criticized, and exposed.

The Church undergoes similar scrutiny and exposure. Chanon Hugh commences the play with a series of secular, pagan addresses; his call to 'Bishop' Valentine is a fascinatingly anti-Laudian oath made in the year that Laud became Archbishop of Canterbury. Hugh's involvement in the wedding appears to be governed purely by financial self-interest.[38] He promises to aid and abet both Squire Tub and Justice Preamble in their machinations, and thus manages to secure payment from both in the distinctly secular coinage of 'angels':

> I thank your Squire's worship,
> Most humbly (for the next, for this I am sure of).
> Oh for a choir of those voices, now,
> To chime in a man's pocket, and cry chink!
> One doth not chirp: it makes no harmony.
> (I.i.88–92)

Local church corruption was one of the problems Laud and Charles sought to rectify in the 1630s. Jonson could be seen to be supporting their calls for stricter regulation; conversely, he could be exposing the futility inherent in any such objective in the locally determined provinces.[39]

Leah Marcus has suggested that *A Tale of a Tub* is an endorsement of the Caroline revival of the policy of royal support for 'rural, holiday pastimes' for political purposes (1633 saw the republication of King James's *Book of Sports*, first published in 1617).[40] In this respect she, like Butler, regards this as an orthodox Caroline text but also acknowledges a potential counter-reading which sees this play exposing the hypocritical appropriation of common pastimes by a government (church and monarchy) essentially uninterested in common rights or matters.⁴¹ Jonson's dramatic celebration of the communal in the play-setting of the bride-ale is a potential challenge to the confused ethics of personal rule.

There were statutory prohibitions in force with regard to the representation on public theatre stages of anything amounting to contemporary Christian ceremony; however, I believe the wedding ceremony of *A Tale of a Tub* needs to be seen in a secular light, like the prayers and procedures of Chanon Hugh. Laud and Charles I encouraged the ceremonies of the Church and yet here the appetite, both sexual and alimentary, reigns, even on the part of the practising Chanon who hopes the bridegroom will keep Audrey 'warm'.

In truth, Audrey grows ever colder and more desperate: 'Husbands, they say, grow thick; but thin are sown./ I care not who it be, so I have one.' (III.vi.43–4). Her anti-pastoral observance on the impotence of potential husbands, thin seed and all, sets the tone for the frosty Valentine's Day proceedings – or lack of proceedings. This is a pastoral, but a negative, inverted one.

Nowhere in Jonson does the weather play such a prominent part in proceedings than in *A Tale of a Tub*, a point beautifully captured in the opening speech:

> Now o'my faith, old Bishop Valentine,
> You ha' brought us nipping weather: *Februere*
> *Doth cut and shear*; your day, and diocese
> Are very cold. All your parishioners,
> As well your laics, as your quiristers,
> Had need to keep to their warm feather-beds,
> If they be sped of loves. This is no season,
> To seek new makes in ....
>
> (I.i.1–8)

A similarly chilly political wind was blowing through the 1630s when Jonson wrote *A Tale of a Tub*. That must be regarded as critically significant, as influential upon Jonson's characterizations as the weather itself. Jonson the 'interhierarchical' author could scarcely have failed to observe and exploit to dramatic effect the paradoxes and dualities of his own age regardless of the play's Tudor setting, just as his Roman tragedies do not fail to explore the tensions of the Jacobean era during which they were commissioned.

The change Jonson registered of 'times trans-shifting'[42] between the Jacobean and the Caroline era cannot be ignored. As Annabel Patterson has convincingly argued, in an essay on poetic collections, the point at which the poems in the posthumously published *Underwood* shift from being those composed under James to those written under Charles is heavily signalled, not only by a date in the margin (interestingly enough not 1625, the year of Charles's accession, but 1629, the year of his prorogation of parliament and the commencement of the eleven-year tyranny) but also by a correlative darkening of mood.[43] The darker shades of this poetic forest bear witness to comparable shifts of register in the dramas of the late 1620s and early 1630s. If a request of the parliaments finally called in 1640 was for a social contract to be negotiated with the monarch, a collective agreement established as it were between the King and his subjects, then the local (vested?) interests of this rarely performed play, written just some seven years earlier, should not be underestimated.

11
Conclusion: 'The End of (T)his Commonwealth Does Not Forget the Beginning'

Ben Jonson was not a republican but he was fiercely involved in a debate over community and communal rights. By now it will be clear the ways in which notions of republicanism in the Jonsonian text and in his 'theatrical republics' shade very obviously into notions of community and the communal. Perhaps the plural 'communities' would be a more accurate term since Jonson – specifically in his generic variety (poetry, prose, criticism, drama, and masques) – celebrates the vast potential of literature for the production of a multiplicity of meanings.

In his interest in, and encouragement of, the participation of audiences in the co-creation of meaning, Jonson demonstrated a vested interest in the theatrical medium. His was evidently not a 'community of the same':[1] his writing constituted a recognition of communities of difference and even of the role of difference and disparity within ostensibly single and homogenized communities.

If at times the claims of this book have themselves seemed a little dispersed, citing sameness and difference, absolutism and republicanism, the individual alongside the communal, this is because it is exactly the dispersal Jonson makes and intends in his texts: the dispersal and displacement of comfortable or fixed notions of 'republic' or 'community'. The strength of any community, as he recognized, is very broadly proportionate to the resistance to it. The seeming disparity of Jonson's canon and his life – with its public theatre productions and their potentiality for subversion, juxtaposed with court-sponsored, supposedly orthodox texts and actions – is also, I believe, a quite self-conscious strategy. Jonson was himself never wholly of one community and often operated on the margins of a number of them.

Yet, this book as a whole testifies to his investment in themes of communality. From marking out specific republican settings in plays, and the employment of specifically or even notionally republican discourse in others, there has been a continued focus on the communities of the plays concerned and related questions about the rights of individuals or institutions, of democracy, rank, and hierarchy – political, sexual, social or otherwise. From this, more philosophical questions of republicanism and community have arisen. In the complex negotiations of the day in Lovewit's Blackfriars house in *The Alchemist*, and at Bartholomew Fair, we see the operations and breakdowns of various notions of community, contract and authority. That is the essence indeed of the 'republic in the fair'.

I have resisted the more usual evolutionary reading of Jonsonian drama (which sees the early years as an aspiration to literary greatness, the 'middle comedies' as the achievement of the same, and post-1616 as a 'falling off')[2] in order to resist a linear or developmental interpretation. For that reason this book lays a greater emphasis than is perhaps usual on the Roman tragedies and on the later Caroline plays. I wish to stress the need to consider Jonson's individual texts and actions within the highly localized and specific context of their own political moment(s), and not necessarily as part of some larger movement. The duration of such 'moments' is itself a highly subjective and locally specific issue. Jonson's texts may not necessarily be seen as part of any general movement towards what has come to be known as the 'English Civil War' and yet specific issues that were of portent in the conflicts that come under that general heading can be traced in individual Jonsonian playtexts.

My argument pivots on an understanding of both the timeless and timely qualities of Jonson's work. There is little doubt that many of his theatrical techniques in the later plays such as *The Devil is an Ass* and *The Staple of News* were conscious reworkings of earlier uses of similar strategies; these were often themselves redeployments of theatrical convention. The onstage audience of *Every Man Out of His Humour* becomes that of the female gossips in *The Staple of News* nearly thirty years later but arguably the technique is re-employed in more salient fashion to comment on the political 'moment' of 1626. Any greater saliency in these later texts is a product I would argue less of Jonson's maturation as a writer (intelligent deployment of theatrical tradition is as true of *Cynthia's Revels* as it is of *The New Inn*) than the nature of their differing political context(s). An onstage audience in the late 1620s and early 1630s provided a means of commentary upon a monarchy increasingly disinterested in public and parliamentary comment and opinion. The late texts are a precise example of the way in which traditional and familiar techniques provide something integral to and subversive of their political moment in Jonson's drama. This paradoxical and potent blend of the timeless and the timely is crucial to an understanding of the Jonsonian canon in its full complexity. His playtexts, I am suggesting, can be read as cultural barometers of particular moments or movements in Jacobean and Caroline England.

Jonson is persistently described as 'paradoxical', 'ambivalent', and 'ambiguous', even as 'neurotic' or 'schizophrenic'.[3] His personal, political and religious fluctuations are perhaps paradigmatic of an early-seventeenth-century fluidity of thought and politics.[4] I have rehearsed elsewhere my oppositions on a number of levels to the movement known as 'historical revisionism': traditional scholars in an effort to retrieve seventeenth-century historical studies from a left-wing emphasis have been so biased in their recuperation of monarchy and in particular the 'Personal Rule' of the 1630s that they have restricted much Jonsonian criticism to orthodox interpretation:[5] that is to say, reducing readings of his texts to straightforward and unnuanced endorsements of monarchy. I am therefore anxious to avoid any over-determined notion of 'Jonson the republican' being argued simply in counter-reaction to more orthodox interpretations of 'Jonson the monarchist'. The fluidity of the man and of the plays themselves within their own respective and occasionally overlapping moments, and communities, is instead emphasized.[6]

That said, there is a clear line traced within this book towards an increased emphasis upon notions of community as opposed to strict republicanism in Jonson's work during the Caroline era. This is seen to occur not solely as a result of personal and professional rejection in this period but as a culmination of Jonson's long-term ruminations on such themes, given particular focus by the political events of that time. In respect of that as well as mere chronology, the later plays have of necessity grouped themselves towards the end of the book as the consideration of republicanism breaks down, via the theatrical republics of Jonson's 'middle comedies', into ideas of community and commonwealth. Earlier interest in ideas of the social contract assume a distinctly parliamentary form in these texts. Theatre is seen as an obvious analogue not only of the social community but of the parliamentary forum itself: a 'House of Commons' indeed. The paradox of a social contract's implication of reciprocal agreement and yet its suggestion of a determinate and limited community of meaning was explored in both the Induction to *Bartholomew Fair* and the play proper. That play exposed the theatrical dichotomy of the veritable autonomy of the paying individual spectator (an autonomy often determined by the amount paid – scarcely an egalitarian or democratic ethos) and the potentially contagious effect of the group or audience (society is seen to have a similarly contagious effect upon Bartholomew Cokes in the play).

Similar ideas are applied to wider communities from *The Devil is an Ass* onwards. In stressing these plays in particular I also hope to reassess literary criticism's concentration upon the Jonsonian Folio of 1616 and its tendency to regard plays after that date as signs of an author in decline.[7] For, as I hope to have demonstrated, these plays, as much as any that precurse them, reveal the indeterminacies of Jonson's relation to literary and political authority.

My account of Jonson's 'republicanism' is intended to bring into view and vex the very notion of contractual meaning and even the notion of community. Nowhere more so does this take place, ironically enough, than in Jonson's last and incomplete work, *The Sad Shepherd* (1637) which is a fascinating embodiment of his interest in communities. Its unusual setting (for Jonson) in Sherwood Forest and on the banks of the Trent, and its English pastoral theme of Robin Hood and his merry men amongst the greensward, has often been remarked upon as a significant departure for the author.[8] He himself marks this supposed departure out in his prologue to the play:

> *He that hath feasted you these forty years, ...*
> *He pray's you would vouchsafe, for your own sake,*
> *To hear him this once more, but, sit awake.*
> *And though he now present you with such wool,*
> *As from mere English Flocks his Muse can pull,*
> *He hopes when it is made up into Cloth;*
> *Not the most curious head here will be loath*

> To wear a Hood of it; it being a Fleece.
> To match,or those of Sicily, or Greece.
> His Scene is Sherwood:
>
> (Prologue, ll. 1, 7–15)

As ever, I think Jonson's Prologue has ambivalent purposes since pastoral, local, English and communal themes have all shown themselves previously in his texts, be it in *The Alchemist, Bartholomew Fair*, or *The Devil is an Ass*. Pastoral features most obviously perhaps in *A Tale of a Tub*, but, as I hope to have demonstrated, the themes and politics of that genre were not a late innovation in Jonson's canon.

The Sad Shepherd, with its magical and pastoral themes, is an interesting glimpse of what work Jonson may have gone on to write, although this game of speculation is always a dangerous one. In fact the play rehearses familiar themes from the preceding canon – in particular of festivity and community, and its disruption by often alien or foreign sources. There is an important comparison here with *Bartholomew Fair*. In the communities of both these plays outsiders are obviously scapegoated. In *The Sad Shepherd* the Sherwood forest community scapegoats the family of Maudlin the witch. A figure of anti-communality as her name suggests, Maudlin is anxious to disturb the merrymaking and festivity of Robin Hood, his merry men and the local shepherds, and in particular to create irrevocable tension in the relationship between Robin and Marian. In doing so she is akin to 'the sowrer sort/Of Shepherds.' (I.iv.18–19) spoken of by those shepherds Robin welcomes to the feast, and therefore to the spirit of puritanism, so often depicted as a hostile and invading force in the communities of Jonson's plays (for example in *The Alchemist* or *Bartholomew Fair*).[9] Yet her treatment by Robin's community is seen as inextricably bound up with her gender and her age and therefore potentially as a venting of their internal tensions on outsiders. Helen Ostovich has remarked on the markedly female derivation of Maudlin's magical powers – transmitted to her via a girdle embroidered by her mother.[10] Female power is imaged in the embroidery and in the alternative phallus of the needle and therefore Ostovich claims 'The belt itself is both a sign and a product of sexual sovereignty.'[11] From this she deduces that Jonson demonstrates misogyny in the majority of his late texts (she makes *The New Inn* her exception to the rule). I would argue however that the misogyny explored in *The Sad Shepherd* and elsewhere in the Jonsonian canon is that of the relevant play-communities and not necessarily of Jonson himself.

Undoubtedly Maudlin's witchcraft and responses to it raise disturbing questions about the operations of community on the level of gender but her difference is marked out in a number of respects, not least her slightly foreign or alien dialect and her ability to shift shapes. She is a powerful figure of female agency but what is extant of Act III indicates that much of her potency derives from the masculine spirit Puck-Hairy. Nor is she the only strong female figure in the play, so simple accusations levelled against Jonson's 'misogyny' are also inadequate: Maid Marian, with her killing of the deer and her witty and humorous deflation of Amie's romantic swooning, is, as I have mentioned (see Chapter 9), a positive female emblem in the Jonsonian canon and in that a descendant of Frances Fitzdotterel, Prudence, and even Dol Common. Simple scapegoating of the female is not the issue here although Jonson recognizes the part it has to play in the superstitions attaching themselves to witchcraft and, interestingly enough, to love. The accusations that so rapidly splinter the Nottingham community's surface harmony are levelled against the women of the group – Marian and the lost Earine – and indicate the bonding of the male society under pressures of this nature. Maudlin knows how she can hit hardest – via the appetite for women and venison. The deer and the women of this play are hunted on an equal basis: this was a familiar conceit of early modern poetry which Jonson exploits to full effect.

Group misogyny clearly has its part to play in notions of witch-craft: yet Jonson carries this consideration a stage further. By depicting in detail the gusto with which Robin's men pursue the 'hag' – Little John declares, 'Rare sport I swear! this hunting of the Witch/Will make us' (II.viii.1–2) – and their stereotypical notion of a witch and how she lives (in stark contrast to the common family feuding we have witnessed between Maudlin, Douce and Lorell) he reveals society's scapegoating of the strange, the other. The men obsessively recount Maudlin's deformed appearance but George-a-Greene quietly records:

> I thought a Witch's banks
> Had inclos'd nothing, but the merry pranks
> Of some old woman.
> (II.viii.36–8)

By using the adjective 'merry', more readily associated with the Sherwood community, George elides the difference between Maudlin and them, and with remarkable insight, for which we must also credit Jonson, recognizes the sexism and ageism that produced so many of the violent and virulent witch-hunts of the age. That the women pursued in this way were mostly old and a little eccentric, if not arthritic, evidences society's need to harmonize itself in opposition to an Other. All of this is also evidence of Jonson's depth of understanding of the operations and potential violations of any community, rural or urban. *The Sad Shepherd* is not therefore a radical late departure in the canon, whether in terms of an interest in misogyny or scapegoating, although its specific operations in the playtext are unique. In investigating the breakdown of this particular alternative community Jonson is pursuing a line of analysis we have mapped out elsewhere in his drama. That in 1637 he was writing about English vagabond and outlaw communities like a number of other playwrights (Richard Brome in *A Jovial Crew* and James Shirley in *The Sisters*)[12] is simply further evidence of the need to view his plays within the context of their individual sociopolitical 'moment' as well as part of a wider analysis.

Vagabond literature has been seen as crypto-monarchist, but perhaps the detailed depictions of alternative societies and communities in Jonson's plays offered an implicit critique of any monarch who failed to recognize and account for such differences within the nation.[13] The harmonizing themes and effects of the masque were exposed as elaborate fantasies in the day-to-day business of policy-making and in truth Jonson had even disrupted that particular generic form by means of the creation of the invading anti-masques; the antimasque invariably constituted signs of difference in the midst of a supposedly orthodox spectacle and was often representative of more subversive social elements. In this way Jonson self-consciously limited the absolutism of the masque and stretched its court-determined boundaries.

In expressing such views Jonson was frequently forced to resort to the cultural discourse and media of the supposed dominant ideology; this may be felt to constitute a hypocritical act if he truly sought the recognition of alternative communities. In recognizing the orality of a culture such as that of Tottenham Court in *A Tale of a Tub* he necessarily imposed his own educated language upon the characters he created. His interest in jargon was both republicanizing and egalitarian, and yet also strangely colonialist and appropriating – such is the nature of the dramatist's art. The paradoxes persist.

The English Commonwealth was not founded until twelve years after Ben Jonson's death and was far from any political future the dramatist may have envisioned. 'Community' and 'republicanism' are words of great valency in contemporary late twentieth-century societies and there is, as ever, the danger of interpreting backwards from our own political discourse and ideologies in order to blur the boundaries between our era and that of the early modern period, to seek comforting parallels as opposed to disjunctions and discontinuities, even to see in the early seventeenth century a precedent for the political upheavals which followed. Yet terms such as 'republic', 'common good', 'common weal' and 'commonwealth' do resonate in the Jonsonian text and in particular in his drama. Within that complex and provocative medium Jonson was able to stretch and strain the boundaries of expectation, theatrical and political. In doing so he was casting responsibility and a sense of personal and communal rights back on to his audiences, be they in the public theatre or at court. That is the most egalitarian and republican act of all: Ben Jonson was a republican in the sense that he registered the potential and difference of all theatrical and literary communities and used his skill as an author to dramatize and mobilize them.

Notes

1. Introduction

1. New Historicist readings of Jonson have tended to concentrate on his masque productions; see, for example, Stephen Orgel, *The Jonsonian Masque* (New York: Columbia University Press, 1965; repr. 1981) and his *The Illusion of Power: Political Theater in the English Renaissance* (Berkeley: University of California Press, 1975). Stephen Greenblatt did write a couple of earlier articles, 'The False Ending in *Volpone*', *Journal of English and Germanic Philology*, 75 (1976), 90–104, and 'Loudun and London' (on *The Devil is an Ass*), *Critical Inquiry*, 12 (1986), 326–46, which are concerned with Jonsonian public theatre drama, but Jonson was a noticeable absence from the complex of figures discussed in *Renaissance Self-Fashioning: From More to Shakespeare* (Chicago: University of Chicago Press, 1980), saving a brief mention of Mosca (p. 233).
2. It should be emphasized from the outset that I am using the term 'radical' in a pre-1650s sense. The complicated ramifications of the term in that later period of political conflict can be seen, for example, in Richard Cust and Ann Hughes (eds), *Conflict in Early Stuart England: Studies in Religion and Politics, 1603–1642* (London and New York: Longman, 1989). Here I am using the term in the 1620s and 1630s sense to suggest an opposition to current governmental practice but not necessarily deep political radicalism in the sense of active republicanism.
3. With current interest in the early modern marketplace, largely influenced by Jean-Christophe Agnew, *Worlds Apart: The Market and the Theater in Anglo-American Thought, 1550–1750* (Cambridge: Cambridge University Press, 1986), Jonson is re-entering the Cultural Materialist debate. Richard Dutton's *Ben Jonson: Authority: Criticism* (London: Macmillan, 1996) engages with related questions. My argument remains, however, that the interest in Jonson as either masquer or as proto-capitalist rarely depicts him in a radical political vein. Martin Butler's recent cluster of articles has proved invaluable in reclaiming Jonson's later plays for socio-historical consideration but has tended to support a rather more traditional, orthodox reading of the author himself. See, for example, 'Stuart Politics in *A Tale of a Tub*', *Modern Language Review*, 85 (1990), 12–28, 'Late Jonson', in Gordon McMullan and Jonathan Hope (eds), *The Politics of Tragicomedy: Shakespeare and*

After (London: Routledge, 1992), pp. 166–88, and 'Ben Jonson and the Limits of Courtly Panegyric', in Kevin Sharpe and Peter Lake (eds), *Culture and Politics in Early Stuart England* (London: Macmillan, 1994) pp. 91–116. Feminist and Queer Theory are just beginning to 'discover' Jonson; see Kate Chedgzoy, Julie Sanders and Susan Wiseman, 'Introduction: Refashioning Ben Jonson', in Julie Sanders with Kate Chedgzoy and Susan Wiseman (eds), *Refashioning Ben Jonson: Gender, Politics, and the Jonsonian Canon* (London: Macmillan, 1998), pp. 1–27.

4. Following precedent and for the purposes of economy I will henceforth refer to James VI and I as James I: this is not to discount the importance of his Scottish title.

5. Thomas Healy's overview of Renaissance theory, *New Latitudes: Theory and English Renaissance Literature* (London: Arnold, 1992) repeats this formulaic reading of Jonson's *Works* (pp. 41–2). For a more nuanced assessment, see Jennifer Brady and W.H. Herendeen (eds), *Ben Jonson's 1616 Folio* (Newark, NJ: University of Delaware Press, 1991). Dutton, *Ben Jonson: Authority: Criticism* argues for a post-1616 'King's Poet'.

6. Recent biographies have tended to confirm this image: see David Riggs, *Ben Jonson: A Life* (Cambridge, MA: Harvard University Press, 1989) and W. David Kay, *Ben Jonson: A Literary Life* (London: Macmillan, 1995).

7. For a detailed examination of these ideas, see David Wootton's introductory essay to his edited collection *Republicanism, Liberty, and Commercial Society, 1649–1776* (Stanford, CA: Stanford University Press, 1994), pp. 1–41 (esp. pp. 1–6). John Morrill, in *The Nature of the English Revolution* (London and New York: Longman, 1993), argues that parliamentarians 'fought the English civil war not to abolish monarchy but to control it' (p. 16).

8. Blair Worden, 'Marchamont Nedham and the Beginnings of English Republicanism, 1649–1656', in Wootton (ed.), *Republicanism, Liberty, and Commercial Society*, pp. 45–81 (p. 50). See also his 'Shakespeare and Politics', *Shakespeare Survey*, 44 (1992), 1–15 (p. 6).

9. Richard Machin and Christopher Norris, *Post-Structuralist Readings of English Poetry* (Cambridge: Cambridge University Press, 1987) pp. 6–7.

10. Markku Peltonen has argued that this is a feature of humanist republican discourse throughout this period; see his *Classical Humanism and Republicanism in English Political Thought, 1570–1640* (Cambridge: Cambridge University Press, 1995), p. 309.

11. Annabel Patterson, *Reading Between the Lines* (London: Routledge, 1993), pp. 210–44 (p. 212).

12. Ibid., p. 221.

13. See Peltonen, *Classical Humanism and Republicanism*. See also Quentin Skinner, *The Foundations of Modern Political Thought*, 2 vols (Cambridge: Cambridge University Press, 1978), and Blair Worden, 'Classical Republicanism and the Puritan Revolution', in Hugh Lloyd-Jones, Valerie Pearl and Blair Worden (eds), *History and Imagination:*

Essays in Honour of Hugh Trevor-Roper (London: Duckworth, 1981), pp. 182–200, and 'English Republicanism', in J.H. Burns and Mark Goldie (eds), *The Cambridge History of Renaissance Political Thought* (Cambridge: Cambridge University Press, 1991), pp. 443–75. See also Jonathan Scott, 'The English Republican Imagination', in John Morrill (ed.), *Revolution and Restoration: England in the 1650s* (London: Collins and Brown, 1992), pp. 35–54.

14. Worden, 'English Republicanism', p. 443.
15. Worden, 'Shakespeare and Politics', p. 6.
16. It is interesting to note that the main expositor of Machiavellian political theory in Dutch writing at this time was Justus Lipsius, the influence of whose writings on Jonson has been charted by Robert C. Evans in *Jonson, Lipsius, and the Politics of Renaissance Stoicism* (Wakefield, NH: Longwood, 1992) and in his article '*Sejanus*: Ethics and Politics in the Early Reign of James', in Sanders, Chedgzoy and Wiseman (eds), *Refashioning Ben Jonson*, pp. 71–92. See also Daniel Boughner, 'Jonson's Use of Lipsius in *Sejanus*', *Modern Language Notes*, 73 (1958), 247–54 and '*Sejanus* and Machiavelli', *Studies in English Literature*, 1 (1960), 81–101.
17. Jonson famously cites Machiavelli's *The Prince* in his commonplace book *Timber; or, Discoveries* and it is a case that *The Prince* largely determined Elizabethan and Jacobean dramatic understanding of Machiavelli. That is not to say that exposure to the more republican text of the *Discourses* was impossible; see Anne Barton, 'Livy, Machiavelli, and Shakespeare's *Coriolanus*', *Shakespeare Survey*, 38 (1985), 115–30, for a related argument on Shakespeare and the *Discourses*. For a more detailed discussion of these issues, see Chapter 2.
18. Part of Jonson's collection of political and religious writings by Lipsius included his translation of and commentary on Polybius. See David McPherson, 'Ben Jonson's Library and Marginalia: An Annotated Catalogue', *Studies in Philology*, 71 (1974), Texts and Studies No. 5.
19. Jonathan Goldberg in *James I and the Politics of Literature: Jonson, Shakespeare, Donne, and their Contemporaries* (Baltimore and London: Johns Hopkins Press, 1983), especially pp. 72–80, explores the republican and absolutist significances of this myth.
20. Eco Haitsma Mulier, 'The Language of Seventeenth-Century Republicanism in the United Provinces: Dutch or European?', in Anthony Pagden (ed.), *The Languages of Political Theory in Early Modern Europe* (Cambridge: Cambridge University Press, 1987), pp. 179–95 (p. 184).
21. Martin van Gelderen, 'The Machiavellian Moment and the Dutch Revolt: The Rise of Neostoicism and Dutch Republicanism', in Gisela Bock, Quentin Skinner, and Maurizio Viroli (eds), *Machiavelli and Republicanism* (Cambridge, Cambridge University Press, 1990), pp. 205–23.
22. Mulier, 'The Language of Seventeenth-Century Republicanism', p. 187.

23. See, for example, Thomas Cogswell, *The Blessed Revolution: English Politics and the Coming of War, 1621–1624* (Cambridge: Cambridge University Press, 1989) and Conrad Russell (ed.), *The Origins of the English Civil War* (London: Macmillan, 1973; repr. 1991). The experience and discourse of republicanism in America is intrinsically linked to the continental European tradition as J.G.A. Pocock points out in *The Machiavellian Moment: Florentine Political Thought and the Atlantic Republican Tradition* (Princeton, NJ: Princeton University Press, 1975).
24. For the more complex reading of that term as covering three distinct revolts and a detailed history of the course of the conflict, see Geoffrey Parker, *The Dutch Revolt*, rev. edn (Harmondsworth: Penguin, 1990).
25. Riggs, *Ben Jonson*, pp. 17–18.
26. There are obvious difficulties in citing as 'truth' Drummond's subsequent gossipy notations of his conversations with Jonson, see Ian Donaldson's introductory essay to his *The Oxford Ben Jonson* (Oxford: Oxford University Press, 1985).
27. Riggs, *Ben Jonson*, p. 18.
28. In IV.iii. Face refers to the 'Spanish Don' (in truth Surly in disguise and hoping to expose the charlatan 'alchemists'), in what is clearly intended as an insult, as 'Egmont's bastard'. Egmont was a Dutch magnate who remained loyal to the crown despite constant disappointment of his political hopes by the Spanish King's underhand methods, but who was eventually executed. Tribulation Wholesome and Ananias, usually described as 'Puritan' visitors to the Blackfriars house are, more accurately, Dutch Anabaptists – a particularly pronounced sect, many of whom fled to London in order to evade Catholic persecution. Subtle's discourse with the emigrants is studded with Dutch references and jokes.
29. Stephen Orgel, 'What is a Text?', *Research Opportunities in Renaissance Drama*, 24 (1981), 3–6.
30. For a thorough investigation of this issue of the Folio and understandings of the canon, see Chedgzoy, Sanders and Wiseman, 'Introduction: Refashioning Ben Jonson'.

2. Roman Frames of Mind

1. See Howard Erskine-Hill, *The Augustan Idea in English Literature* (London: Arnold, 1983). See also Tom Cain's introductory essay to his edition of *Poetaster* (Manchester: Manchester University Press, 1995).
2. The phrase is self-consciously borrowed from Katherine Eisaman Maus's seminal text, *Ben Jonson and the Roman Frame of Mind* (Princeton, NJ: Princeton University Press, 1984).
3. Franco Moretti, 'The Great Eclipse: Tragic Form as the Deconsecration of Sovereignty', in John Drakakis (ed.), *Shakespearean Tragedy* (London and New York: Longman, 1992), pp. 45–83.
4. See Angela G. Dorenkamp, 'Jonson's *Catiline*: History as the Trying Faculty', *Studies in Philology*, 67 (1970), 210–20 and Michael J.C.

Echeruo, 'The Conscience of Politics and Jonson's *Catiline*', *Studies in English Literature*, 6 (1966), 341–56.
5. See McPherson, 'Ben Jonson's Library and Marginalia'.
6. For a detailed and scholarly account of Jonson's engagement with Lipsius, see Robert C. Evans, *Habit of Mind: Evidence and Effects of Ben Jonson's Reading* (New Jersey and London: Associated Universities Press, 1995). See also Daniel C. Boughner, 'Jonson's Use of Lipsius in *Sejanus*', *Modern Language Notes*, 75 (1960), 545–50. Lipsius's edition of Tacitus, published in 1574, was standard. Jonson shared his qualified understanding about the possibility for employing Tacitean theory in contemporary politics, feeling that what the *Annals* did demonstrate was the evil of tyrannical government. See Kenneth Schellhase, *Tacitus in Renaissance Political Thought* (Chicago: University of Chicago Press, 1976). For a detailed investigation of these linguistic concurrences, see Evans, '*Sejanus*: Ethics and Politics in the Early Reign of James'.
7. See McPherson, 'Ben Jonson's Library and Marginalia'.
8. See Titus Livy, *The Early History of Roma: Books I–V* trans. Aubrey De Selincourt; intro. D.M. Ogilvie (Harmondsworth: Penguin, 1971); Tacitus, *The Annals of Imperial Rome*, trans. and intro. Michael Grant (Harmondsworth: Penguin, 1971 [1956]); and Niccolò Machiavelli, *The Discourses*, trans. Leslie J. Walker; intro. Bernard Crick (Harmondsworth: Penguin, 1970).
9. See Peltonen, *Classical Humanism and Republicanism*. On the influence of Italian political humanism on English Renaissance drama, see, for example, G.K. Hunter, 'English Folly and Italian Vice: The Moral Landscape of John Marston', in *Jacobean Theatre*, Stratford-upon-Avon Studies (London: Arnold, 1960), pp. 85–112; J.W. Lever, *The Tragedy of State* (London: Methuen, 1971); and Barton, 'Livy, Machiavelli, and Shakespeare's *Coriolanus*'.
10. Niccolò Machiavelli, *The Prince*, trans. and ed. Quentin Skinner and Russell Price (Cambridge: Cambridge University Press, 1988).
11. Quentin Skinner has indeed argued that Machiavelli's language can be regarded as Ciceronian rather than Tacitean, which has important implications for Jonson's characterization of Cicero in *Catiline*. See Quentin Skinner, *Machiavelli* (Oxford: Oxford University Press, 1981). See also Ronald Syme, *Tacitus* 4 vols (Oxford: Oxford University Press, 1958).
12. Machiavelli, *Discourses*, p. 522.
13. It is from this observational point that Daniel C. Boughner moves out to consider the specific instances of Machiavellian influence on the language and structures of Jonson's *Sejanus*. See his '*Sejanus* and Machiavelli'; plus 'Juvenal, Horace and *Sejanus*', *Modern Language Notes*, 73 (1958), 247–54.
14. See Skinner, *Machiavelli*. See also Bock, Skinner and Viroli (eds), *Machiavelli and Republicanism*, and Pocock, *The Machiavellian Moment*.
15. See Daniel Waley, *The Italian City-State Republics* 3rd edn (London and New York: Longman, 1988).
16. B.N. DeLuna, *Jonson's Romish Plot: A Study of 'Catiline' and its Contexts*

(Oxford: Clarendon Press, 1967). For a related reading of Shakespeare, see Garry Wills, *Witches and Jesuits: Shakespeare's 'Macbeth'* (Oxford: Oxford University Press, 1995).
17. See Skinner, *Machiavelli*, esp. pp. 48–77.
18. Machiavelli, *Discourses*, I.58, p. 255.
19. Blair Worden, 'Ben Jonson Among the Historians', in Sharpe and Lake (eds), *Culture and Politics in Early Stuart England*, pp. 67–90 (p. 82).
20. David Stockton, *Cicero the Politician* (Oxford: Oxford University Press, 1971).
21. Geoffrey Hill, 'The World's Proportion: Jonson's Dramatic Poetry in *Sejanus* and *Catiline*', in *Jacobean Theatre*, Stratford-upon-Avon Studies (London: Arnold, 1960), pp. 113–32.
22. Maus, *Ben Jonson and the Roman Frame of Mind*, p. 10.
23. Ibid., p. 14.
24. Goldberg, *James I and the Politics of Literature*, esp. pp. 176–86.
25. Ibid., p. 177.
26. See Goldberg, *James I and the Politics of Literature*, who discusses James's relationship to the 'spectacle of power' and see Leonard Tennenhouse, *Power on Display: The Politics of Shakespeare's Genres* (London and New York: Methuen, 1986). On Anne of Denmark's involvement with the Jacobean court masque, see Barbara Kiefer Lewalski, 'Enacting Opposition: Queen Anne and the Subversion of Masquing', in her *Writing Women in Jacobean England* (Cambridge, MA: Harvard University Press, 1993) and Marion Wynne-Davies, 'The Queen's Masque: Renaissance Women and the Seventeenth-Century Court Masque', in S.P. Cerasano and Marion Wynne-Davies (eds), *Gloriana's Face: Women, Public and Private, in the English Renaissance* (Hemel Hempstead: Harvester, 1992), pp. 79–104.
27. Moretti, 'The Great Eclipse', p. 58.
28. Ibid., p. 70.
29. See Goldberg, *James I and the Politics of Literature*, p. 183 and Peter Womack, *Ben Jonson* (Oxford: Blackwell, 1986), pp. 9–14.
30. See Worden, 'Among the Historians', p. 68.
31. Anthony Miller, 'The Roman State in *Julius Caesar* and *Sejanus*', in Ian Donaldson (ed.), *Jonson and Shakespeare* (London: Macmillan, in association with the Humanities Research Centre, Australian National University, Canberra, 1983), pp. 179–201 (p. 194). Christopher Ricks relates this to a general theme of political and sexual dismemberment in the play: '*Sejanus* and Dismemberment', *Modern Language Notes*, 76 (1961), 301–7.
32. Miller, 'The Roman State', p. 194.
33. Tullius Cicero, *The Speeches*, trans. R. Gardner (Chicago: Loeb Classical Library, 1958).
34. John Fletcher and Philip Massinger wrote a play about the tragic fate of United Provinces' populist leader Jan van Oldenbarneveldt at the hands of those he supposedly represented in 1619. It is also worth registering here that the secretary to Margaret of Parma, the appointed Catholic ruler of the Spanish-controlled Low Countries

was Justus Lipsius. He was, as we have seen, one of Jonson's major political influences.
35. Annabel Patterson, *Shakespeare and the Popular Voice* (Oxford: Blackwell, 1989).
36. Ibid., p. 2.
37. Christopher Hill, 'The Many-Headed Monster', in *Change and Continuity in Seventeenth-Century England*, 2nd edn (London: Weidenfeld and Nicolson, 1991), pp. 181–204 (p. 181).
38. Alexander Leggatt, *Ben Jonson, His Vision and His Art* (London and New York: Methuen, 1981), p. 58.
39. Michel Foucault, *Discipline and Punish: The Birth of the Prison* (Harmondsworth: Penguin, 1977), p. 59.
40. Ibid., p. 59.

3. 'Saying Something About Venice'

1. The title of this chapter is a conscious allusion to Italo Calvino's *Invisible Cities* (London: Picador, 1979) where the journeying Marco Polo claims that whenever he describes a city he has seen he is 'saying something about Venice' (p. 69).
2. Recent essays cover the bibliographical ground which asserts this; see Anne Barton, *Ben Jonson, Dramatist* (Cambridge: Cambridge University Press, 1984), pp. 105–19; and Brian Parker, 'Jonson's Venice', in J.R. Mulryne and Margaret Shewring (eds), *Theatre of the English and Italian Renaissance* (London: Macmillan, 1991), pp. 92–112. See also Jonathan Bate, 'The Elizabethans in Italy', in Jean-Pierre Maquerlot and Michèle Willems (eds), *Travel and Drama in the Age of Shakespeare* (Cambridge: Cambridge University Press, 1996), pp. 55–74 and Roberta Mullini, 'Streets, Squares, and Courts: Venice as a Stage in Shakespeare and Ben Jonson', in Michele Marrapodi and others (eds), *Shakespeare's Italy: Functions of Italian Locations in Renaissance Drama* (Manchester: Manchester University Press, 1993), pp. 158–84.
3. Many other texts, dramatic or otherwise, have elected to use Venice as their centre, amongst them Shakespeare's *The Merchant of Venice*, Thomas Otway's *Venice Preserved*, Henry James's *The Wings of the Dove*, Thomas Mann's *Death in Venice*, and Jeanette Winterson's *The Passion*. Catherine Belsey reflects that most of these stories indicate that 'Venice is no place for lovers', see her 'Love in Venice', in Deborah E. Barker and Ivo Kamps (eds), *Shakespeare and Gender: A History* (London: Verso, 1995), pp. 196–213 (p. 196).
4. See, amongst others, Richard Burt, *Licensed by Authority: Ben Jonson and the Discourses of Censorship* (Ithaca, NY: Cornell University Press, 1993), and '(Un)Censoring in Detail: Thomas Middleton, Fetishism, and the Regulation of Dramatic Discourse' (forthcoming); Janet Clare, *Art Made Tongue-Tied by Authority: Elizabethan and Jacobean Dramatic Censorship* (Manchester: Manchester University Press, 1990); Richard Dutton, *Mastering the Revels: The Regulation and Censorship of English Renaissance Drama* (London: Macmillan, 1991); and Blair Worden,

'Literature and Political Censorship in Early Modern Europe', in A.C. Duke and C.A. Tamse (eds), *Too Mighty to be Free: Censorship and the Press in Britain and the Netherlands* (Zutphen: De Walburg Press, 1987), pp. 45–62.
5. Leah Marcus, in *Puzzling Shakespeare: Local Reading and its Discontents* (Berkeley: University of California Press, 1988), proffers a similar argument in relation to Vienna in Shakespeare's *Measure for Measure*, suggesting that the city of that play is 'not only London. It can also be taken as Vienna, or some more generalized depiction of a European city under absolutist or imperial rule. The conflict between local liberties and emerging authority was not London's problem alone' (p. 184).
6. Greenblatt, 'The False Ending in *Volpone*'.
7. Barton, *Ben Jonson, Dramatist*, p. 108.
8. For the political history of the Venetian republic, see, amongst others, John Hale (ed.), *Renaissance Venice* (London: Faber, 1973) and W.J. Bouwsma, *Venice and the Defense of Republican Liberty* (Berkeley: University of California Press, 1968). On the social politics of the city, see Brian Pullan, *Rich and Poor in Renaissance Venice: The Social Institutions of a Catholic State* (Oxford: Blackwell, 1971).
9. Goldberg, *James I and the Politics of Literature*, p. 75.
10. Richard Mackenney, *The City-State, 1500–1700: Republican Liberty in an Age of Princely Power* (London: Macmillan, 1989), p. 1.
11. See McPherson, 'Ben Jonson's Library and Marginalia'.
12. C.J. Gianakaris, 'Jonson's Use of "Avocatori" in *Volpone*', *English Language Notes*, 12 (1974–75), 8–14, suggests that Jonson displays 'a sophisticated grasp of Venetian justice as it existed during the republican period of that city' (p. 14); this is a problematic idea since the republican period in Venice was a lengthy one and the particular period in the *Avocatori*'s history Gianakaris is discussing is a far more restricted one.
13. Goldberg, *James I and the Politics of Literature*, p. 78.
14. One of the more spectacular Venetian events recounted by Wotton was the lavish reception ceremonies staged in the city to welcome the French monarch Henri III in 1574. Volpone claims to have participated in these celebrations as an actor, telling Celia:
> I am, now, as fresh,
> As hot, as high, and in as jovial plight,
> As when (in that so celebrated scene,
> At recitation of our comedy,
> For entertainment of the great Valois)
> I acted young Antinous;
> (III.vii.157–62).
15. Lady Would-be here proves herself prone to another 'myth of Venice', one which saw sensuality as a crucial element in the city's operations. There was indeed a flourishing homosexual subculture devoted to cross-dressing and involving young men lounging in gondolas in women's dress, see Richard Sennett, *Flesh and Stone: The Body and the City in Western Civilization* (London: Faber, 1992), p. 223,

but here Lady Would-be believes Peregrine is a woman in disguise: the irony is of course that on the stage Lady Would-be would have been performed by a boy actor in female dress.
16. Goldberg, *James I and the Politics of Literature*, p. 79.
17. A number of the essays collated in Harold Bloom (ed.), *Modern Critical Interpretations: Ben Jonson's Volpone, or the Fox* (New Haven and New York: Chelsea House Publishers, 1988), including Bloom's own introduction, repeat the formula that the harsh sentences imposed on Volpone and Mosca are neither Venice's nor London's but Jonson's own castigation of the indulgences of the theatre. These essays acknowledge the energies of the play but refuse to ascribe them to Jonson. Such readings miss the nuances and subtlety of the Jonsonian creation; witness Barton's observation (first made in *Ben Jonson Dramatist*) that 'The sentences themselves ... are unashamedly those of the dramatist rather than the obtuse magistrates of Venice' (p. 110). If so, why then is not Volpone's ultimate act of transgression, the epilogue, also unashamedly Jonson's? The 1995 Royal National Theatre production of *Volpone*, directed by Matthew Warchus, elected to omit the epilogue and to end with both Mosca and Volpone onstage in their respective states of incarceration: this was a considerable rewriting of the play.
18. Michel de Certeau, *The Practice of Everyday Life*, trans. Steven Rendall (Berkeley: University of California Press, 1984), p. 128. For de Certeau, whilst the language of power 'is in itself urbanizing ... the city is left prey to contradictory movements that counterbalance and combine themselves outside the reach of panoptic power. The city becomes the dominant theme in political legends, but it is no longer a field of programmed and regulated operations' (p. 95).
19. Richard Sennett, *The Fall of Public Man* (London: Faber, 1986), p. 38.
20. Ibid., p. 3.
21. Ibid., p. 38. Sennett focuses on the cities of the eighteenth and nineteenth centuries but his theories of public performance and public space seem equally applicable to the rise of the city in the seventeenth century and to dramatic treatments of the same by city-comedy writers such as Jonson and Middleton. For related reflections on the Renaissance city, see Sennett, *Flesh and Stone*.
22. A welcome exception is William W.E. Slights, 'The Play of Conspiracies in *Volpone*', in Bloom (ed.), *Volpone*, pp. 113–30. He relates the play's various competing and conflicting conspiracies as a product of a post-Gunpowder plot and paranoid Britain.
23. Skills which Jonas Barish rightfully recognizes as Volpone's in 'The Double-Plot in *Volpone*', in Jonas A. Barish (ed.), *Ben Jonson: A Collection of Critical Essays* (Englewood Cliffs, NJ; Prentice-Hall, 1963), pp. 93–105.
24. Agnew, *Worlds Apart*, pp. 23–4.
25. See Greenblatt, 'The False Ending in *Volpone*', and for a detailed exposition of the opening scene of *Volpone*, see Martin Butler, *Ben Jonson: Volpone: A Critical Study* (Harmondsworth: Penguin, 1987), pp. 20–36.
26. J. Hillis Miller, 'The Critic as Host', in Harold Bloom and others (eds),

Deconstruction and Criticism (London: Routledge and Kegan Paul, 1979), pp. 217–53 (p. 219). Although this article makes no direct reference to *Volpone* I am indebted to it for its invaluable insight into the related theme of parasitism.
27. Michael McCanles, *Jonsonian Discriminations: The Humanist Poet and the Praise of True Nobility* (Toronto: University of Toronto Press, 1992), p. 184. On the Jonsonian engagement with Seneca, see also Chapter 2 in Evans, *Habits of Mind*.
28. Miller, 'The Critic as Host', p. 219.
29. Stephen Greenblatt and Giles Gunn (eds), *Redrawing the Boundaries: The Transformation of English and American Literary Studies* (New York: MLA, 1992), p. 7.
30. Ibid., p. 6.
31. Ian Donaldson, 'Jonson's Tortoise', in Jonas A. Barish (ed.), *Jonson: Volpone: A Casebook* (London: Macmillan, 1977), pp. 189–94 (p. 193).
32. Goldberg, *James I and the Politics of Literature*, p. 72.
33. It was standard practice at Venetian *festa* to display banners at household windows; Celia is then making a social, participatory gesture from her imprisoned position. The relevance of this for issues of gender are self-evident.
34. Dutton, *Ben Jonson: Authority: Criticism*, p. 49.
35. Michael Anderson examines the proximity of performance styles and space between *commedia* and mountebanks in 'Making Room: Commedia and the Privatization of the Theatre', in Christopher Cairns (ed.), *The Commedia Dell'Arte: From the Renaissance to Dario Fo*, (Lewiston, NY: Edwin Mellen Press, 1989), pp. 74–97.
36. See Siro Ferrone, 'La vendita del teatro: Tipologie Europee tra cinque e seicento', in Cairns (ed.), *The Commedia dell'Arte*, pp. 35–73, which makes the point that theatre licences were often granted as a means of spying on the movement of foreigners since not only did they often comprise the performing troupes but a large proportion of the audiences. Government agents were thus able to act as regular paying spectators.
37. See Hale (ed.), *Renaissance Venice* and Innocenzo Cervelli, *Machiavelli e la crisi dello stato veneziano* (Naples: Guido Editore, 1974).

4. The Alternative Commonwealth of Women

1. Plato, *Republic*, ed. and trans. Desmond Lee, 2nd edn (Harmondsworth: Penguin, 1974; repr. 1987). The banishment of poets is in truth a belated and small part of the whole.
2. See part six of the Penguin translation of the *Republic*, p. 236. Plato's sense of female participation is strongly related to the myth of Sparta that was a potent one in contemporary Athens, namely that women took an active role in military and athletic preparations, and did so naked like the men; the sexually voyeuristic undertones of this 'liberation' of women should not therefore be underestimated.
3. In 'Ben Jonson's Library and Marginalia', McPherson lists Jonson's

possession of a three-volume edition of Plato, printed in Paris in 1578. The copy, which unfortunately contains no attributable markings, lies in the Chetham Library in Manchester.
4. John Donne, *The Sermons of John Donne*, ed. George Potter and Evelyn Simpson, 10 vols (Berkeley: University of California Press, 1953–1962), II. 17. pp. 347–8.
5. Juliet Dusinberre, *Shakespeare and the Nature of Women* (London: Macmillan, 1975), explored the impact of Puritanism upon attitudes towards women. The book has since faced considerable academic opposition and revision, not least at the hands of historicist critics such as Lisa Jardine, see *Still Harping on Daughters: Women and Drama in the Age of Shakespeare*, 2nd edn (Brighton: Harvester, 1983). Dusinberre's central thesis, however, remains a valuable one to work with.
6. Mary Beth Rose, *The Expense of Spirit: Love and Sexuality in English Renaissance Drama* (Ithaca, NY: Cornell University Press, 1988). Rose offers a fairly traditional misogynist reading of *Epicoene* but I am here applying the more liberatory terms she accords to Shakespeare in order to re-evaluate Jonson.
7. Helen Ostovich, '"Jeered by Confederacy": Group Aggression in Jonson's Comedies', *Medieval and Renaissance Drama in England*, 3 (1986), 115–28.
8. Ibid., p. 120.
9. William Flesch has suggested that the renaissance act/ritual of gift-giving was inextricably bound up with Foucauldian notions of power, see *Generosity and the Limits of Authority: Shakespeare, Herbert, Milton* (Ithaca, NY: Cornell University Press, 1992).
10. Critics, such as Mary Beth Rose in *The Expense of Spirit*, have tended to stress the personal anxiety theme. She establishes a rather odd opposition between the 'extreme conservatism' of Jonson's text and the proto-feminism of Dekker and Heywood's *The Roaring Girl* (c.1611). I would suggest that the latter play's stress on the sheer uniqueness of Moll, the female protagonist's, personality, and the juxtaposed existence of the more traditional, and therefore marriageable, heroine in the shape of Mary Fitzallard, is as conservative as anything Rose chooses to highlight in *Epicoene*. Moll's individuality annuls any real sense of social threat whereas by contrast the group operations of the Ladies' Collegiate are potentially more lasting and subversive. See also Mark Breitenberg, *Anxious Masculinity in Early Modern England* (Cambridge: Cambridge University Press, 1996).
11. Feminist academics have done much to recuperate the canon of women's writing at this time, see, for example, Germaine Greer and others (eds), *Kissing the Rod: An Anthology of Seventeenth-Century Women's Verse* (London: Virago, 1988). On Mary Wroth's work in particular, see Helen Hackett, '"Yet Tell Me Some Such Fiction": Lady Mary Wroth's *Urania* and the "Femininity" of Romance', in Clare Brant and Diane Purkiss (eds), *Women, Texts, and Histories, 1575–1760* (London: Routledge, 1992), pp. 39–68; and Kim F. Hall, '"I Rather Would Wish to be a Black-Moor": Beauty, Race, and Rank in Lady

Mary Wroth's *Urania'*, in Margo Hendricks and Patricia Parker (eds), *Women, 'Race', and Writing in the Early Modern Period* (London: Routledge, 1994), pp. 178–94. Hackett points out that in criticizing the *Urania* for its allusions to his own family Edward Denny accused Wroth of hermaphroditism. This was then a common attack on educated women.

12. In his recent anthology of Renaissance verse David Norbrook admirably elected to include extensive extracts from Wroth's work. The verses indicate her complicated love-life. See David Norbrook and H.R. Woudhuysen (eds), *The Penguin Book of Renaissance Verse, 1509–1659* (Harmondsworth: Penguin, 1992). She was in love with William Herbert, Earl of Pembroke by whom she would bear two children after her husband's death; see Gary Waller, *The Sidney Family Romance* (Detroit: Wayne State University Press, 1993). An articulate and lettered woman effectively silenced by the traditional process of arranged marriage, Wroth must have presented a poignant image for Jonson:

> In this strange labyrinth, how shall I turn?
> Ways are on all sides, while the way I miss:
> If to the right hand, there, in love I burn;
> Let me go forward, therein danger is; ...
> Yet that which most my troubled sense doth move
> Is to leave all, and take the thread of love.
> (*Pamphilia*, 'A Crown of Sonnets ...' I.1–4, 13–14).

13. On Wroth and theatricality, see Michael Shapiro, 'Lady Mary Wroth Describes a "Boy Actress"', *Medieval and Renaissance Drama in England*, 4 (1989), 187–93 and Ann Rosalind Jones, 'Designing Women: The Self as Spectacle in Mary Wroth and Veronica Franco', in Naomi J. Miller and Gary Waller (eds), *Reading Mary Wroth: Representing Alternatives in Early Modern England* (Knoxville: University of Tennessee Press, 1991), pp. 135–53.

14. See Lewalski, *Writing Women in Jacobean England*, pp. 15–44.

15. Stephen Orgel describes it as 'providing a martial context for womanly virtue'; see his 'The Role of the King', in H. Aram Veeser (ed.), *The New Historicism Reader* (London: Routledge, 1994), pp. 35–45 (p. 36). See also his *Impersonations: The Performance of Gender in Shakespeare's England* (Cambridge: Cambridge University Press, 1996). Lynda E. Boose remarks that 'one can only guess at the extent to which the subversiveness of this performance was intentional' in '"The Getting of a Lawful Race": Racial Discourse in Early Modern England and the Unrepresentable Black Woman', in Hendricks and Parker (eds), *Women, 'Race', and Writing in the Early Modern Period*, pp. 35–54 (p. 51). See also Kim F. Hall, 'Sexual Politics and Cultural Identity in *The Masque of Blackness*', in Sue-Ellen Case and Janelle Reinelt (eds), *The Performance of Power: Theatrical Discourse and Politics* (Iowa City: University of Iowa Press, 1991), pp. 3–18, and her *Things of Darkness: Economies of Race and Gender in Early Modern England* (Ithaca, NY: Cornell University Press, 1995).

16. Riggs, *Ben Jonson*, p. 119. He even goes so far as to suggest (in a not

entirely convincing thesis) that the Queen's personal antagonism towards the King may have influenced the scandalous references to the Scottish favourites in *Eastward Ho* for which Jonson and his fellow playwrights Marston and Chapman were temporarily imprisoned. The play was performed by the controversial Children of the Queen's Revels.

17. See David Lindley (ed.), *Court Masques* (Oxford: Oxford University Press, 1995).
18. Richard Dutton has a chapter on the play and the masques in *Ben Jonson: To the First Folio* (Cambridge: Cambridge University Press, 1983). I am also indebted to Jeremy Maule for discussion of these themes.
19. David Lindley, *The Trials of Frances Howard: Fact and Fiction at the Court of King James* (London: Routledge, 1993) and Anne Somerset, *Unnatural Murder* (London: Weidenfeld and Nicolson, 1996).
20. Martin Butler and David Lindley, 'Restoring Astraea: Jonson's Masque for the Fall of Somerset', *English Literary History*, 61 (1994), 807–27.
21. See my '"Twill Fit the Players Yet": Women and Theatre in Jonson's Later Drama', forthcoming, and Helen Ostovich, '"Hell for Lovers": Shades of Adultery in *The Devil is an Ass*', in Sanders, Chedgzoy and Wiseman (eds), *Refashioning Ben Jonson*, pp. 155–82.
22. See Gail Kern Paster, *The Body Embarrassed: Drama and the Disciplines of Shame in Early Modern England* (Ithaca, NY: Cornell University Press, 1993).
23. The play at least ends on an optimistic note with the marriages of Compass and Pleasance, and Captain Ironside and Lady Loadstone, partnerships dictated by magnetic theory according to Helen Ostovich's illuminating account of the play in 'The Appropriation of Pleasure in *The Magnetic Lady*', *Studies in English Literature*, 34 (1994), 425–42.
24. See Juvenal, 'Satire VI', in *Juvenal and Persius*, trans. G.G. Ramsey (Cambridge, MA: Harvard University Press, 1979).
25. This is the understanding of virtuous nobility that Markku Peltonen amongst others has argued for as central to early modern English understandings of 'republicanism'. See his *Classical Humanism and Republicanism*.
26. Once again Jonson could have found a real-life parallel to this in Lady Anne Clifford's lengthy legal struggle to reclaim her father's land. Clifford herself recorded these struggles in her diaries, see D.J.H. Clifford (ed.), *The Diaries of Lady Anne Clifford* (Stroud: Alan Sutton, 1990).
27. On the potency of female action within the domain of sexuality, see Kate Millett, *Sexual Politics* (London: Virago, 1977).
28. Kathleen McLuskie, in *Renaissance Dramatists* (Hemel Hempstead: Harvester, 1989), argues that whilst women do play an integral role in the politics of this play this is merely a mark of how the political situation has deteriorated in the republic. This is not a view I feel is borne out by the text.

29. Cited in Barton, *Ben Jonson, Dramatist*, p. 156.
30. Barton, *Ben Jonson, Dramatist*, p. 157.
31. Sallust, *Bellum Catilinae*, in *Works*, trans. J.C. Rolfe (Cambridge, MA: Harvard University Press, 1921). My thanks also to the library at Clare College, Cambridge for allowing me to work with Jonson's own copy of this text, one of the few extant from his personal library which contain annotations clearly in his hand, both underlining and commenting (in Latin) on the passages he employed in the construction of *Catiline*. Jonson's other major source was Cicero.
32. Like virtue, an active political life was seen as a central tenet of republicanism in the Renaissance – see Peltonen, *Classical Humanism and Republicanism*.
33. Ann Hughes, 'Gender and Politics in Leveller Literature', in Susan D. Amussen and Mark Kishlansky (eds), *Political Culture and Cultural Politics in Early Modern England* (Manchester: Manchester University Press, 1995), pp. 162–88.
34. See my '"The Days's Sports Devised in the Inn": Jonson's *The New Inn* and Theatrical Politics', *Modern Language Review*, 91 (1996), 545–60.
35. Marina Warner, *From the Beast to the Blonde: On Fairytales and their Tellers* (London: Chatto and Windus, 1994).
36. I have explored these ideas and this play in greater depth in .'Midwives and the New Science in the Seventeenth Century: Language, Print and Theatre', in Erica Fudge, Ruth Gilbert and Susan Wiseman (eds), *At the Borders of the Human: Science and Culture in the Seventeenth Century* (London: Macmillan, forthcoming).
37. Ostovich, 'The Appropriation of Pleasure', p. 427.
38. See Stephen Orgel, 'Shakespeare and the Cannibals', in Marjorie Garber (ed.), *Cannibals, Witches, and Divorce: Estranging the Renaissance* (Baltimore and London: Johns Hopkins Press, 1987), pp. 40–66, where Orgel discusses colonial issues and a culture of consent whereby European versions of Indians were offered, such as the tendency to anglicize the figure of Pocahontas.
39. Thomas Cogswell, 'England and the Spanish Match', in Cust and Hughes (eds), *Conflict in Early Stuart England*, pp. 107–33.
40. Ostovich, 'The Appropriation of Pleasure', p. 425.
41. Ibid., p. 426.

5. Republicanism and Theatre

1. Mackenney, *The City-State*, pp. 28–9.
2. I am indebted for some of my thinking on this matter to Andrew Gurr and his keynote address to the 'Ben Jonson and Theatre' conference, University of Reading, January 1996.
3. Steven Mullaney, *The Place of the Stage: Licence, Play, and Power in Renaissance England* (Chicago and London: University of Chicago Press, 1980), p. 38. Mullaney's account does oversimplify the tripartite status of theatre at this time, with the co-existence of public, private and court theatre. All three forms are potentially invoked in the

course of *The Alchemist*: with public theatre evoked by the city community, private theatre represented by the Blackfriars itself, and court masque being represented by Lovewit's Act V intervention.
4. Mullaney, *The Place of the Stage*, p. viii.
5. I make related claims for the transitional charge of the Blackfriars theatre in 'The Day's Sports Devised in the Inn'.
6. Sennett, *The Fall of Public Man*.
7. Robert Smallwood, '"Here in the Friars": Immediacy and Theatricality in *The Alchemist'*, *Review of English Studies*, 32 (1981), 142–60 (p. 142).
8. Some excellent recent research has begun to blur the previously distinct boundary line between 1590s history plays and early Jacobean city comedies. The nascent capitalism of the latter is becoming traceable in the former. My thanks to Tom Healy and to Chris Pye for discussions on this issue; see Thomas Healy, 'Remembering with Advantage: Nation and Ideology in *Henry V'*, in Michael Hattaway and Boika Sokolova (eds), *Shakespeare in the New Europe* (Sheffield: Sheffield Academic Press, 1994), pp. 174–93; and Christopher Pye, 'The Theater, the Market, and the Subject of History', unpublished article.
9. Agnew, *Worlds Apart*, p. 11.
10. Ibid., p. 12.
11. Tom Hayes, in *The Birth of Popular Culture: Ben Jonson, Maid Marian, and Robin Hood* (Pittsburgh, PA: Duquesne University Press, 1992), somewhat unfairly sees her as a brutalized and virilized capitalist who is more successful in the 'male' business world than the men themselves (pp. 21–2).
12. See Stephen Greenblatt, *Marvelous Possessions: The Wonder of the New World* (Oxford: Clarendon Press, 1991). My thanks to Stephen Greenblatt for reading an earlier draft of this chapter.
13. Burt, *Licensed by Authority*, p. 92.
14. See, for example, David Mann, *The Elizabethan Player* (London: Routledge, 1991).
15. Anne Righter, *Shakespeare and the Idea of the Play* (Harmondsworth: Penguin, 1962).
16. Jonson had himself acted in this play and was commissioned by Philip Henslowe to write additions to it for the Rose theatre, adding to the metatheatricality; see Carol Chillington Rutter (ed.), *Documents of the Rose Playhouse* (Manchester: Manchester University Press, 1984), and Barton, *Ben Jonson, Dramatist*.
17. Mullaney, *The Place of the Stage*, p. 69.
18. Sennett, *The Fall of Public Man*.
19. This subtle distinction is often lost in performance since directors recognize humorous potential in the twinning of the religious fanatics; in addition, Tribulation's role in terms of lines spoken and time present onstage is relatively small, certainly by comparison with the cozeners.
20. Niccolò Machiavelli, *The Prince*, trans. and intro. George Bull (Harmondsworth: Penguin, 1961; repr. 1981), p. 100. Quentin Skinner and Russell Price (eds), *The Prince* (Cambridge: Cambridge University

Press, 1988) elect to translate '*principe*' as 'ruler' which gives a greater sense of the political subtlety of the text. I have used the Penguin translations of Machiavelli throughout, however, for ease of access.
21. Ibid., p. 101.
22. See Greenblatt, *Marvelous Possessions* and, for the antithesis of my argument, see Harry Levin, 'Two Magian Comedies: *The Tempest* and *The Alchemist*', *Shakespeare Survey*, 22 (1969), 47–58, where he argues that, whereas Shakespeare's contemporaneous play takes account of New World developments, Jonson's play is firmly rooted in London; I would question the imaginative scope of this.
23. Greenblatt, *Marvelous Possessions*, p. 25.
24. See R.W. Van Fossen's introduction to his edition of *Eastward Ho* (Manchester: Manchester University Press, 1979), pp. 1–58. On 'colonial transformations' in Jonson's drama, see also Rebecca Ann Bach, 'Ben Jonson's "Civill Savages"', *Studies in English Literature*, 37 (1997), 277–93 and my 'The Politics of Escapism: Fantasies of Travel and Power in Ben Jonson's *The Alchemist* and Richard Brome's *The Antipodes*', in Ceri Sullivan and Barbara White (eds), *Writing and Fantasy* (London and New York: Longman, forthcoming).
25. In his edition of the play, in *Selected Plays of Ben Jonson* II, Martin Butler stresses his careful adherence to Jonson's punctuation of this play, as seen into print for the 1616 Folio *Works*; he is right to stress the significance of the often complex and unusual punctuation for a fuller understanding of this playtext.
26. John S. Mebane, 'Renaissance Magic and the Return of the Golden Age: Utopianism and Religious Enthusiasm in *The Alchemist*', *Renaissance Drama*, n.s. 10 (1979), 117–39 (128–9).
27. In the theatre this can have a remarkably tangible effect – the sudden, possibly unnoticed removal of the few props required by those earlier scenes leaving an audience quite literally out in the cold, feeling the air of an empty stage. The occurrence in Sam Mendes's 1991–92 RSC production provoked a spontaneous round of applause. Ian Donaldson makes a related point in *Jonson's Magic Houses: Essays in Interpretation* (Oxford: Clarendon Press, 1997), p. 74.
28. Peter Holland, 'The Resources of Characterization in *Othello*', *Shakespeare Survey*, 41 (1989), 119–32.
29. This would also characterize his crowd-driven play *Bartholomew Fair* and has, mistakenly I believe, led Leo Salingar to deny the Bartholomew birds the right to the label 'community' in his article, 'Crowd and Public in *Bartholomew Fair*', *Renaissance Drama*, n.s. 10 (1979), 141–59.
30. William W.E. Slights, 'Unfashioning the Man of Mode: A Comic Countergenre in Marston, Jonson and Middleton', *Renaissance Drama*, n.s. 15 (1984), 69–91.
31. Interestingly enough, Jonson himself would be granted the reversion of this office by James in 1624, see Richard Dutton, 'Ben Jonson and the Master of the Revels', in J.R. Mulryne and Margaret Shewring (eds), *Theatre and Government under the Early Stuarts* (Cambridge: Cambridge University Press, 1993), pp. 57–86. Jonson plays on this

idea in *The Magnetic Lady* where Compass is granted the reversion to the office of Surveyor of the Projects General; he actually inherits the title during the play when the current holder Thin-wit dies. This was another barely concealed thrust at Inigo Jones, whose office this was in actuality.

32. Stephen Greenblatt, 'Martial Law in the Land of Cockaigne', in *Shakespearean Negotiations* (Oxford: Clarendon Press, 1988), pp. 129–63.

6. The Republic in the Fair

1. Peter Stallybrass and Allon White, *The Politics and Poetics of Transgression* (London: Methuen, 1986), p. 27.
2. See, for example, Barton, *Ben Jonson, Dramatist*, p. 218, and Womack, *Ben Jonson*, p. 159.
3. See Stanley Fish, 'Authors-Readers: Jonson's Communities of the Same', in Stephen Greenblatt (ed.), *Representing the English Renaissance* (Berkeley: University of California Press, 1988), pp. 231–64. Whilst I prefer to argue for Jonson's diverse communities, not least of readers, Fish's provocative essay is a useful tool to work with.
4. See Stallybrass and White, *The Politics and Poetics of Transgression*. See also Mikhail Bakhtin, *Rabelais and his World*, trans. Hélène Iswolsky (Bloomington: Indiana University Press, 1984). For a concise summary of Bakhtin's theories of the carnivalesque and their subsequent applications to the theatrical form, see Simon Dentith (ed.), *Bakhtinian Thought: An Introductory Reader* (London: Routledge, 1995). On Bakhtin, carnival, and theatre, see Michael Bristol, *Carnival and Theater: Plebeian Culture and the Structure of Authority in Renaissance England* (London and New York: Methuen, 1985). On Bakhtin, language and the heteroglossia and its relevance to Jonson studies, see Womack, *Ben Jonson*, pp. 15–16.
5. See, for example, Jonathan Dollimore and Alan Sinfield (eds), *Political Shakespeare: New Essays in Cultural Materialism* (Manchester: Manchester University Press, 1985). See also Jonathan Dollimore, *Radical Tragedy: Religion, Ideology and Power in the Drama of Shakespeare and his Contemporaries*, 2nd edn (London: Harvester Wheatsheaf, 1989), and Stallybrass and White, *The Politics and Poetics of Transgression*.
6. Burt, *Licensed by Authority*, suggests that the application of a Bakhtinian model to *Bartholomew Fair* is a critical fallacy, a misunderstanding of the term 'popular tradition'. Whilst Bakhtin himself made only limited application of his own theory of the 'carnivalesque' to early modern drama, it has been one of the most fruitful areas of his influence.
7. Jonathan Dollimore, 'Transgression and Surveillance in *Measure for Measure*', in Dollimore and Sinfield (eds), *Political Shakespeare*, pp. 72–87.
8. The arbitrary nature of the marriage contract is also a feature of the

plot of *The Magnetic Lady* with Compass's marriage to Pleasance.
9. Benjamin Bennett, *Hugo von Hofmannsthal: The Theatres of Consciousness* (Cambridge: Cambridge University Press, 1988), p. 222.
10. I follow both George Hibbard's (New Mermaid) and Martin Butler's (Cambridge University Press) editorial lead here in spelling 'Ursla' thus, in respect of early modern pronunciation.
11. James Knowles, 'The Spectacle of the Realm: Civic Consciousness, Rhetoric, and Ritual in Early Modern London', in Mulryne and Shewring (eds), *Theatre and Government Under the Early Stuarts*, pp. 157–89; plus Richard Dutton (ed.), *Jacobean Civic Pageants* (Keele: Keele University Press, 1996).
12. Dutton, *Ben Jonson: Authority: Criticism*, p. 2.
13. See Keith Sturgess, *Jacobean Private Theatre* (London and New York: Routledge, 1987). See also Dutton, *Mastering the Revels*. Kathleen McLuskie challenged Sturgess's argument in a paper she gave at the 'Refashioning Ben Jonson' conference at Warwick University in January 1995: '"Base Detractors and Illiterate Apes": Jonson and his Audiences', My thanks to Kate for allowing me to work with a draft version of this paper and for her comments on this chapter. See also her 'Making and Buying: Ben Jonson and the Commercial Theatre Audience', in Sanders, Chedgzoy and Wiseman (eds), *Refashioning Ben Jonson*, pp. 134–54.
14. See Susan Wiseman, '"The Eccho of Uncertaintie": Jonson, Classical Drama, and the Civil War', in Sanders, Chedgzoy and Wiseman (eds), *Refashioning Ben Jonson*, pp. 208–9.
15. John Creaser, 'Enigmatic Ben Jonson', in Michael Cordner, Peter Holland and John Kerrigan (eds), *English Comedy* (Cambridge: Cambridge University Press, 1994), pp. 100–18.
16. See Dentith (ed.), *Bakhtinian Thought*, pp. 195–224.
17. The notion of the burgeoning seventeenth-century capital city being re-created amidst the recreative booths of the fair feeds Brian Gibbons's interpretation in *Jacobean City Comedy* 2nd edn (London: Methuen, 1980). The *Bartholomew Fair* chapter is one of the important additions to the revised version of Gibbons's book.
18. See Fish, 'Authors-Readers'.
19. See Patterson, *Shakespeare and the Popular Voice* and *Reading Between the Lines*.
20. In Adam Overdo, Jonson is parodying the disguised duke motif, which Shakespeare and Marston amongst others, in plays such as *Measure for Measure* and *The Malcontent*, had popularized to the extent of creating a genre.
21. See Greenblatt, *Shakespearean Negotiations*.
22. Ian Archer has suggested that London aldermen frequently took a mediatory position in altercations in the city between controlling authorities and the populace. See *The Pursuit of Stability: Social Relations in Elizabethan London* (Cambridge: Cambridge University Press, 1991), p. 5.
23. In the 1987 production at the Regents Park Open Air Theatre, London, Peter Barnes, the adaptor and director, not only chose to add

dialogue and balladry of his own but he omitted the entire Induction scene. This seems to me to entirely miss the point. The critical framework to the play is vital here as it is in *The Magnetic Lady*. Recent productions of *Bartholomew Fair* all appear to have done injustice to the text. Richard Eyre's 1989 production at the (now Royal) National Theatre, London transposed events to nineteenth-century London, in the process cutting the dense topicality of the Jonsonian text and eschewing its central politics. In December 1997, Laurence Boswell's production at the Royal Shakespeare Company moved events to the Notting Hill Carnival. The production did omit the Induction (possibly due to sheer economies and time – the production ran at 3^1/$_2$ hours as it was) but in many other respects was true to the spirit and indeed the language of the text. I am indebted to Peter Holland's programme notes for this production for reflections on the play.

24. Gillian Beer, 'Circulatory Systems: Money, Gossip, and Blood in *Middlemarch*', in her *Arguing with the Past; Essays in Narrative from Woolf to Sidney* (London: Routledge, 1989), pp. 99–116.
25. In the *Discourses*, he describes how the tension between the patricians and the plebeians led to the formation of the offices of the tribunes; this he said made the republic 'more perfect', see I.4., 'That Discord between the Plebs and the Senate of Rome made this Republic both Free and Powerful', p. 219.
26. Agnew, *Worlds Apart*, pp. 110–11.
27. John Gordon Sweeney, *Jonson and the Psychology of Public Theater* (Princeton, NJ: Princeton University Press, 1985), p. 7.
28. See Susan Bennett, *Theatre Audiences: A Theory of Production and Reception* (London: Routledge, 1990).
29. Creaser, 'Enigmatic Ben Jonson', p. 102.
30. Burt, *Licensed by Authority* effects a fascinating comparison between Shakespeare's and Jonson's attitudes towards theatre in *The Winter's Tale* and *Bartholomew Fair* respectively. He dwells at length on the Autolycus scene and the difference between the new songs he is selling and Shakespeare's 'old tale' in order to suggest Shakespeare seeks a transcendence for his art, and yet does not draw the parallel wtih the Nightingale scene in *Bartholomew Fair*, instead citing the puppet play as the entertainment Jonson sought to delegitimize. The comparison of the two song-selling scenes would open wider questions of the Jonson–Shakespeare interaction rather than difference – a point Burt is anxious to make.
31. Bennett, *Hofmannsthal*, p. 201.
32. Richard Dutton has implied in *Ben Jonson: Authority: Criticism* that Jonson in some senses became a timeserver at court after the *Eastward Ho* scandal of 1605, citing the masques as proof of this reading. Implicitly subversive readings of court performances by characters such as Nightingale suggest that Jonson's career is by no means as clear-cut, nor as linear as this might suggest.
33. See Tessa Watt, *Cheap Print and Popular Piety, 1550–1640* (Cambridge: Cambridge University Press, 1991), esp. pp. 1–127.
34. Paster, *The Body Embarrassed*, makes the interesting point that urina-

tion appears in the text to be a peculiarly female problem. She examines the literary connection between urination, release and prostitution through such figures as Ursla and Dol Common.
35. A parody which Jonathan Bate argues is present in *Poetaster*: see his *Shakespeare and Ovid* (Oxford: Clarendon Press, 1993), pp. 167–70.
36. Christopher Marlowe, *The Complete Poems and Translations*, ed. Stephen Orgel (Harmondsworth: Penguin, 1971).
37. Bennett, *Theatre Audiences*, p. 77.
38. Although Thomas Dekker in *The Gulls Hornbook* suggested that theatre's very danger lay in its levelling potential. See Kathleen McLuskie, *Dekker and Heywood* (London: Macmillan, 1994), pp. 4, 6.
39. In *The Illusion of Power*, Stephen Orgel argues for the notion of a 'democratic' theatre in the Renaissance. The description seems at odds with observations made elsewhere in the same text that, for example: 'The Elizabethan public theater established a hierarchy that was primarily economic ...' (p. 8). He achieves doublethink of Orwellian proportions when he goes on to declare that 'Within these categories, all spectators were equal [but some were more equal than others?]; nothing in the structure of the play-house or the quality of the theatrical experience distinguished the lord who paid his threepence from the merchant who paid his.' (p. 8). Cokes's wrangle over admission fees in *Bartholomew Fair* surely proves the opposite, that theatre fostered bourgeois aspirations of upward mobility and was far from being a 'democratizing institution'.
40. Archer, *The Pursuit of Stability*, p. 260.

7. The Commonwealth of Hell: *The Devil is an Ass*

1. See Leah Marcus, *The Politics of Mirth: Jonson, Herrick, Milton, Marvell and the Defence of Old Holiday Pastimes* (Chicago: Chicago University Press, 1986), esp, pp. 64–105; Robert C. Evans, 'Contemporary Contexts of Jonson's *The Devil is an Ass*', *Comparative Drama*, 26 (1992), 140–76; and my 'The Trials of Frances Fitzdottrel in *The Devil is an Ass*', unpublished conference paper, Northern Renaissance Seminar: Historicisms Conference, Sheffield Hallam University, 1996.
2. Archer, *The Pursuit of Stability*, p. 58.
3. *Bartholomew Fair* was not included in the 1616 *Works*; it was intended for inclusion in a second volume which was eventually published posthumously under the oversight of Sir Kenelm Digby in 1641. The texts that comprise this second volume make a considerable contribution towards challenging the 'orthodox' reading of Jonson that is regularly produced from readings of the *Works*.
4. See William Empson, *The Structure of Complex Words* (London: Chatto and Windus, 1964). He does not look specifically at 'devil' although the working premise and the chapter on 'dog' are revealing.
5. The Gamini Salgado edition of *The Devil is an Ass* contained within his *Jacobean City Comedies* (Harmondsworth: Penguin, 1985), has 'holidays' for 'holy-days' which reduces the statement's impact somewhat.

6. This was seen as dependent on the election and regular rotation of office-holding; see Peltonen, *Classical Humanism and Republicanism*, esp. pp. 119–89.
7. Greenblatt, 'Loudun and London', and 'Shakespeare and the Exorcists', in *Shakespearean Negotiations*, pp. 44–128.
8. Greenblatt, *Shakespearean Negotiations*, p. 94.
9. Ibid., p. 96.
10. The 1616 wholesale rewriting of *Every Man In His Humour* allows me to equate that text with these later examinations of community by Jonson. In the Folio version of the play he made the significant geographical transposition from Florence to contemporary London, emphasizing his interest at this time in the urban communities of the Jacobean capital.
11. See Marcus, *The Politics of Mirth*, pp. 89–92.
12. See Evans, 'Contemporary Contexts of Jonson's *The Devil is an Ass*', where he examines Jonson's own (no longer extant) contribution of speeches to a welcoming dinner held for James by Cockayne. The King too is implicit in the rapid turnaround of establishment attitudes to the Alderman's project; this makes *The Devil is an Ass*'s language of projection less obvious in its consolidation of James.
13. Riggs, *Ben Jonson*. References are also to be found in Jonson's own play *Catiline*. See DeLuna, *Jonson's Romish Plot*. See also Richard Dutton, 'The Lone Wolf', in Sanders, Chedgzoy and Wiseman (eds), *Refashioning Ben Jonson*, pp. 114–33.
14. See my 'A Parody of Lord Chief Justice Popham in *The Devil is an Ass*', *Notes and Queries*, 44 (1997), 528–30.
15. Kevin Sharpe, *The Personal Rule of Charles I* (London and New Haven: Yale University Press, 1992), explores the significance for the 1630s of fen drainage and forest law disputes from a revisionist, pro-Caroline angle. For accounts that suggest a potential at least for a deeper oppositional political significance to popular protest of this nature, see C. Holmes, 'Drainers and Fenmen: The Problem of Popular Political Consciousness in the Seventeenth Century', in Anthony Fletcher and John Stevenson (eds), *Order and Disorder in Early Modern England* (Cambridge: Cambridge University Press, 1985), pp. 166–95, and Keith Lindley, *Fenland Riots and the English Revolution* (London: Heinemann, 1982). Peter Happé's edition of *The Devil is an Ass* (Manchester: Manchester University Press, 1994) is disappointingly one-sided in its reading of the fen-drainage theme, saying that 'Like so much of the play this is ambivalent, for draining the fens was useful, and it was ultimately achieved ...' (p. 7). As we shall see, both of these statements require considerable qualification.
16. There is also an important question as to whether Jonson would have had any awareness of ecology when framing his critique; the danger of imposing late twentieth-century concerns on his work is paramount. An interesting comparison might be Jonathan Bate's application of similar 'green' theorizing to the work of Wordsworth in *Romantic Ecology: Wordsworth and the Environmental Tradition* (London: Routledge, 1991). Issues of community related to land development

were, however, crucial in the early seventeenth century, see Buchanan Sharp, *In Contempt of All Authority: Rural Artisans and Riot in the West of England, 1586–1660* (Berkeley: University of California Press, 1980) and my 'Seeing the Seventeenth-Century Forest for the Woods and the Trees', unpublished paper, 'Literature and Ecology' conference, University of Swansea, March 1997.
17. Interesting then to record that in the 1990s the Netherlands themselves are in the process of reconverting vast farmland sites into wetland habitats in order to preserve a number of rare species as well as the delicate ecobalance of wetland and flatland marshes.
18. On Jonson's problematic associations with the Catholic faith, see Ian Donaldson, 'Jonson's Duplicity: The Catholic Years', in his *Jonson's Magic Houses*, pp. 47–65.
19. Jeremy Purseglove, *Taming the Flood* (Oxford: Oxford University Press, 1989), p. 47.
20. A real-life model for Jonson's theme here of a woman's involvement in a land-rights case may be Lady Anne Clifford, whose diaries record her ongoing legal efforts at this time to resecure her father's land for her personal management. See D.J.H. Clifford (ed.), *The Diaries of Lady Anne Clifford* and my 'The Trials of Frances Fitzdottrel in *The Devil is an Ass*'.
21. Andrew Motion, 'Inland', in *The Pleasure Steamers* (Manchester: Carcanet, 1978). In Wicken Fen, near Ely in Cambridgeshire, one of the few remaining protected wetland sites in Great Britain and the National Trust's first acquisition, there is still a section known as 'Adventurers' Fen'.
22. Riggs, *Ben Jonson*, p. 244.
23. See L.C. Knights, *Drama and Society in the Age of Jonson* (Harmondsworth: Penguin in assoc. with Chatto and Windus, 1962) and Don E. Wayne's reassessment of Knights in his 'Drama and Society in the Age of Jonson: An Alternative View', *Renaissance Drama*, n.s. 13 (1982), 103–29.
24. Riggs, *Ben Jonson*, p. 224. See also Butler and Lindley, 'Restoring Astraea'.
25. See *Conversations* in Donaldson, *The Oxford Ben Jonson*, p. 604 (ll. 350–5).
26. See A.R. Braunmuller, 'Robert Carr, Earl of Somerset, as Collector and Patron', in Linda Levy Peck (ed.), *The Mental World of the Jacobean Court* (Cambridge: Cambridge University Press, 1992), pp. 230–50.
27. See David Lindley, 'Embarrassing Ben: Masques for Frances Howard', *English Literary Renaissance*, 16 (1986), 345–59.
28. See Hayes, *The Birth of Popular Culture*, pp. 126–8. Marcus, *The Politics of Mirth*, sees *The Devil is an Ass* as intricately connected to the highly topical Overbury scandal, pp. 89–90.
29. See Ostovich, 'Hell for Lovers'.
30. Purseglove, *Taming the Flood*, p. 32.
31. Lindley, *Fenland Riots*, p. 107.
32. Richard Brome, *The Court Beggar* in *Dramatic Works* (London: Pearson, 1873), I, V.ii. p. 267.

33. Cited in Purseglove, *Taming of the Flood*, p. 56. Interestingly, in the same year as Thomas Randolph's play was printed, a sneering comment in the royalist press referred to Oliver Cromwell as 'Lord of the Fens', a later variation on Jonson's notion of the 'Duke of Drowned Land' as being the lord of nothing. John Morrill credits this labelling of Cromwell for the subsequent apocryphal belief that he had been active in fen-drainage protests in his constituency of Ely (an idea reiterated by Purseglove in *Taming the Flood*); see Morrill, *The Nature of the English Revolution*, pp. 136–7.

8. The Commonwealth of Paper: Print, News and *The Staple of News*

1. See David Norbrook, '*Areopagitica*, Censorship and the Early Modern Public Sphere', in Richard Burt and John Archer (eds), *The Administration of Aesthetics: Censorship, Political Criticism and the Public Sphere* (Minneapolis: University of Minnesota Press, 1994), pp. 3–33 (pp. 7–8).
2. See Barish, *The Anti-theatrical Prejudice* which has been employed in quasi-doctrinal fashion to label Jonson as anti-theatrical and elitist in his politics. For a persuasive refutation of this reading, see Creaser, 'Enigmatic Ben Jonson'.
3. I am indebted here to the work of Ian Atherton on manuscript news in this period and for our lively discussions on this theme. See also Richard Cust, 'News and Politics in Seventeenth-Century England', *Past and Present*, 112 (1986), 60–90. Karen Newman's 'Engendering the News' in A. L. Magnusson and C.E. McGee (eds), *The Elizabethan Theater XIV* (Toronto: P.D. Meany, 1996), pp. 49–69, reached me too late to figure in my discussions here but provides an interesting counterpoint to my argument.
4. Hayes, *The Birth of Popular Culture*, p. 49.
5. Leah S. Marcus, 'Renaissance/Early Modern Studies', in Greenblatt and Gunn (eds), *Redrawing the Boundaries*, pp. 41–63 (p. 50). The work of Elizabeth Eisenstein is seminal here. See, for example, *The Printing Press as an Agent of Change* (Cambridge: Cambridge University Press, 1980).
6. See the introductory essay to Anthony Parr's Revels edition of *The Staple of News* (Manchester: Manchester University Press, 1988), p. 22.
7. The issue is expertly weighed in Natalie Zemon Davis, 'The Print and the People', in her *Society and Culture in Early Modern France* (London: Duckworth, 1975).
8. Eisenstein, *The Printing Press as an Agent of Change*, p. 80.
9. See McKenzie, '*The Staple of News*', although he registers considerable doubt as to Jonson's participation in any such movement.
10. Parr, *The Staple of News*, p. 25.
11. I am indebted to Nigel Smith's forthcoming work on the Levellers and print culture here. On the issue of illiteracy and print culture, see R.A. Houston, *Literacy in Early Modern Europe* (London and New York:

Longman, 1988), and Davis, *Society and Culture in Early Modern France*.
12. He nevertheless concedes that Jonson is an interesting case for any consideration of the effects of censorship in the Stuart period. See Worden, 'Literature and Political Censorship', p. 45. For examples of texts which present the monolithic understandings of censorship which Worden attacks, see Annabel Patterson, *Censorship and Interpretation: The Conditions of Writing and Reading in Early Modern England* (Madison: University of Wisconsin Press, 1984) and Clare, *Art Made Tongue-Tied by Authority*. For an argument sympathetic to Worden, see S.L. Lambert, 'The Printers and the Government, 1604–1640', in Robin Myers and Michael Harris (eds), *Aspects of Printing from 1600* (Oxford: Oxford Polytechnic Press, 1987), pp. 1–29.
13. See Burt, *Licensed by Authority* and '(Un)Censoring in Detail': I am grateful to Richard Burt for making an advance copy of this article available to me, and for reading and offering comments upon an earlier draft of this chapter.
14. See Fish, 'Authors-Readers'.
15. McKenzie, *'The Staple of News'*, p. 111.
16. Ibid., p. 113.
17. Marcus, *Puzzling Shakespeare*, p. 21.
18. See Healy, *New Latitudes*, pp. 41–2.
19. Joseph Loewenstein, 'For a History of Literary Property: John Wolfe's Reformation', *English Literary Renaissance*, 18 (1988), 389–412.
20. See Ayres, 'The Iconography of Jonson's *Sejanus*' and Lindley, 'Embarrassing Ben'.
21. See Burt, '(Un)Censoring in Detail', p. 5.
22. Parr, *The Staple of News*, p. 24.
23. Martin Butler, in '"We Are One Man's All": Jonson's *The Gipsies Metamorphosed*', *Yearbook of English Studies*, 21 (1991), 253–73, suggests that one of the motives behind Jonson's composition of the 1621 masque *The Gypsies Metamorphosed* may have been to seek the support and patronage of Charles I and the Duke of Buckingham (who commissioned the piece) in the waning years of James. The course of events, however, and subsequent references in Jonson's plays imply that the bid was unsuccessful.
24. For an interesting discussion of this masque, see Patricia Fumerton, *Cultural Aesthetics: Renaissance Literature and the Practice of Social Ornament* (Chicago: University of Chicago Press, 1991). She examines the way in which masques displaced the consumption of sweets and confectionery following a banquet – 'consuming the void' as it was known – and how the idea of that ritual – a withdrawal into privacy – was replaced by an act of exposure, the masque. The banqueting halls for the purpose accordingly grew in size. Fumerton discusses the masque and its 'trivial' themes in terms not of the Spanish match but an aristocratic 'aestheticization' of foreign trade, pp. 141–68.
25. The phrase is Louis MacNiece's and describes his own work as a war propagandist at the BBC: see *Collected Poems* (London: Faber, 1979).

26. See Cogswell, *The Blessed Revolution*, and 'England and the Spanish Match'.
27. Alastair Bellany, '"Rayling Rymes and Vaunting Verse": Libellous Politics in Early Stuart England, 1603–1628', in Sharpe and Lake (eds), *Culture and Politics in Early Stuart England*, pp. 285–310, rightly suggests the need for greater literary-historical attention to be paid to the content of popular ballads. Cogswell, *Blessed Revolution*, makes a similar observation with particular reference to the Spanish match.
28. See Kevin Sharpe, 'The King's Writ: Royal Authors and Royal Authority in Early Modern England', in Sharpe and Lake (eds), *Culture and Politics in Early Stuart England*, pp. 117–38.
29. See Roy Strong, *Henry, Prince of Wales, and England's Lost Renaissance* (London: Thames and Hudson, 1986).
30. See *News from the New World*, ll. 53–6. The lines in *The Staple of News* are clearly derivative, as they are elsewhere in the text. *Neptune's Triumph* is also a regular source – an indication of Jonson's dealings with the problematic ephemerality of these masques and their particular brand of 'news' in this ephemerality-focused public theatre play.
31. See McKenzie, '*The Staple of News*'.
32. Sara Pearl, '"Sounding to Present Occasions": Jonson's Masques of 1620–25', in David Lindley (ed.), *The Court Masque* (Manchester: Manchester University Press, 1984), pp. 60–77.
33. Fumerton, *Cultural Aesthetics*, in a section entitled 'Tearing Down the Masque: Towards an Aesthetics of Consumerism', suggests that the masque form underwent a process of self-combustion or deconstruction as the age of capitalism took hold, pp. 159–68.
34. Commentaries on the play since Herford and the Simpsons have made this point but have produced it as confirmation of Jonson's opposition to news-offices such as the Staple and the dissolution therefore as an act of wish-fulfilment. I take issue with this reading; see McKenzie, '*The Staple of News*'.
35. Fascinatingly, one of the popular genres of books borne out of the increased output by printing presses in England was that of 'fashion manuals', books depicting the national costumes of other countries and detailing the trends and styles of its own.
36. Jonson was fascinated with this stage in life. Bartholomew Cokes is another example of a prodigal ward. Cokes has a moral tutor in Humphrey Wasp; Jonson, having himself been tutor to Sir Walter Raleigh's problematic son Wat during some well-documented adventures in Paris, was personally acquainted with the theme.
37. Richard Levin, '*The Staple of News*, the Society of Jeerers and Canters' College', *Philological Quarterly*, 44 (1965), 445–53. Richard Brome would also exhibit an interest in the language of canting in *A Jovial Crew* (1641). McKenzie, '*The Staple of News*' observes a link between emergent print culture and expanding academic institutions, comparing the Canters' College with the universities of the 1620s at which a large number of new lectureships were being created, and in opposition to which both Charles I and Archbishop Laud would speak.
38. This speech derives *verbatim* from the text of *Neptune's Triumph*, see ll.

69–71. Its implicit comparison of the art of cookery and the art of war can be compared with that of Furnace, the choleric cook in Massinger's *A New Way to Pay Old Debts* (c. 1625), (I.ii.23–31).
39. Food frequently provided a masque theme for Jonson. See in particular *Pleasure Reconciled to Virtue*, with Comus as God of the belly, the masque reappropriated in more strictly republican (and Protestant) terms by Milton in *Comus, A Masque presented at Ludlow Castle* (1634). See also Leah Marcus, 'The Occasion of Ben Jonson's *Pleasure Reconciled to Virtue*', *Studies in English Literature*, 19 (1979), 271–94.
40. See *Neptune's Triumph*, ll. 134–40.
41. See Jean Wilson, *Entertainments for Elizabeth I* (Woodbridge: Brewer, 1980).
42. McKenzie, '*The Staple of News*', posits Pennyboy Junior as another of Jonson's quasi-monarchs. Perhaps in his growth towards awareness of the populace's opinion(s), he acts as a paradigm of the need for limited monarchy.
43. See *News from the New World*, ll. 48–51.
44. John Milton, *Areopagitica; For the Liberty of Unlicenc'd Printing, To the Parlament of England* (1644), ed. William Haller in *The Works of John Milton* IV, gen. ed. Frank Allen Patterson (New York: Columbia University Press, 1931), ll. 16–22, p. 328. Spelling modernized.
45. See Norbrook, '*Areopagitica*'. See also George Orwell and Reginald Reynolds (eds), *British Pamphleteers* (London: Wingate, 1948), 1.
46. See *News from the New World*, ll. 57–9.
47. One of the major difficulties with the censorship debate and the early modern period is that we lose sight of the brevity of the performance life of these texts. *Bartholomew Fair* was performed only twice during Jonson's life and this may explain why censorship was more a response to the moment than a coordinated, coercive policy.
48. See Burt, '(Un)Censoring in Detail'.
49. Devra Kifer, 'Too Many Cookes: An Addition to the Printed Text of *The Staple of News*', *English Language Notes*, 11.4 (1973), 264–71.

9. Alternative Societies: *The New Inn* and the Late Plays

1. Essentially 'absolutist' readings of Jonson include Richard Helgerson's *Self-Crowned Laureates: Jonson, Spenser, Milton, and the Literary Tradition* (Berkeley: University of California Press, 1983) and his 'Ben Jonson', in Thomas N. Corns (ed.), *The Cambridge Companion to English Renaissance Poetry: Donne to Marvell* (Cambridge: Cambridge University Press, 1983), pp. 148–70. See also Robert N. Watson, *Ben Jonson's Parodic Strategy: Literary Imperialism in the Comedies* (Cambridge, MA: Harvard University Press, 1987).
2. Richard Allen Cave looks at the communities of the late plays in *Ben Jonson* (London: Macmillan, 1991), pp. 144–71.
3. See Anne Barton, '*The New Inn* and the Problem of Jonson's Late Style', *English Literary Renaissance*, 9 (1979), 395–418.
4. Bach, 'Ben Jonson's "Civill Savages"'.

5. See Peter Clark, *The English Alehouse, 1200–1830* (London and New York: Longman, 1983); and 'The Alehouse and the Alternative Society', in Donald Pennington and Keith Thomas (eds), *Puritans and Revolutionaries* (Oxford: Clarendon Press, 1978), pp. 47–72; S.K. Roberts, 'Alehouses, Brewing and Government under the Early Stuarts', *Southern History*, 2 (1980), 45–71; and Keith Wrightson, 'Alehouses, Order and Reformation in Rural England, 1590–1660', in Eileen and Stephen Yeo (eds), *Popular Culture and Class Conflict, 1590–1914* (Brighton: Harvester Press, 1981), pp. 1–27.
6. It is interesting that Prudence is her title only in the printed text of the play: in first performances she was called Cicely and the alteration may have been an effort on Jonson's part to further signify her important position within the play.
7. See Bakhtin, *Rabelais and his World*.
8. See Clark, 'The Alehouse and Alternative Society'. Ian Archer has emphasized the importance of the parish boundaries in establishing and defining communities in the Elizabethan period; see *The Pursuit of Stability*.
9. See Graham Parry, *The Golden Age Restored: The Culture of the Stuart Court, 1603–42* (Manchester: Manchester University Press, 1981).
10. Martin Butler, 'Late Jonson', p. 172. In fact, the 1629 parliament was the crucial second session of the 1628 parliament, dissolved amidst heated debate over the Petition of Right. Summoned on 20 January 1629, it was dissolved on 2 March. For a detailed account, see Sharpe, *The Personal Rule of Charles I*, pp. 40–1, 61. *The New Inn* was registered on 19 January 1629 (1628 in seventeenth-century terms since New Year began 25 March) and performed in March.
11. Watson, *Ben Jonson's Parodic Strategy*, p. 210.
12. See Clark, *The English Alehouse*, and Wrightson, 'Alehouses, Order and Reformation'.
13. See Richard Dutton, '*Hamlet, An Apology for Actors* and the Sign of the Globe', *Shakespeare Survey*, 41 (1989), 35–43.
14. Clark, *The English Alehouse*, p. 7.
15. Charles Nicholl, in *The Reckoning* (London: Jonathan Cape, 1992), his recent book of ruminations upon the death of Christopher Marlowe, records how similar prejudice and cultural stereotyping has led to the popular notion of the Deptford establishment where Marlowe died or was murdered as a sleazy pub, when in truth it was a highly reputable inn and lodgings house run by an eminent citizen's widow.
16. See Marcus, *The Politics of Mirth*, pp. 106–39. See also David Underdown, *Revel, Riot and Rebellion: Popular Politics and Culture in England, 1603–1660* (Oxford: Oxford University Press, 1987).
17. Michael Hattaway's edition opts for the even more magniloquent:

> If a great person do me an affront,
> A giant of the time, sure I will bear it
> Or out of the time, sure I will bear it
> Or cut of patience or necessity.
> (IV.iv.190–3)

18. Barton, *Ben Jonson, Dramatist*, invokes the latter only in order to discuss nostalgia, pp. 258–84.
19. See Richard S. Peterson, *Imitation and Praise in the Poems of Ben Jonson* (New Haven: Yale University Press, 1981).
20. Simon Hornblower, 'Creation and Development of Democratic Institutions in Ancient Greece', in John Dunn (ed.), *Democracy: The Unfinished Journey, 508 BC to AD 1993* (Oxford: Oxford University Press, 1993), pp. 1–6 (p. 1). See also Quentin Skinner, *The Foundations of Modern Political Thought*, 2 vols (Cambridge: Cambridge University Press, 1978).
21. Thomas Hobbes would cite Sparta as a paradigm in his more absolutist political writings. See Thomas Hobbes, *Leviathan*, ed. Richard Tuck (Cambridge: Cambridge University Press, 1991; repr. 1994).
22. Clark, 'The Alehouse and Alternative Society', p. 48.
23. See Evans, *Jonson, Lipsius*.
24. Clark, 'The Alehouse and Alternative Society', p. 159.
25. Ibid., p.159.
26. Roberts, 'Alehouses, Brewing and Government', p. 48.
27. See Martin Butler, '*A New Way to Pay Old Debts*: Massinger's Grim Comedy', in Cordner, Holland and Kerrigan (eds), *English Comedy*, pp. 119–36.
28. See Paul Christianson, 'Royal and Parliamentary Voices on the Ancient Constitution, c. 1604–1621', in Peck (ed.), *The Mental World of the Jacobean Court*, pp. 71–95.
29. The terms are Barton's; see *Ben Jonson, Dramatist*, p. 346.
30. The proceedings of a court of love are set out in the *locus classicus*, the *Aresta Amorum, sive Processus inter Amantes cum Decisionibus Parlamenti* of Martial d'Auvergne, written circa 1455, and which went through more than 35 editions between 1500 and 1734. Actual assemblies as described here had been held in Europe, although there are no records of such proceedings in England: however, a number of the entertainments devised for Elizabeth I bore obvious resemblance (in that respect this particular choice of motif could be seen as another nostalgic strategy). Certainly a number of playtexts at this time recognized the stage potential of such events – Heywood's *Play of Love*, Marston's *The Faun*, and Massinger's *The Parliament of Love* amongst them (unfortunately the latter survives only in mutilated form and we are unsure if it was ever performed). See Michael Hattaway's introductory essay to his Revels edition of *The New Inn* (Manchester: Manchester University Press, 1984).
31. Hattaway, *The New Inn*, p. 30.
32. See Parry, *The Golden Age Restored* and Erica Veevers, *Images of Love and Religion: Queen Henrietta Maria and Court Entertainments* (Cambridge: Cambridge University Press, 1989).
33. Henrietta Maria herself took part in many of these productions and is credited with having presaged the advent of female actors on the stage at the time of her son's 1660 restoration. See Sophie Tomlinson, 'She that Plays the King: Henrietta Maria and the Threat of the Actress in Caroline Culture', in McMullan and Hope (eds), *The Politics*

of *Tragicomedy*, pp. 189–207. See also Elizabeth Howe, *The First English Actresses: Women and Drama, 1660–1700* (Cambridge: Cambridge University Press, 1992). I expand on these ideas in '"The Day's Sports Devised in the Inn": Jonson's *The New Inn* and Theatrical Politics', *Modern Language Review*, 91 (1996), 545–60, and in '"Twill Fit the Players Yet": Women and Theatre in Jonson's Late Plays', forthcoming.

34. Hattaway, *The New Inn*, p. 31.
35. Butler, 'Late Jonson', p. 173.
36. Conrad Russell, 'Parliament and the King's Finances', in Russell (ed.), *The Origins of the English Civil War*, pp. 91–116 (p. 91). See also Martin Butler, *Theatre and Crisis, 1632–42* (Cambridge: Cambridge University Press, 1984), pp. 72–4.
37. I am aware in making this observation that I am producing an essentially 'Whig' version of seventeenth-century history which revisionist historians would challenge. See, for example, Russell (ed.), *The Origins of the English Civil War*. For more tempered accounts of the Ship Money debate, see Michael J. Braddick, *The Nerves of State: Taxation and the Financing of the English State, 1558–1714* (Manchester: Manchester University Press, 1996), esp. pp. 83–6 and pp. 180–99; Peter Lake, 'The Collection of Ship Money in Cheshire during the 1630s: A Case Study of Relations between Central and Local Government', *Northern History*, 17 (1981), 44–71; K. Fincham, 'The Judges' Decision on Ship Money in February 1637: The Reaction of Kent', *Bulletin of the Institute of Historical Research*, 57 (1984), 230–7; and Cust and Hughes, 'Introduction', pp. 31–2. On other prerogative taxes, see Richard Cust, *The Forced Loan and English Politics, 1626–1628* (Oxford: Oxford University Press, 1987).
38. See Cust, *The Forced Loan*.
39. Jonson's Epigram #64: 'To Our Great and Good K[ing] Charles on His Anniversary Day, 1629' does appear to lay the blame for the failure of the 1629 Parliament at the feet of the King's subjects:

>O times! O manners! surfeit bred of ease,
>The truly epidemical disease!
>'Tis not alone the merchant, but the clown
>Is bankrupt turned; the cassock, cloak, and gown
>Are lost upon account! and none will know
>How much to heaven for thee, great Charles they owe!
>(ll.17–22)

but the political leanings of the epigrams are rarely so simple or clearcut, as Michael McCanles has shown in *Jonsonian Discriminations*. For an erudite exposition of the relative merits of Whiggish and revisionist historical accounts of this period, see Cust and Hughes, 'Introduction'. I am indebted to Ann Hughes for her guidance in this and other matters.
40. Margot Heinemann, '"God Help the Poor: The Rich Can Shift": The World Upside-Down and the Popular Tradition in the Theatre', in McMullan and Hope (eds), *The Politics of Tragicomedy*, pp. 151–65 (p. 151).

10. Local Government and Personal Rule in *A Tale of a Tub*

1. Marcus, *The Politics of Mirth*, makes a similar point, pp. 132–5.
2. Butler, 'Stuart Politics', acknowledges the potential for the alternative reading I am explicating in this chapter.
3. Sharpe, *The Personal Rule of Charles I*, pp. 52–62. Sharpe records that Charles's proclamation on the dissolution of parliament in 1629 made it clear that no parliament was to meet imminently, but suggests that this did not constitute a renunciation of parliamentary government. James I had ruled for a lengthy period without parliament, 1614–21, but the atmosphere in 1629 was markedly distinct.
4. There has been some critical debate over the exact dating of the play, prompted largely by Herford and the Simpsons' now ostensibly discredited decision to position the playtext as Jonson's earliest extant script, including it therefore in their volume of early plays (III), placed before even *The Case is Altered*. They argued for later additions and revisions as a means of explaining references within the text that would have been impossible to write in the 1590s. For a wholly convincing refutation of that argument, see Barton, *Ben Jonson, Dramatist*, p. 321.
5. These names are related to the trades and histories of the respective characters' godfathers – for example, Rasi Clench or To-Pan the tinker – a further instance of patriarchs writing sons. The Plato-derived argument that names reveal the essence of things was expressed by Jonson's own father-figure and Westminster School educator, William Camden, in his historical work *Britannia*. In Jonson's epigram to Camden (Epigram #14), Martin Elsky has demonstrated how the poet uses naming nouns and adjectives with Augustan Virgilian Latin etymologies in describing his tutor; he thus identifies Camden's moral nature with classical values, see his *Authorizing Words: Speech, Writing and Print in the English Renaissance* (Ithaca, NY: Cornell University Press, 1989).
6. A similar argument is forwarded by Butler in 'Stuart Politics'.
7. Butler, 'Late Jonson', p. 171.
8. Ann Hughes discusses the 'burgeoning genre of county surveys and histories' at this time; see her 'Local History and the Origins of the Civil War', in Cust and Hughes (eds), *Conflict in Early Stuart England*, pp. 224–53. See also her *The Causes of the English Civil War* (London: Macmillan, 1991), p. 20, and Graham Parry, *The Trophies of Time* (Oxford: Oxford University Press, 1997).
9. Burt, *Licensed By Authority*, makes this point. He also describes how Jonson scarcely capitulated to the censor when criticisms were made of his satire of Inigo Jones in the character of Vitruvius Hoop. Jonson changed the offending name but the substitute, In-and-In Medlay, is hardly less suggestive; he also retained Medlay's 'Motion' at the end, a clear parody of the masque form.
10. See *Underwood*, 14, 'An Epistle to Master John Selden'. Butler, 'Late Jonson', argues that Jonson had distanced himself from more radical figures such as Cotton and Selden by this time (p. 171).

11. This play effects numerous puns on 'coats' of various kinds, emphasizing how the signs of office have become all-powerful: when feigning the role of 'pursuivant', Miles Metaphor is instructed by Justice Preamble to wear the coat as well as the badge of office (I.v.43); see Butler, 'Stuart Politics', p. 24.
12. Martin Butler, 'Private and Occasional Drama', in A.R. Braunmuller and Michael Hattaway (eds), *The Cambridge Companion to English Renaissance Drama* (Cambridge: Cambridge University Press, 1990), pp. 127–60. Of course, this 'Motion' is a comic version of the masque achieved by means of shadow-puppetry although, as Butler stresses in 'Stuart Politics', the social ranks and hierarchies of quotidian life are scrupulously maintained in the seating of the audience (p. 27). See also the puppet-play admissions scene in *Bartholomew Fair* V.iii. 1–45.
13. The lottery motif for the selection of marital partnerships was also employed in *Bartholomew Fair*: Grace decides to choose between Quarlous and Winwife as prospective husbands by means of the lottery. In truth her strategy is designed to keep both men at bay until she is well clear of the fair and her responsibilities; as it is her plot is skilfully circumvented by Quarlous. Rebecca Ann Bach has made an intriguing connection between these lotteries and actual London lotteries in the Jacobean period that financed the Virginia Company's colonial operations, see her 'Ben Jonson's "Civill Savages"', p. 280.
14. Butler, 'Stuart Politics', p. 18.
15. Margot Heinemann makes the point that although parliament only met in this period when summoned by the monarch, nevertheless parliamentary consent over taxes was important and bitter disputes over the same provided dramatic substance from *Woodstock* in the early 1590s through to Massinger's *King and the Subject* in 1638; see her 'Political Drama', in Braunmuller and Hattaway (eds), *The Cambridge Companion to English Renaissance Drama*, pp. 161–205. On the forced loan, see Cust, *The Forced Loan*.
16. Valerie Pearl, 'Social Policy in Early Modern London', in Hugh Lloyd-Jones, Valerie Pearl and Blair Worden (eds), *History and Imagination: Essays in Honour of Hugh Trevor-Roper* (London: Duckworth, 1981), pp. 115–31 (p. 116).
17. L.M. Hill, 'County Government in Caroline England, 1625–1640', in Russell (ed.), *The Origins of the English Civil War*, pp. 66–90 (p. 66).
18. Butler, 'Stuart Politics', suggests that *A Tale of a Tub* is condescending in its approach to those who are not of the parish gentry and that the latter have all the wit (p. 13), but I would suggest that such figures as Tub and his mother and the Justice are seen as manipulative and disruptive forces in the play. That this disruption comes from crown-appointed officials or aristocracy is significant for the politics of this play which I see in a more subversive vein than Butler.
19. Pearl, 'Social Policy in Early Modern London', p. 116.
20. The phrase is Joan Kent's from *The English Village Constable, 1580–1642: A Social and Administrative Study* (Oxford: Clarendon Press, 1986).

Notes 219

21. Ian Donaldson, *The World Upside-Down: Comedy from Jonson to Fielding* (Oxford: Clarendon Press, 1970), p. 65.
22. Marcus, *The Politics of Mirth*, suggests they represent, along with Overdo, such figures as Chief Justice Coke who sought at this time to curb and constrain royal prerogative by asserting their legal rights (p. 54). Bristle and Haggis are confused in the pursuit of their office by the absence of legitimizing authority, that is to say the local Justice of the Peace, Adam Overdo. In this they are akin to the madman Trouble-all, who will do nothing without the Justice's warrant: we have in Peter Womack's terms in *Ben Jonson*, a state of 'suspended magistracy' (pp. 110–13); Womack traces a series of patterns in Jonson's plays, such as *Poetaster, Sejanus* and *Every Man In His Humour*, which he articulates in terms of the absence and return of legitimate authority.
23. See Kent, *The English Village Constable*.
24. Sharpe, *The Personal Rule of Charles I.*
25. Heinemann, 'Political Drama', is at pains to stress that although the House of Commons was made up of elected representatives, it was nevertheless a far from public forum. See also Conrad Russell, *Parliaments and English Politics, 1621–29* (Oxford: Oxford University Press, 1979).
26. In truth Justices rarely fare well in Jonson; as well as poor Overdo in *Bartholomew Fair*, we have the easily gulled and personally ambitious (if somewhat equivocal) figure of Sir Paul Eitherside in *The Devil is an Ass*. In the Folio version of *Every Man In His Humour* we have Justice Clement who, despite the implications of his name, produces famously arbitrary sentencing. Preamble is of course as machinatory as those he is meant to prosecute and holds little respect for his rustic neighbours and colleagues; as he tells Chanon Hugh:
    > You are my learned, and canonic neighbour,
    > I would not have you stray; but the incorrigible
    > Nott-headed beast, the clowns, or constables,
    > Still let them graze; eat salads, chew the cud:
    > (I.v. 20–3)
27. Keith Wrightson, 'Two Concepts of Order: Justices, Constables and Jurymen in Seventeenth-Century England', in John Brewer and John Styles (eds), *An Ungovernable People: The English and their Law in the Seventeenth and Eighteenth Centuries* (London: Hutchinson, 1980), pp. 21–46 (p. 26).
28. Ibid., p. 25.
29. Hill, 'County Government in Caroline England,' p. 74.
30. Ibid., p. 75.
31. See McCanles, *Jonsonian Discriminations*.
32. Pearl, 'Social Policy in Early Modern London', p. 116. Hill, 'County Government in Caroline England', says of the Quarter Sessions, 'The sessions were the judicial and administrative meetings of the Commission of the Peace four times each year in principal towns throughout the county. The meetings were limited by a fourteenth century statute to a duration of three days although two day sessions

were the norm ... [They were] the *omnium gatherum* of the Shires ... the quarter days were among the great events of the provincial calendar. Grand juries and juries of presentment [the presentment of accused criminals], the sheriff, undersheriffs [offices almost extinct by 1620 but revived under Caroline rule – another piece of present-minded "nostalgia"], bailiffs, constables, and so on throughout the petty hierarchy of the county; all of these would be present to wait upon the Justices of the Peace.' (p. 69).

33. Wrightson, 'Two Concepts of Order'. On Essex, see also William Hunt, *The Puritan Moment: The Coming of Revolution in an English County* (Cambridge, MA: Harvard University Press, 1983). Hughes, in 'Local History and the Origins of the Civil War', offers the counterbalancing suggestion that case studies of localities should not be used to generalize outwards to the nation, but rather as unique and distinct examples (pp. 237–9).

34. Cust, *The Forced Loan*, offers an alternative, and convincing, reading of the late 1620s as the period in which local antagonism towards centralized coercive policies found a definite political voice. See also Hughes, *The Causes of the English Civil War*, pp. 162–3, and Braddick, *The Nerves of State*.

35. Hughes, 'Local History and the Origins of the Civil War', p. 249.

36. Butler, 'Stuart Politics', p. 28.

37. Butler mentions the possible critique embedded in the play's insistence on the source of Tub family wealth in a footnote to 'Stuart Politics', n. 13, remarking that eventual complaints against the saltpetre men who carried out searches for the mineral made their way into the Grand Remonstrance in Parliament, but he does not go on to trace the direct implications of this for our understanding of the Tub family, except to say that this sourcing of their wealth in animal dung undermines Lady Tub's self-importance and grandeur.

38. John Lemly, '"Make Odde Discoveries!": Disguises, Masques and Jonsonian Romance', in A.R. Braunmuller and J.C. Bulman (eds), *Comedy from Shakespeare to Sheridan: Change and Continuity in the English and European Dramatic Tradition* (Newark, NJ and London: Associated Universities Press, 1986), pp. 131–47, regards Hugh as an example of 'beneficent authority' subjected only to a 'genial unveiling', like that of Adam Overdo's, but I find him far more equivocal and his statements far more spurious than that reading would imply.

39. Butler's 'Stuart Politics', and his 'Ecclesiastical Censorship of Early Stuart Drama: The Case of Jonson's *The Magnetic Lady*', *Modern Philology*, 89 (1991–2), 469–81, suggest a Jonson largely sympathetic to Laudian religious policy.

40. See Marcus, *The Politics of Mirth*, pp. 106–39; and Underdown, *Revel, Riot and Rebellion*.

41. Historical debate rages over contemporary attitudes to Laud's policies. Revisionists such as Sharpe and Russell have disagreed sharply over the extent to which Laud can be credited with initiating the policies associated with him (see Sharpe, *The Personal Rule of Charles I*). Andrew Foster calls for a more orthodox understanding of Laud's

coercive approach in 'Church Policies of the 1630s', in Cust and Hughes (eds), *Conflict in Early Stuart England*, pp. 193–223. Jonson seems to place himself in the midst of such ambiguities.
42. The phrase is from Robert Herrick's *Hesperides* (1648).
43. Annabel Patterson, 'Jonson, Marvell, and Miscellaneity', in Neil Freistat (ed.), *Poems in their Place: The Intertextuality and Order of Poetic Collections* (Chapel Hill and London: University of North Carolina Press, 1986), pp. 95–118.

11. Conclusion: 'The End of (T)his Commonwealth Does Not Forget the Beginning'

1. The phrase is Stanley Fish's, see 'Author-Readers'. Richard Helgerson has recently claimed for Jonson a 'double sense of community', classical, and contemporary and aristocratic, see his 'Ben Jonson'. In doing so Helgerson effectively agrees with Fish, suggesting that Jonson wrote for a select coterie audience and in publishing his 1616 Folio demonstrated a resistance to the emergent print culture. I have argued against this notion in Chapter 8.
2. John Dryden's categorization of the late Jonson plays as 'dotages' has held critical sway in this respect (see Barton, *Ben Jonson, Dramatist*, p. 263). Ian Donaldson has, however, recently suggested an important kinship between the two authors; see his 'Fathers and Sons: Jonson, Dryden, and *Mac Flecknoe*', in *Jonson's Magic Houses*, pp. 162–79. See also Jennifer Brady, 'Dryden and the Negotiations of Literary Succession and Precession', in Earl Miner and Jennifer Brady (eds), *Literary Transmission and Authority: Dryden and Other Writers* (Cambridge: Cambridge University Press, 1993), pp. 27–54, and Wiseman, 'The Eccho of Uncertaintie'.
3. See Burt, *Licensed by Authority*, and Arthur F. Marotti, 'All About Jonson's Poetry', *English Literary History*, 39 (1972), 208–37.
4. See similar suggestions of fluidity in David Norbrook's account of Thomas May in his 'Lucan, Thomas May and the Creation of a Republican Literary Culture', in Sharpe and Lake (eds), *Culture and Politics in Early Stuart England*, pp. 45–66.
5. See, for example, Sharpe, *The Personal Rule of Charles I*; Russell (ed.), *The Origins of the English Civil War*; and for a counter-reaction, Cust and Hughes, 'Introduction', pp. 1–46. The revisionist manifesto of retrieving seventeenth-century historical study from a damaging over-concentration on parliament has never really been fulfilled but has led to selective interpretation of parliamentary proceedings in its resistance to the notion of a gradual move towards civil war. See Kevin Sharpe and Peter Lake's own introductory essay to *Culture and Politics in Early Stuart England*, pp. 1–20. Jonson's careful reworking of the political debates of his times into his drama suggests a wholly more subtle approach than that of an either/or decision and his response to Personal Rule was wholly more complex than the rosy hue awarded the same period in Sharpe's lengthy account.

6. Ann Hughes has very usefully suggested that we need to think of a network of overlapping rather than discrete communities in this period; see her 'Local History and the Origins of the Civil War'.
7. Martin Butler is an obvious exception here and I readily acknowledge the influence of his own research upon mine. See for example, 'Late Jonson' and 'Stuart Politics'. See also Kate Chedgzoy, Julie Sanders and Susan Wiseman's introductory essay in Sanders, Chedgzoy and Wiseman (eds), *Refashioning Ben Jonson*, pp. 1–27.
8. See Hayes, *The Birth of Popular Culture*.
9. Marcus, *The Politics of Mirth*, makes just this case for the play, pp. 24–63. Marcus has, however, recently challenged her own earlier reading in 'Of Mire and Authorship', in David L. Smith, Richard Strier and David Bevington (eds), *The Theatrical City: Culture, Theatre, and Politics in London, 1576–1649* (Cambridge: Cambridge University Press, 1995), pp. 170–82.
10. See Ostovich, 'The Appropriation of Pleasure', p. 426.
11. Ibid., p. 426.
12. See Rosemary Gaby, 'Of Vagabonds and Commonwealths: *Beggars' Bush*, *A Jovial Crew*, and *The Sisters*', *Studies in English Literature*, 34 (1994), 401–24.
13. Butler, *Theatre and Crisis*, accords a more subversive role to the drama of writers such as Richard Brome (see esp. pp. 269–79).

Bibliography

Abraham, Lyndy, *Marvell and Alchemy* (Aldershot: Scolar Press, 1990)
Aers, Lesley and Nigel Wheale (eds), *Shakespeare and the Changing Curriculum* (London: Routledge, 1991)
Agnew, Jean-Christophe, *Worlds Apart: The Market and the Theater in Anglo-American Thought, 1550–1750* (Cambridge: Cambridge University Press, 1986)
Anderson, Michael, 'Making Room: Commedia and the Privatization of the Theatre,' in Christopher Cairns (ed.), *The Commedia Dell'Arte: From the Renaissance to Dario Fo* (Lewiston, NY: Edwin Mellen Press, 1989), pp. 74–97
Armstrong, Elizabeth, *Before Copyright: The French Book-Privilege System, 1498–1526* (Cambridge: Cambridge University Press, 1991)
Ayres, Philip, 'The Iconography of Jonson's *Sejanus* 1605: Copy-Text for the Revels Edition', in J.C. Eade (ed.), *Editing Texts: Papers from a Conference of the Humanities Research Centre, May 1984*, (Canberra: Humanities Research Centre, Australian National University, 1985), pp. 47–53
—— 'Jonson, Northampton, and the "Treason" in *Sejanus*,' *Modern Philology*, 80 (1982-3), 356–63
—— (ed.), *Sejanus, His Fall* (Manchester: Manchester University Press, 1990)
Bach, Rebecca Ann, 'Ben Jonson's "Civill Savages"', *Studies in English Literature*, 37 (1997) 277–93
Bakhtin, Mikhail, *Rabelais and his World*, trans. Hélène Iswolsky (Bloomington: Indiana University Press, 1984)
Barber, C.L., *Shakespeare's Festive Comedy* (Princeton, NJ: Princeton University Press, 1959)
Barish, Jonas, *The Antitheatrical Prejudice* (Berkeley: University of California Press, 1981)
—— (ed.), *Ben Jonson: Volpone: A Casebook* (London: Macmillan, 1977)

—— (ed.), *Ben Jonson: A Collection of Critical Essays* (Englewood Cliffs, NJ: Prentice-Hall, 1963)
——, *Ben Jonson and the Language of Prose Comedy* (Berkeley: University of California Press, 1960)
——, 'The Double-Plot in *Volpone*', in Jonas Barish (ed.), *Ben Jonson: A Collection of Critical Essays* (Englewood Cliffs, NJ: Prentice-Hall, 1963)
——, 'Ovid, Juvenal, and *The Silent Woman*', *Proceedings of the Modern Language Association*, 71 (1956), 213–24
Barthes, Roland, *Image, Music, Text*, ed. and trans. Stephen Heath (London: Fontana, 1977)
Barton, Anne, *Ben Jonson, Dramatist* (Cambridge: Cambridge University Press, 1984)
——, 'Livy, Machiavelli and Shakespeare's *Coriolanus*', *Shakespeare Survey*, 38 (1985), 115-30.
——, *The Names of Comedy* (Oxford: Clarendon Press, 1990)
——, '*The New Inn* and the Problem of Jonson's Late Style', *English Literary Renaissance*, 9 (1979), 395–418
——, 'The Road from Penshurst: Wordsworth, Ben Jonson, and Coleridge in 1802', *Essays in Criticism*, 37 (1987), 209–34
——, 'Shakespeare and Jonson', in Kenneth Muir, Jay L. Halio and D.J. Palmer (eds), *Shakespeare, Man of the Theater*, Proceedings of the Second Congress of the International Shakespeare Association, 1981 (Newark, NJ: University of Delaware Press, 1983), pp. 151–72
Bate, Jonathan, 'The Elizabethans in Italy', in Jean-Pierre Maquerlot and Michèle Willems (eds), *Travel and Drama in the Age of Shakespeare* (Cambridge: Cambridge University Press, 1996), pp. 55–74
——, *Romantic Ecology: Wordsworth and the Environmental Tradition* (London: Routledge, 1991)
——, *Shakespeare and Ovid* (Oxford: Clarendon, 1993)
Beer, Gillian, *Arguing with the Past: Essays in Narrative from Woolf to Sidney* (London: Routledge, 1989)
Bellany, Alastair, '"Rayling Rymes and Vaunting Verse": Libellous Politics in Early Stuart England, 1603–1628', in Kevin Sharpe and Peter Lake (eds), *Culture and Politics in Early Stuart England* (London: Macmillan, 1994), pp. 285–310
Belsey, Catherine, 'Love in Venice', in Deborah E. Barker and Ivo Kamps (eds), *Shakespeare and Gender: A History* (London: Verso, 1995), pp. 196–213

Benet, Diana, '"The Master-Wit is the Master-Fool": Jonson's *Epicoene* and the Moralists', *Renaissance Drama*, n.s. 16 (1985), 121–40

Benjamin, Walter, 'The Work of Art in the Age of Mechanical Reproduction', in Hannah Arendt (ed.), *Illuminations* (London: Fontana, 1992)

Bennett, Benjamin, *Hugo von Hofmannsthal: The Theatres of Consciousness* (Cambridge: Cambridge University Press, 1988)

Bennett, Susan, *Theatre Audiences: A Theory of Production and Reception* (London: Routledge, 1990)

Berg, Sara J. van den, *The Action of Ben Jonson's Poetry* (Newark, NJ: University of Delaware Press, 1987)

Bergeron, David M., '"Lend me your Dwarf": Romance in *Volpone*', *Medieval and Renaissance Drama in England*, 3 (1986), 93–113

Berman, Marshall, *All that is Solid Melts into Air: The Experience of Modernity* (New York: Verso, 1982)

Bernauer, James and David Rasmussen (eds), *The Final Foucault* (Cambridge, MA: Harvard University Press, 1987)

Blissett, William, Julian Patrick and R.W. Van Fossen (eds), *A Celebration of Ben Jonson* (Toronto: University of Toronto Press, 1973)

Bloom, Harold, *The Anxiety of Influence* (Oxford: Oxford University Press, 1973)

—— (ed.), *Modern Critical Interpretations: Ben Jonson's Volpone, or the Fox* (New Haven and New York: Chelsea House Publishers, 1988)

Boccaccio, Giovanni, *The Decameron*, trans. Mark Musa and Peter Bondanella (New York and London: Norton, 1982)

Bock, Gisela, Quentin Skinner and Maurizio Viroli (eds), *Machiavelli and Republicanism* (Cambridge: Cambridge University Press, 1991)

Bond, Edward, *Bingo: Scenes of Money and Death*, in *Plays* III (London: Methuen, 1987)

Boughner, Daniel C., 'Jonson's Use of Lipsius in *Sejanus*', *Modern Language Notes*, 75 (1960), 545–50.

——, 'Juvenal, Horace, and *Sejanus*', *Modern Language Notes*, 73 (1958), 247–54

——, 'Sejanus and Machiavelli', *Studies in English Literature*, 1 (1960), 81–100

Bouwsma, W.J., *Venice and the Defense of Republican Liberty* (Berkeley: University of California Press, 1968)

Braddick, Michael J., *The Nerves of State: Taxation and the Financing of the English State, 1558–1714* (Manchester: Manchester University Press, 1996)

Brady, Jennifer, 'Dryden and the Negotiations of Literary Succession and Precession', in Earl Miner and Jennifer Brady (eds), *Literary Transmission and Authority: Dryden and Other Writers* (Cambridge: Cambridge University Press, 1993), pp. 27–54

——'Jonson's 'To King James': Plain Speaking in the *Epigrammes* and the *Conversations'*, *Studies in Philology*, 82 (1985), 380–98

Brady, Jennifer and W.H. Herendeen (eds), *Ben Jonson's 1616 Folio* (Newark, NJ: University of Delaware Press, 1991)

Brant, Clare and Diane Purkiss (eds), *Women, Texts and Histories, 1575–1760* (London: Routledge, 1992)

Braunmuller, A.R., 'Robert Carr, Earl of Somerset, as Collector and Patron', in Linda Levy Peck (ed.), *The Mental World of the Jacobean Court* (Cambridge: Cambridge University Press, 1992), pp. 230–50

Braunmuller, A.R. and J.C. Bulman (eds), *Comedy from Shakespeare to Sheridan: Change and Continuity in the English and European Tradition* (Newark, NJ and London: Associated Universities Press, 1986)

Braunmuller, A.R. and Michael Hattaway (eds), *The Cambridge Companion to English Renaissance Drama* (Cambridge: Cambridge University Press, 1990)

Bray, Alan, *Homosexuality in Renaissance England* (London: Gay Men's Press, 1982)

Breitenberg, Mark, *Anxious Masculinity in Early Modern England* (Cambridge: Cambridge University Press, 1996)

Bristol, Michael D., *Carnival and Theater: Plebeian Culture and the Structure of Authority in Renaissance England* (London and New York: Methuen, 1985)

——, 'Carnival and the Institutions of Theater in Elizabethan England', *English Literary History*, 50 (1983), 637–54

Brome, Richard, *The Antipodes*, ed. Ann Haaker (London: Arnold, 1967)

——, *The Court Beggar*, in *Dramatic Works* (London: Pearson, 1873)

——, *A Jovial Crew*, ed. Ann Haaker (London: Arnold, 1968)

——, *A Jovial Crew*, adapt. Stephen Jeffreys (London: Warner Chappell, 1992)

Bruster, Douglas, *Drama and the Market in the Age of Shakespeare* (Cambridge: Cambridge University Press, 1992)

Bryant Jr, J.A., 'Jonson's Revision of *Every Man In His Humour*',

Studies in Philology, 59 (1962), 641–50

Burke, Peter, *The Italian Renaissance: Culture and Society in Italy* (Oxford: Polity Press, 1986)

Burt, Richard, *Licensed by Authority: Ben Jonson and the Discourses of Censorship* (Ithaca, NY: Cornell University Press, 1993)

——, 'Licensed by Authority: Ben Jonson and the Politics of Early Stuart Theater', *English Literary History*, 54 (1987), 529–60.

——, '(Un)Censoring in Detail: Thomas Middleton, Fetishism, and the Regulation of Dramatic Discourse', forthcoming.

Butler, Martin, 'Ben Jonson and the Limits of Courtly Panegyric', in Kevin Sharpe and Peter Lake (eds), *Culture and Politics in Early Stuart England* (London: Macmillan, 1994), pp. 91–116

——, 'Ben Jonson's *Pan's Anniversary* and the Politics of Early Stuart Pastoral', *English Literary Renaissance*, 22 (1992), 369–404

——, *Ben Jonson: Volpone: A Critical Study* (Harmondsworth: Penguin Masterstudies, 1987)

——, 'Ecclesiastical Censorship of Early Stuart Drama: The Case of Jonson's *The Magnetic Lady*', *Modern Philology*, 89 (1991–2), 469–81

——, 'Late Jonson', in Gordon McMullan and Jonathan Hope (eds), *The Politics of Tragicomedy: Shakespeare and After* (London: Routledge, 1992), pp. 166–88

——, 'Private and Occasional Drama', in A.R. Braunmuller and Michael Hattaway (eds), *The Cambridge Companion to English Renaissance Drama* (Cambridge: Cambridge University Press, 1990), pp. 127–60

——, 'Royal Slaves?: The Stuart Court and the Theatres', *Renaissance Drama Newsletter*, Supplement 2 (University of Warwick: Graduate School for Renaissance Studies, 1984)

——, 'Stuart Politics in *A Tale of a Tub*', *Modern Language Review*, 85 (1990), 12–28

——, *Theatre and Crisis, 1632–1642* (Cambridge: Cambridge University Press, 1984)

——, '"We Are One Man's All": Jonson's *The Gipsies Metamorphosed*', *Yearbook of English Studies*, 21 (1991), 253–73

Butler, Martin, and David Lindley, 'Restoring Astraea: Jonson's Masque for the Fall of Somerset', *English Literary History*, 61 (1994), 807–27

Cain, Tom (ed.), *Ben Jonson's Poetaster* (Manchester: Manchester University Press, 1995)

Cairns, C. (ed.), *The Commedia Dell'Arte: From the Renaissance to Dario Fo* (Lewiston, NY: Edwin Mellen Press, 1989)

Calvino, Italo, *Invisible Cities* (London: Picador, 1979)
Cantor, Paul, *Shakespeare's Rome: Republic and Empire* (Ithaca, NY: Cornell University Press, 1978)
Cartelli, Thomas, '*Bartholomew Fair* as Urban Arcadia: Jonson Responds to Shakespeare', *Renaissance Drama*, n.s. 14 (1983), 151–72
Cave, Richard Allen, *Ben Jonson* (London: Macmillan, 1991)
Cave, Terence, *The Cornucopian Text: Problems of Writing in the French Renaissance* (Oxford: Clarendon Press, 1979)
Certeau, Michel de, *The Practice of Everyday Life*, trans. Steven Rendall (Berkeley: University of California Press, 1984)
Cervelli, Innocenzo, *Machiavelli e la crisi dello stato veneziano* (Naples: Guido Editore, 1974)
Chaudhuri, Una, 'The Spectator in Drama/Drama in the Spectator', *Modern Drama*, 27.3 (1984), 281–98
Chedgzoy, Kate, Julie Sanders and Susan Wiseman, 'Introduction: Refashioning Ben Jonson,' in Julie Sanders, with Kate Chedgzoy and Susan Wiseman (eds), *Refashioning Ben Jonson: Gender, Politics, and the Jonsonian Canon* (London: Macmillan, 1998), pp. 1–27
Cheney, Patrick, 'Jonson's *The New Inn* and Plato's Myth of the Hermaphrodite', *Renaissance Drama*, n.s. 14 (1983), 173–94
Cicero, Tullius, *The Speeches*, trans. R. Gardner (Chicago: Loeb Classical Library, 1958)
Clare, Janet, *Art Made Tongue-Tied by Authority: Elizabethan and Jacobean Dramatic Censorship* (Manchester: Manchester University Press, 1990)
Clark, Peter, 'The Alehouse and the Alternative Society', in Donald Pennington and Keith Thomas (eds), *Puritans and Revolutionaries* (Oxford: Clarendon Press, 1978), pp. 47–72
——, *The English Alehouse: A Social History, 1200–1830* (London and New York: Longman, 1983)
Clark, Sandra, '*Hic Mulier, Haec Vir*, and the Controversy over Masculine Women', Studies in Philology, 82 (1985), 157–83
Clifford, D.J.H. (ed.), *The Diaries of Lady Anne Clifford* (Stroud: Alan Sutton, 1990)
Cogswell, Thomas, *The Blessed Revolution: English Politics and the Coming of War, 1621–1624* (Cambridge: Cambridge University Press, 1989)
——, 'England and the Spanish Match', in Richard Cust and Ann Hughes (eds), *Conflict in Early Stuart England: Studies in Religion*

and Politics, 1603–1642 (London and New York: Longman, 1989), pp. 107–33

Contarini, Gaspario, *De Magistratibus et Republica Venetorum*, in *Gasparis Contareni Cardinalis Opera* (Farnborough: Gregg, 1968)

Cope, Jackson I., 'Bartholomew Fair as Blasphemy', *Renaissance Drama*, n.s. 8 (1965), 127–52

Cordner, Michael, Peter Holland and John Kerrigan (eds), *English Comedy* (Cambridge: Cambridge University Press, 1994)

Coward, Barry, *Profiles in Power: Cromwell* (London and New York: Longman, 1991)

Creaser, John, 'Enigmatic Ben Jonson,' in Michael Cordner, Peter Holland, and John Kerrigan (eds), *English Comedy* (Cambridge: Cambridge University Press, 1994), pp. 100-18

Cust, Richard, *The Forced Loan and English Politics, 1626–1628* (Oxford: Oxford University Press, 1987)

——, 'News and Politics in Seventeenth-Century England', *Past and Present*, 112 (1986), 60-90

Cust, Richard and Ann Hughes (eds), *Conflict in Early Stuart England: Studies in Religion and Politics, 1603–1642* (London and New York: Longman, 1989)

——, 'Introduction', in Richard Cust and Ann Hughes (eds), *Conflict in Early Stuart England: Studies in Religion and Politics, 1603–1642* (London and New York: Longman, 1989), pp. 1–46

Davis, Natalie Zemon, *Society and Culture in Early Modern France* (London: Duckworth, 1975)

DeLuna, B.N., *Jonson's Romish Plot: A Study of 'Catiline' and its Historical Context* (Oxford: Clarendon Press, 1967)

Dentith, Simon (ed.), *Bakhtinian Thought: An Introductory Reader* (London: Routledge, 1995)

Dollimore, Jonathan, 'Transgression and Surveillance in *Measure for Measure*', in Jonathan Dollimore and Alan Sinfield (eds), *Political Shakespeare: New Essays in Cultural Materialism* (Manchester: Manchester University Press, 1985)

Dollimore, Jonathan, and Alan Sinfield (eds), *Political Shakespeare: New Essays in Cultural Materialism* (Manchester: Manchester University Press, 1985)

Donaldson, Ian (ed.), *Jonson and Shakespeare* (London: Macmillan, in association with the Humanities Research Centre, Australian National University, Canberra, 1983)

——, *Jonson's Magic Houses: Essays in Interpretation* (Oxford: Clarendon Press, 1997)

——, 'Jonson's Tortoise', in Jonas A. Barish (ed.), *Jonson: Volpone: A Casebook* (London: Macmillan, 1977), pp. 189–94
——, (ed.), *The Oxford Ben Jonson* (Oxford: Oxford University Press, 1985)
——, *The World Upside-Down: Comedy from Jonson to Fielding* (Oxford: Clarendon Press, 1970)
Donne, John, *The Sermons of John Donne*, ed. George Potter and Evelyn Simpson, 10 vols (Berkeley: University of California Press, 1953–1962)
Dorenkamp, Angela G., 'Jonson's *Catiline*: History as the Trying Faculty', *Studies in Philology*, 67 (1970), 210–20
Drakakis, John (ed.), *Alternative Shakespeares* (London and New York: Methuen, 1988)
Drew-Bear, Annette, 'Face-Painting Scenes in Ben Jonson's Plays', *Studies in Philology*, 77 (1980), 388–401
Dryden, John, *Of Dramatic Poesy and Other Critical Essays*, ed. George Watson (London: Everyman, 1962), I
Duffy, Eamon, *The Stripping of Altars: Traditional Religion in England, c.1400–c.1580* (New Haven and London: Yale University Press, 1992)
Duncan, Douglas, *Ben Jonson and the Lucianic Tradition* (Cambridge: Cambridge University Press, 1979)
——, 'A Guide to *The New Inn*', *Essays in Criticism*, 20 (1970), 311–26
Dunn John (ed.), *Democracy: The Unfinished Journey, 508 BC to AD 1993* (Oxford: Oxford University Press, 1993)
Dusinberre, Juliet, *Shakespeare and the Nature of Women* (London: Macmillan, 1975)
Dutton, Richard, *Ben Jonson: Authority: Criticism* (London: Macmillan, 1996)
——, *Ben Jonson: To The First Folio* (Cambridge: Cambridge University Press, 1982)
——, 'Hamlet, An Apology for Actors and the Sign of the Globe', *Shakespeare Survey* 41 (1989), 35-43
——, (ed.) *Jacobean Civic Pageants* (Keele: Keele University Press, 1996)
——, 'The Lone Wolf', in Julie Sanders, with Kate Chedgzoy and Susan Wiseman (eds), *Refashioning Ben Jonson: Gender, Politics, and the Jonsonian Canon* (London: Macmillan, 1998), pp. 114–33
——, *Mastering the Revels: The Regulation and Censorship of English Renaissance Drama* (London: Macmillan, 1991)
——, 'The Significance of Jonson's Revision of *Every Man In His*

Humour', *Modern Language Review*, 69 (1974), 241–9

Echeruo, Michael J.C., 'The Conscience of Politics and Jonson's *Catiline*', *Studies in English Literature*, 6 (1996), 341–56

Eisenstein, Elizabeth, *The Printing Press as an Agent of Change* (Cambridge: Cambridge University Press, 1980)

Elam, Keir, *The Semiotics of Theatre and Drama* (London and New York: Methuen, 1980)

Elsky, Martin, *Authorizing Words: Speech, Writing, and Print in the English Renaissance* (Ithaca, NY: Cornell University Press, 1989)

Empson, William, *Seven Types of Ambiguity* (London: Chatto and Windus, 1951)

——, *Some Versions of Pastoral: A Study of Pastoral Form in Literature* (Harmondsworth: Penguin, 1968)

——, *The Structure of Complex Words* (London: Chatto and Windus, 1964)

Engle, Lars, *Shakespearean Pragmatism: Market of his Time* (Chicago and London: University of Chicago Press, 1993)

Erickson, Peter and Coppelia Kahn (eds), *Shakespeare's Rough Magic: Renaissance Essays in Honour of C.L. Barber* (Newark, NJ: Princeton University Press, 1985)

Erskine-Hill, Howard, *The Augustan Idea in English Literature* (London: Arnold, 1983)

Evans, Robert C., 'Ben Jonson's Chaucer', *English Literary Renaissance*, 19 (1989), 324–45

——, *Ben Jonson and the Poetics of Patronage* (Lewisburg, PA and London: Bucknell University Press, 1989)

——, 'Contemporary Contexts of Jonson's *The Devil is an Ass*', *Comparative Drama*, 26 (1992), 140–76

——, *Habits of Mind: Evidence and Effects of Ben Jonson's Reading* (New Jersey and London: Associated Universities Press, 1995)

——, *Jonson, Lipsius, and the Politics of Renaissance Stoicism* (Wakefield, NH: Longwood, 1992)

——, '*Sejanus*: Ethics and Politics in the Early Reign of James', in Julie Sanders, with Kate Chedgzoy and Susan Wiseman (eds), *Refashioning Ben Jonson: Gender, Politics, and the Jonsonian Canon* (London: Macmillan, 1998), pp. 71–92

Ferrone, Siro, 'La vendita del teatro: Tipologie Europee tra cinque e seicento', in Christopher Cairns (ed.), *The Commedia dell'Arte: From the Renaissance to Dario Fo* (Lewiston, NY: Edwin Mellen Press, 1989), pp. 35–73

Fincham, K., 'The Judges' Decision on Ship Money in February

1637: The Reaction of Kent', *Bulletin of the Institute of Historical Research*, 57 (1984), 230–7

Fish, Stanley, 'Authors-Readers: Jonson's Communities of the Same', in Stephen Greenblatt (ed.), *Representing the English Renaissance* (Berkeley: University of California Press, 1988), pp. 231–64

Flesch, William, *Generosity and the Limits of Authority: Shakespeare, Herbert, Milton* (Ithaca, NY: Cornell University Press, 1992)

Fletcher, Anthony and John Stevenson (eds), *Order and Disorder in Early Modern England* (Cambridge: Cambridge University Press, 1985)

Florio, John, *A Worlde of Words* (Hildesheim and New York: Georg Olms, 1972)

Foakes, R.A., 'The Descent of Iago: Satire, Ben Jonson, and Shakespeare's *Othello*', in E.A.J. Honigmann (ed.), *Shakespeare and his Contemporaries: Essays in Comparison* (Manchester: Manchester University Press, 1986), pp. 16–30

Foster, Andrew, 'Church Policies of the 1630s', in Richard Cust and Ann Hughes (eds), *Conflict in Early Stuart England: Studies in Religion and Politics, 1603–1642* (London and New York: Longman, 1989), pp. 193–223

Foucault, Michel, *Discipline and Punish: The Birth of the Prison* (Harmondsworth: Penguin, 1977)

——, 'What is an Author?,' in Paul Rabinow (ed.), *The Foucault Reader* (Harmondsworth: Penguin, 1984), pp. 101–20

French, Peter J., *John Dee: The World of an Elizabethan Magus* (London: Routledge and Kegan Paul, 1972)

Freund, Elizabeth, *The Return of the Reader: Reader-Response Criticism* (London: Methuen, 1987)

Friedberg, Harris, 'Ben Jonson's Poetry: Pastoral, Georgic, Epigram', *English Literary Renaissance*, 4 (1974), 111–35

Fumerton, Patricia, *Cultural Aesthetics: Renaissance Literature and the Practice of Social Ornament* (Chicago: University of Chicago Press, 1991)

Gaby, Rosemary, 'Of Vagabonds and Commonwealths: *Beggars' Bush*, *A Jovial Crew*, and *The Sisters*', *Studies in English Literature*, 34 (1994), 401–24

Gair, Reavely, *The Children of Paul's* (Cambridge: Cambridge University Press, 1982)

Garber, Marjorie (ed.), *Cannibals, Witches, and Divorce: Estranging the Renaissance* (Baltimore and London: Johns Hopkins Press, 1987)

——, *Shakespeare's Ghost Writers: Literature as Uncanny Causality* (New York and London: Methuen, 1987)
——, *Vested Interests: Cross-Dressing and Cultural Anxiety* (London and New York: Routledge, 1992)
Gelderen, Martin van, 'The Machiavellian Moment and the Dutch Revolt: The Rise of Neostoicism and Dutch Republicanism', in Gisela Bock, Quentin Skinner and Maurizio Viroli (eds), *Machiavelli and Republicanism* (Cambridge: Cambridge University Press, 1990), pp. 205–23
Geertz, Clifford, *The Interpretation of Cultures* (London: Fontana Press, 1993)
Gianakaris, C.J., 'Jonson's Use of "Avocatori" in *Volpone*', *English Language Notes*, 12 (1974–5), 8–14
Giannotti, Donato, *Opere Politiche* (Milan: Marzorati, 1979)
Gibbons, Brian, *Jacobean City Comedy*, 2nd edn (London: Methuen, 1980)
Gilbert, Felix, *The Pope, His Banker, and Venice* (Cambridge, MA: Harvard University Press, 1980)
Giuseppi, Montague S., 'Gunpowder', in H.E. Malden (ed.), *The Victoria History of the Counties of England: Surrey* (London: James Street, 1905), II, pp. 306–28
Goldberg, Jonathan, 'Fatherly Authority: The Politics of Stuart Family Images', in Margaret W. Ferguson, Maureen Quilligan and Nancy J. Vickers (eds), *Rewriting the Renaissance: The Discourses of Sexual Difference in Early Modern Europe* (Chicago and London: University of Chicago Press, 1986), pp. 3–32
——, *James I and the Politics of Literature* (Baltimore, MD: Johns Hopkins University Press, 1983)
Goody, Jack and Ian Watt, 'The Consequences of Literacy', *Comparative Studies in Society and History*, 5 (1963), 304–45
Greenblatt, Stephen, 'The False Ending in *Volpone*', *Journal of English and Germanic Philology*, 75 (1976), 90–104
——, (ed.), *The Forms of Power and the Power of Forms in the Renaissance* (Norman, OK: Pilgrim Books, 1982)
——, *Learning to Curse: Essays on Early Modern Culture* (London: Routledge, 1990)
——, 'Loudun and London', *Critical Inquiry*, 12 (1986), 326–46
——, *Marvelous Possessions: The Wonder of the New World* (Oxford: Clarendon Press, 1991)
——, (ed.), *New World Encounters* (Berkeley: University of California Press, 1993)

——, *Renaissance Self-Fashioning: From More to Shakespeare* (Chicago: University of Chicago Press, 1980)
——, (ed.), *Representing the English Renaissance* (Berkeley: University of California Press, 1988)
——, *Shakespearean Negotiations: The Circulation of Social Energy in Renaissance England* (Oxford: Clarendon Press, 1988)
——, *Sir Walter Raleigh: The Renaissance Man and his Roles* (New Haven: Yale University Press, 1973)
Greenblatt, Stephen and Giles Gunn (eds), *Redrawing the Boundaries: The Transformation of English and American Literary Studies* (New York: Modern Language Association, 1992)
Greenblatt, Stephen and others (eds), *The Norton Shakespeare* (London and New York: Norton, 1997)
Greene, Thomas, *The Light in Troy: Imitation and Discovery in Renaissance Poetry* (New Haven and London: Yale University Press, 1982)
——, *The Vulnerable Text: Essays on Renaissance Literature* (New York: Columbia University Press, 1986)
Greer, Germaine and others (eds), *Kissing the Rod: An Anthology of Seventeenth-Century Women's Verse* (London: Virago, 1988)
Guicciardini, Francesco, *History of Italy*, trans. Sidney Alexander (London: Macmillan, 1967)
Gurr, Andrew, *The Shakespearean Stage, 1547–1642*, 2nd edn (Cambridge: Cambridge University Press, 1987)
Haaker, Ann, 'The Plague, the Theater, and the Poet', *Renaissance Drama*, n.s. 1 (1968), 283–306
Hackett, Helen, '"Yet Tell Me Some Such Fiction": Lady Mary Wroth's *Urania* and the "Femininity" of Romance', in Clare Brant and Diane Purkiss (eds), *Women, Texts and Histories, 1575–1760* (London: Routledge, 1992), pp. 39–68
Hale, J.R. (ed.), *Encyclopedia of the Italian Renaissance* (London: Thames and Hudson, 1989)
——, (ed.), *Renaissance Venice* (London: Faber, 1973)
Hall, Kim F., ' "I Rather Would Wish to be a Black-moor": Beauty, Race, and Rank in Lady Mary Wroth's *Urania*', in Margo Hendricks and Patricia Parker (eds), *Women, 'Race', and Writing in the Early Modern Period* (London: Routledge, 1994), pp. 178–94
——, 'Sexual Politics and Cultural Identity in *The Masque of Blackness*', in Sue-Ellen Case and Janelle Reinelt (eds), *The Performance of Power: Theatrical Discourse and Politics* (Iowa City: University of Iowa Press, 1991), pp. 3–18

——, *Things of Darkness: Economies of Race and Gender in Early Modern England* (Ithaca, NY: Cornell University Press, 1995)

Hampton, Timothy, *Writing from History: The Rhetoric of Exemplarity in Renaissance Literature* (Ithaca, NY: Cornell University Press, 1990)

Happé, Peter (ed.), *Ben Jonson's The Devil is an Ass* (Manchester: Manchester University Press, 1994)

Hattaway, Michael (ed.), *Ben Jonson's The New Inn* (Manchester: Manchester University Press, 1984)

Hawkins, Harriet, 'The Idea of the Theater in Jonson's *The New Inn*', *Renaissance Drama*, n.s. 9 (1966), 205–26

Hayes, Tom, *The Birth of Popular Culture: Ben Jonson, Maid Marian, and Robin Hood* (Pittsburgh, PA: Duquesne University Press, 1992)

Haynes, Jonathan, *The Social Relations of Jonson's Theater* (Cambridge: Cambridge University Press, 1992)

Healy, Thomas, *New Latitudes: Theory and English Renaissance Literature* (London: Arnold, 1992)

——, 'Remembering with Advantages: Nation and Ideology in *Henry V*', in Michael Hattaway and Boika Sokolova (eds), *Shakespeare in the New Europe* (Sheffield: Sheffield Academic Press, 1994), pp. 174–93

Healy, Thomas, and Jonathan Sawday (eds), *Literature and the English Civil War* (Cambridge: Cambridge University Press, 1990)

Heinemann, Margot, ' "God Help the Poor: The Rich Can Shift": The World Upside-Down and the Popular Tradition in the Theatre', in Gordon McMullan and Jonathan Hope (eds), *The Politics of Tragicomedy: Shakespeare and After* (London: Routledge, 1992), pp. 151–65

——, 'Political Drama', in A.R. Braunmuller and Michael Hattaway (eds), *The Cambridge Companion to English Renaissance Drama* (Cambridge: Cambridge University Press, 1990), pp. 161–205

——, *Puritanism and Theatre: Thomas Middleton and Opposition Drama under the Early Stuarts* (Cambridge: Cambridge University Press, 1980)

Helgerson, Richard, 'Ben Jonson', in Thomas N. Corns (ed.), *The Cambridge Companion to English Poetry: Donne to Marvell* (Cambridge: Cambridge University Press, 1994), pp. 148-70

——, *Self-Crowned Laureates: Jonson, Spenser, Milton, and the Literary Tradition* (Berkeley: University of California Press, 1983)

Henderson, Katherine Usher, and Barbara F. McManus (eds), *Half-*

Humankind: Contexts and Texts of the Controversy About Women in England, 1540–1640 (Urbana and Chicago: University of Illinois Press, 1985)

Hendricks, Margo, and Patricia Parker (eds), *Women, 'Race', and Writing in the Early Modern Period* (London: Routledge, 1994)

Herford, C.H., and Percy and Evelyn Simpson (eds), *Ben Jonson*, 11 vols (Oxford: Clarendon Press, 1925–52)

Hibbard, G.R. (ed.), *Ben Jonson's Bartholomew Fair* (London: Benn (New Mermaids), 1977)

Hill, Christopher, 'The Many-Headed Monster', in *Change and Continuity in Seventeenth-Century England*, 2nd edn (London: Weidenfeld and Nicolson, 1991), pp. 181–204

——, *Puritanism and Revolution* (London: Secker, 1958)

——, *The World Turned Upside Down: Radical Ideas During the English Revolution* (London: Temple Smith, 1972)

Hill, Geoffrey, 'The World's Proportion: Jonson's Dramatic Poetry in *Sejanus* and *Catiline*', in *Jacobean Theatre*, Stratford-Upon-Avon Studies I (London: Arnold, 1960), pp. 113–32

Hirst, Derek, *The Representative of the People? Voters and Voting in England under the Early Stuarts* (Cambridge: Cambridge University Press, 1975)

Hobbes, Thomas, *Leviathan*, ed. Richard Tuck (Cambridge: Cambridge University Press, 1991; repr. 1994)

Hogg, James (ed.), *Recent Research on Ben Jonson* (Salzburg: University of Salzburg Press, 1978)

Holland, Peter, 'The Resources of Characterization in *Othello*', *Shakespeare Survey*, 41 (1989), 119–32

Holmes, C., 'The County Community in Stuart Historiography', *Journal of British Studies*, 19 (1980), 54–73

——, 'Drainers and Fenmen: The Problem of Popular Political Consciousness in the Seventeenth Century', in Anthony Fletcher and John Stevenson (eds), *Order and Disorder in Early Modern England* (Cambridge: Cambridge University Press, 1985), pp. 166–95

Horace, *The Complete Works of Horace*, trans. Lord Dunsay and Michael Oakley (London and New York: Dent, 1961)

Houston, R.A., *Literacy in Early Modern Europe* (London and New York: Longman, 1988)

Howard, Douglas (ed.), *Philip Massinger: A Critical Reassessment* (Cambridge: Cambridge University Press, 1985)

Howard, Jean E., 'Scripts and/versus Playhouses: Ideological

Production and the Renaissance Stage', *Renaissance Drama*, n.s. 20 (1989), 31–49
——, *Shakespeare's Art of Orchestration: Stage Technique and Audience Response* (Chicago: University of Chicago Press, 1984)
——, *The Stage and Social Struggle in Early Modern England* (London and New York: Routledge, 1994)
Howard, Jean E. and Marion F. O'Connor (eds), *Shakespeare Reproduced: The Text in History and Ideology* (London and New York: Methuen, 1987; repr. 1990)
Huebert, Ronald, ' "A Shrew Yet Honest": Manliness in Jonson', *Renaissance Drama*, n.s. 15 (1984), 31–68
Hughes, Ann, *The Causes of the English Civil War* (London: Macmillan, 1991)
——, 'Gender and Politics in Leveller Literature', in Susan D. Amussen and Mark Kishlansky (eds), *Political Culture and Cultural Politics in Early Modern England* (Manchester: Manchester University Press, 1995), pp. 162–88
——, 'Local History and the Origins of the Civil War', in Richard Cust and Ann Hughes (eds), *Conflict in Early Stuart England: Studies in Religion and Politics, 1603–1642* (London and New York: Longman, 1989), pp. 224–53
——, *Politics, Society and Civil War in Warwickshire, 1620–1660* (Cambridge: Cambridge University Press, 1987)
Hunt, William, *The Puritan Moment: The Coming of Revolution in an English County* (Cambridge, MA: Harvard University Press, 1983)
Hunter, G.K., 'English Folly and Italian Vice: The Moral Landscape of John Marston', in *Jacobean Theatre*, Stratford-Upon-Avon Studies I (London: Arnold, 1960), pp. 85–112
Jackson, Gabriele Bernhard, *Vision and Judgement in Ben Jonson's Drama* (New Haven and London: Yale University Press, 1968)
Jardine, Lisa, *Still Harping on Daughters: Women and Drama in the Age of Shakespeare*, 2nd edn (Brighton: Harvester, 1983)
Jones, Ann Rosalind, 'Designing Women: The Self as Spectacle in Mary Wroth and Veronica Franco', in Naomi J. Miller and Gary Waller (eds), *Reading Mary Wroth: Representing Alternatives in Early Modern England* (Knoxville: University of Tennessee Press, 1991), pp. 135–53
Jones, Robert C., 'Jonson's *The Staple of News*'s Gossips and Fulwell's *Like Will to Like*: "The Old Way" in a "New Morality Play"', *Yearbook of English Studies*, 3 (1973), 74–7.
Juvenal, 'Satire VI', in *Juvenal and Persius*, trans. G.G. Ramsey

(Cambridge, MA: Harvard University Press, 1979)

Kastan, David Scott and Peter Stallybrass (eds), *Staging the Renaissance: Reinterpretations of Elizabethan and Jacobean Drama* (London: Routledge, 1991)

Kay, W. David, *Ben Jonson: A Literary Life* (London: Macmillan, 1995)

——, 'Jonson's Urbane Gallants: Humanistic Contexts for *Epicoene*', *Huntington Library Quarterly*, 39 (1975–6), 251–66

Kent, Joan, *The English Village Constable, 1580–1642: A Social and Administrative Study* (Oxford: Clarendon Press, 1986)

Kifer, Devra, 'Too Many Cookes: An Addition to the Printed Text of *The Staple of News*', *English Language Notes*, 11 (1973–4), 264–71

Kinney, A.F., and Dan S. Collins (eds), *Renaissance Historicism: Selections from English Literary Renaissance* (Amherst, MA: University of Massachusetts Press, 1987)

Kishlansky, Mark, *Parliamentary Selection: Social and Political Choice in Early Modern England* (Cambridge: Cambridge University Press, 1986)

Knapp, Jeffrey, *An Empire Nowhere: England, America, and Literature from 'Utopia' to 'The Tempest'* (Berkeley: University of California Press, 1992)

Knights, L.C., *Drama and Society in the Age of Jonson* (Harmondsworth: Penguin in association with Chatto and Windus, 1962)

Knowles, James, 'The Spectacle of the Realm: Civic Consciousness, Rhetoric and Ritual in Early Modern London', in J.R. Mulryne and Margaret Shewring (eds), *Theatre and Government Under the Early Stuarts* (Cambridge: Cambridge University Press, 1993), pp. 157–89

Lake, Peter, 'The Collection of Ship Money in Cheshire during the 1630s: A Case Study of Relations between Central and Local Government', *Northern History*, 17 (1981), 44–71

Lambert, Sheila, 'The Printers and the Government, 1604–1640', in Robin Myers and Michael Harris (eds), *Aspects of Printing from 1600* (Oxford: Oxford Polytechnic Press, 1987), pp. 1–29

Lauinger, Anne, '"It Makes the Father Lesse to Rue": Resistance to Consolation in Jonson's "On My First Daughter"', *Studies in Philology*, 86 (1989), 219–34

Leggatt, Alexander, *Ben Jonson, His Vision and His Art* (London and New York: Methuen, 1981)

——, 'The Suicide of Volpone', *University of Toronto Quarterly*, 39 (1969), 19–32

Lemly, John, ' "Make Odde Discoveries!": Disguises, Masques and Jonsonian Romance', in A.R. Braunmuller and J.C. Bulman (eds), *Comedy from Shakespeare to Sheridan: Change and Continuity in the English and European Dramatic Tradition* (Newark, NJ and London: Associated Universities Press, 1986), pp. 131–47

Lentricchia, Frank and Thomas McLaughlin (eds), *Critical Terms for Literary Study* (Chicago and London: University of Chicago Press, 1990)

Lenz, Carolyn Ruth Swift, Gayle Greene and Carol Thomas Neely (eds), *The Woman's Part: Feminist Criticism of Shakespeare* (Urbana: University of Illinois Press, 1980)

Lever, J.W. (ed.), *Every Man In His Humour: A Parallel Text Edition of the 1601 Quarto and the 1616 Folio* (London: Arnold, 1971)

——, *The Tragedy of State: A Study of Jacobean Drama* (London: Methuen, 1957; repr. 1971)

Levin, Harry, 'Two Magian Comedies: *The Tempest* and *The Alchemist*', *Shakespeare Survey*, 22 (1969), 47–58

Levin, Richard, 'The New *New Inn* and the Proliferation of Good Bad Drama', *Essays in Criticism*, 22 (1972), 41–7

——, *New Readings vs. Old Texts: Recent Trends in the Reinterpretations of Renaissance Drama* (Chicago and London: University of Chicago Press, 1979)

——, '*The Staple of News*, the Society of Jeerers and Canters' College', *Philological Quarterly*, 44 (1965), 445–53

Levith, Murray J., *Shakespeare's Italian Settings and Plays* (London: Macmillan, 1989)

Lewalski, Barbara Kiefer, *Writing Women in Jacobean England* (Cambridge, MA: Harvard University Press, 1993)

Limon, Jerzy, *Dangerous Matter: English Drama and Politics, 1623–4* (Cambridge: Cambridge University Press, 1986)

Lindley, David (ed.), *Court Masques* (Oxford: Oxford University Press, 1995)

——, (ed.), *The Court Masque* (Manchester: Manchester University Press, 1984)

——, 'Embarrassing Ben: Masques for Frances Howard', *English Literary Renaissance*, 16 (1986), 343–59

——, *The Trials of Frances Howard: Fact and Fiction at the Court of King James* (London: Routledge, 1993)

Livy, Titus, *The Early History of Rome: Books I–IV*, trans. Aubrey de Selincourt; intro. D.M. Ogilvie (Harmondsworth: Penguin, 1971)

Loewenstein, Joseph, 'For a History of Literary Property: John

Wolfe's Reformation', *English Literary Renaissance*, 18 (1988), 389–412

——, *Responsive Readings: Versions of Echo in Pastoral, Epic and the Jonsonian Masque* (New Haven: Yale University Press, 1984)

Lyly, John, *The Dramatic Works*, ed. F.W. Fairholt (London: Reeves and Turner, 1892), I

Machiavelli, Niccolò, *The Discourses*, trans. and ed. Leslie J. Walker; intro. Bernard Crick (Harmondsworth: Penguin, 1970)

——, *The Prince*, trans. and ed. George Bull (Harmondsworth: Penguin, 1961; repr. 1981)

——, *The Prince*, trans. and ed. Quentin Skinner and Russell Price (Cambridge: Cambridge University Press, 1988)

Machin, Richard and Christopher Norris, *Post-Structuralist Readings of English Poetry* (Cambridge: Cambridge University Press, 1987)

Mackenney, Richard, *The City-State, 1500–1700: Republican Liberty in an Age of Princely Power* (London: Macmillan, 1989)

MacNeice, Louis, *Collected Poems* (London: Faber, 1979)

Maltby, Edward, *Waterlogged Wealth* (London: Earthscan, 1986)

Mann, David, *The Elizabethan Player* (London: Routledge, 1991)

Marcus, Leah S., 'Levelling Shakespeare: Local Customs and Local Texts', *Shakespeare Quarterly*, 42 (1991), 168–78

——, 'Masquing Occasions and Masque Structure', *Research Opportunities in Renaissance Drama*, 24 (1981), 7–16

——, 'The Occasion of Ben Jonson's *Pleasure Reconciled to Virtue*', *Studies in English Literature*, 19 (1979), 271–94

——, 'Of Mire and Authorship', in David L. Smith, Richard Strier and David Bevington (eds), *The Theatrical City: Culture, Theatre and Politics in London, 1576–1649* (Cambridge: Cambridge University Press, 1995), pp. 170–82

——, *The Politics of Mirth: Jonson, Herrick, Milton, Marvell and the Defence of Old Holiday Pastimes* (Chicago: University of Chicago Press, 1986)

——, *Puzzling Shakespeare: Local Reading and its Discontents* (Berkeley: University of California Press, 1988)

——, 'Renaissance/Early Modern Studies', in Stephen Greenblatt and Giles Gunn (eds), *Redrawing the Boundaries: The Transformation of English and American Literary Studies* (New York: MLA, 1992), pp. 41–63

Marlowe, Christopher, *The Complete Poems and Translations*, ed. Stephen Orgel (Harmondsworth: Penguin, 1971)

Marotti, Arthur F., 'All About Ben Jonson's Poetry', *English Literary History*, 39 (1972), 208–37
——, 'Patronage, Poetry and Print', in *Yearbook of English Studies*, 21 (1991), 1–26
Martial, *Epigrams*, ed. and trans. James Michie (Harmondsworth: Penguin, 1978)
Massinger, Philip, *Selected Plays*, ed. by Colin Gibson (Cambridge: Cambridge University Press, 1978)
Massinger, Philip and John Fletcher, *The Tragedy of Sir John van Oldenbarnevelt* (London: Malone Society Reprint, 1980)
Maus, Katherine Eisaman, *Ben Jonson and the Roman Frame of Mind* (Princeton, NJ: Princeton University Press, 1984)
McCanles, Michael, *Jonsonian Discriminations: The Humanist Poet and Praise of True Nobility* (Toronto: University of Toronto Press, 1992)
McDonald, Russ, *Shakespeare and Jonson: Jonson and Shakespeare* (Lincoln and London: University of Nebraska Press, 1988)
McLuskie, Kathleen, *Dekker and Heywood* (London: Macmillan, 1994)
——, 'Making and Buying: Ben Jonson and the Commercial Theatre Audience', in Julie Sanders, with Kate Chedgzoy and Susan Wiseman (eds), *Refashioning Ben Jonson: Gender, Politics, and the Jonsonian Canon* (London: Macmillan, 1998), pp. 134–54
——, 'The Poets' Royal Exchange: Patronage and Commerce in Early Modern Drama', *Yearbook of English Studies*, 21 (1991), 53–62
——, *Renaissance Dramatists* (Hemel Hempstead: Harvester Wheatsheaf, 1989)
McMillin, Scott, 'Jonson's Early Entertainments: New Information from Hatfield House', *Renaissance Drama*, n.s. 1 (1968), 153–66
McMullan, Gordon and Jonathan Hope (eds), *The Politics of Tragicomedy: Shakespeare and After* (London: Routledge, 1992)
McPherson, David, 'Ben Jonson's Library and Marginalia: An Annotated Catalogue', *Studies in Philology*, 71 (1974), Texts and Studies Supplement, 1–106
Mebane, John S., 'Renaissance Magic and the Return of the Golden Age: Utopianism and Religious Enthusiasm in *The Alchemist*', *Renaissance Drama*, n.s. 10 (1979), 117–39
Middleton, Thomas, *A Game at Chess*, ed. J.W. Harper (London: Ernest Benn, 1966)
Middleton, Thomas and Thomas Dekker, *The Roaring Girl*, ed. Paul Mulholland (Manchester: Manchester University Press, 1987)

Miles, Rosalind, *Ben Jonson: His Craft and Art* (London: Methuen, 1990)
——, *Ben Jonson: His Life and Work* (London: Methuen, 1986)
Millard, Barbara C., '"An Acceptable Violence": Sexual Contest in Jonson's *Epicoene*', *Medieval and Renaissance Drama in England* 1 (1984), 143–58
Miller, Anthony, 'The Roman State in *Julius Caesar* and *Sejanus*', in Ian Donaldson (ed.), *Jonson and Shakespeare* (London: Macmillan, in association with the Humanities Research Centre, Australian National University, Canberra, 1983), pp. 179–201
Miller, J. Hillis, 'The Critic as Host', in Harold Bloom and others (eds), *Deconstruction and Criticism* (London: Routledge and Kegan Paul, 1979), pp. 217–53
Miller, Naomi J., '"Nott Much to be Marked": Narrative of the Woman's Part in Lady Mary Wroth's *Urania*', *Studies in English Literature*, 29 (1989), 121–38
Millett, Kate, *Sexual Politics* (London: Virago, 1977)
Milton, John, *Areopagitica; for the Liberty of Unlicenc'd Printing, To the Parlament of England*, in *The Works of John Milton*, gen.ed. Frank Allen Patterson (New York: Columbia University Press, 1931), IV
Mitchell, W.J.T. (ed.), *The Politics of Interpretation* (Chicago and London: University of Chicago Press, 1982)
Morretti, Franco, 'The Great Eclipse: Tragic Form as the Deconsecration of Sovereignty', in John Drakakis (ed.), *Shakespearean Tragedy* (London and New York: Longman, 1992), pp. 45–83
Morrill, John, *The Nature of the English Revolution* (London and New York: Longman, 1993)
——, (ed.), *Revolution and Restoration: England in the 1650s* (London: Collins and Brown, 1992)
Morse, David, *England's Time of Crisis: From Shakespeare to Milton: a Cultural History* (London: Macmillan, 1989)
Mortimer, Anthony, 'The Feigned Commonwealth in the Poetry of Ben Jonson', *Studies in English Literature*, 13 (1973), 69–79
Motion, Andrew, *The Pleasure Steamers* (Manchester: Carcanet, 1978)
Mouffe, Chantal (ed.), *Dimensions of a Radical Democracy: Pluralism, Citizenship and Community* (London: Verso, 1992)
Mulier, Eco Haitsma, 'The Language of Seventeenth-Century Republicanism in the United Provinces: Dutch or European?', in

Anthony Pagden (ed.), *The Languages of Political Theory in Early Modern Europe* (Cambridge: Cambridge University Press, 1987), pp. 179–95

Mullaney, Steven, *The Place of the Stage: Licence, Play, and Power in Renaissance England* (Chicago: University of Chicago Press, 1988)

Mullini, Roberta, 'Streets, Squares, and Courts: Venice as a Stage in Shakespeare and Ben Jonson', in Michele Marrapodi and others (eds), *Shakespeare's Italy: Functions of Italian Locations in Renaissance Drama* (Manchester: Manchester University Press, 1993), pp. 158–84

Mulryne, J.R., and Margaret Shewring (eds), *Theatre and Government under the Early Stuarts* (Cambridge: Cambridge University Press, 1993)

——, (eds), *This Golden Round* (Stratford-upon-Avon: Mulryne and Shewring, 1989)

Mulvihill, James D., 'Jonson's *Poetaster* and the Ovidian Debate', *Studies in English Literature*, 22 (1982), 239–55

Murray, Timothy, *Theatrical Legitimations: Allegories of Genius in Seventeenth-Century England and France* (Oxford: Oxford University Press, 1987)

Newman, Karen, 'Engendering the News', in A.L. Magnusson and C.E. McGee (eds), *The Elizabethan Theater XIV* (Toronto: P.D. Meany, 1996), pp. 49–69

——, *Fashioning Femininity and English Renaissance Drama* (Chicago and London: University of Chicago Press, 1991)

Newton, Richard C., 'Goe Quit 'hem All: Ben Jonson and Formal Verse Satire', *Studies in English Literature*, 16 (1976), 105-16

Nicholl, Charles, *The Chemical Theatre* (London and Boston: Routledge and Kegan Paul, 1980)

——, *The Reckoning: The Murder of Christopher Marlowe* (London: Jonathan Cape, 1992)

Nichols, J.G., *The Poetry of Ben Jonson* (New York: Barnes and Noble, 1969)

Norbrook, David, '*Areopagitica*, Censorship and the Early Modern Public Sphere', in Richard Burt and John Archer (eds), *The Administration of Aesthetics: Censorship, Political Criticism, and the Public Sphere* (Minneapolis: University of Minnesota Press, 1994), pp. 3–33

——, 'Lucan, Thomas May and the Creation of a Republican Literary Culture', in Kevin Sharpe and Peter Lake (eds), *Culture and Politics in Early Stuart England* (London: Macmillan, 1994), pp. 45–66

——, *Poetry and Politics in the English Renaissance* (London: Routledge, 1984)
——, 'The Politics of Milton's Early Poetry', in Annabel Patterson (ed.), *John Milton* (London and New York: Longman, 1992), pp. 46–64
Norbrook, David, and H.R. Woudhuysen (eds), *The Penguin Book of Renaissance Verse* (Harmondsworth: Penguin, 1992)
Orgel, Stephen, *The Illusion of Power: Political Theater in the English Renaissance* (Berkeley: University of California Press, 1975)
——, *The Jonsonian Masque* (New York: Columbia University Press, 1965; repr. 1981)
——, 'The Role of the King', in H. Aram Veeser (ed.), *The New Historicism Reader* (London: Routledge, 1994), pp. 35–45
——, 'Shakespeare and the Cannibals', in Marjorie Garber (ed.), *Cannibals, Witches and Divorce: Estranging the Renaissance* (Baltimore and London: Johns Hopkins Press, 1987), pp. 40–66
——, '"To Make Boards to Speak": Inigo Jones's Stage and the Jonsonian Masque', *Renaissance Drama*, n.s. 1 (1968), 121–52
——, 'What is a Text?,' *Research Opportunities in Renaissance Drama*, 24 (1981), 3–6
Ornstein, Robert, 'Shakespeare and Jonsonian Comedy', *Shakespeare Survey*, 22 (1969), 43–46
Orwell, George and Reginald Reynolds (eds), *British Pamphleteers* (London: Wingate, 1948), I
Ostovich, Helen, 'The Appropriation of Pleasure in *The Magnetic Lady*', *Studies in English Literature*, 34 (1994), 425–42
——, 'Hell for Lovers: Shades of Adultery in *The Devil is an Ass*', in Julie Sanders, with Kate Chedgzoy and Susan Wiseman (eds), *Refashioning Ben Jonson: Gender, Politics, and the Jonsonian Canon* (London: Macmillan, 1998), pp. 155–82
——, '"Jeered by Confederacy": Group Aggression in Jonson's Comedies', *Medieval and Renaissance Drama in England*, 2 (1986), 115–28
——, '"So Sudden and Strange a Cure": A Rudimentary Masque in *Every Man Out of His Humour*', *English Literary Renaissance*, 22 (1992), 315–32
Parfitt, George, *English Poetry of the Seventeenth Century* (London and New York: Longman, 1992)
——, 'History and Ambiguity: Jonson's 'A Speech According to Horace', *Studies in English Literature*, 19 (1979), 85–92
Parker, Brian, 'An English View of Venice: Ben Jonson's *Volpone*

(1606)', in Sergio Rossi and Dianella Savoia (eds), *Italy and the English Renaissance* (Milan: Edizioni Unicopoli, 1989), pp. 187–202
——, 'Jonson's Venice', in J.R. Mulryne and Margaret Shewring (eds), *Theatre of the English and Italian Renaissance* (London: Macmillan, 1991), pp. 92–112
Parker, Geoffrey, *The Dutch Revolt*, rev. edn (Harmondsworth: Penguin, 1990)
Parr, Anthony (ed.), *Ben Jonson's The Staple of News* (Manchester: Manchester University Press, 1988)
Parry, Graham, *The Golden Age Restored: The Culture of the Stuart Court, 1603–42* (Manchester: Manchester University Press, 1981)
——, *The Trophies of Time* (Oxford: Oxford University Press, 1997)
Paster, Gail Kern, *The Body Embarrassed: Drama and the Disciplines of Shame in Early Modern England* (Ithaca, NY: Cornell University Press, 1993)
——, *The Idea of the City in the Age of Shakespeare* (Athens: University of Georgia Press, 1985)
Patterson, Annabel, 'Against Polarization: Literature and Politics in Marvell's Cromwell Poems', *English Literary Renaissance*, 5 (1975), 251-72
——, *Censorship and Interpretation: The Conditions of Writing and Reading in Early Modern England* (Madison: University of Wisconsin Press, 1984)
——, 'Jonson, Marvell and Miscellaneity', in Neil Freistat (ed.), *Poems in Their Place: The Intertextuality and Order of Poetic Collections* (Chapel Hill and London: University of North Carolina Press, 1986), pp. 95-118
——, *Pastoral and Ideology: Virgil to Valéry* (Oxford: Clarendon Press, 1988)
——, *Reading Between the Lines* (London: Routledge, 1993)
——, *Shakespeare and the Popular Voice* (Oxford: Blackwell, 1984)
Pearl, Valerie, 'Social Policy in Early Modern London', in Hugh Lloyd-Jones, Valerie Pearl and Blair Worden (eds), *History and the Imagination: Essays in Honour of Hugh Trevor-Roper* (London: Duckworth, 1981), pp. 115–31
Pechter, Edward, '*Julius Caesar* and *Sejanus*: Roman Politics, Inner Selves and the Powers of the Theatre', in E.A.J. Honigmann (ed.), *Shakespeare and his Contemporaries: Essays in Comparison* (Manchester: Manchester University Press, 1986), pp. 60–78
Peck, Linda Levy (ed.), *The Mental World of the Jacobean Court* (Cambridge: Cambridge University Press, 1992)

Peltonen, Markku, *Classical Humanism and Republicanism in English Political Thought, 1570–1640* (Cambridge: Cambridge University Press, 1995)
Pennington, Donald and Keith Thomas (eds), *Puritans and Revolutionaries* (Oxford: Clarendon Press, 1978)
Peterson, Richard S., *Imitation and Praise in the Poems of Ben Jonson* (New Haven: Yale University Press, 1981)
Pierce, Robert B., 'Ben Jonson's Horace and Horace's Ben Jonson', *Studies in Philology*, 78 (1981), 20–31
Pitkin, Hanna Fenichel, *Fortune is a Woman: Gender and Politics in the Thought of Niccolò Machiavelli* (Berkeley: University of California Press, 1984)
Plato, *The Republic*, ed. and trans. Desmond Lee (Harmondsworth: Penguin, 1987)
——, *The Symposium*, trans. W. Hamilton (Harmondsworth: Penguin, 1952)
Pocock, J.G.A., *The Machiavellian Moment: Florentine Political Thought and the Atlantic Republican Tradition* (Princeton, NJ: Princeton University Press, 1975)
Pullan, Brian, *Rich and Poor in Renaissance Venice: The Social Institutions of a Catholic State* (Oxford: Blackwell, 1971)
Purseglove, Jeremy, *Taming the Flood: A History and Natural History of Rivers and Wetlands* (Oxford: Oxford University Press, 1989)
Pye, Christopher, *The Regal Phantasm: Shakespeare and the Politics of Spectacle* (London: Routledge, 1990)
——, 'The Theater, the Market and the Subject of History', unpublished article
Rackin, Phyllis, 'Androgyny, Mimesis and the Marriage of the Boy Heroine on the English Renaissance Stage', in Elaine Showalter (ed.), *Speaking of Gender* (London: Routledge, 1989), pp. 113–33
Rady, Martin, *From Revolt to Independence: The Netherlands, 1550–1650* (London: Hodder and Stoughton, 1990)
Randall, Dale B., *Jonson's Gipsies Unmasked* (Durham, NC: Duke University Press, 1975)
Ricks, Christopher, '*Sejanus* and Dismemberment', *Modern Language Notes*, 76 (1961), 301–7
Riggs, David, *Ben Jonson: A Life* (Cambridge, MA: Harvard University Press, 1989)
Righter, Anne, *Shakespeare and the Idea of the Play* (Harmondsworth: Penguin, 1962)

Roberts, S.K., 'Alehouses, Brewing and Government under the Early Stuarts', *Southern History*, 2 (1980), 45–71

Rose, Mary Beth, *The Expense of Spirit: Love and Sexuality in English Renaissance Drama* (Ithaca, NY: Cornell University Press, 1988)

Rowe, George C., *Distinguishing Jonson: Imitation, Rivalry and the Direction of a Dramatic Career* (Lincoln and London: University of Nebraska Press, 1988)

Russell, Conrad (ed.), *The Origins of the English Civil War* (London: Macmillan, 1973; repr. 1991)

——, *Parliaments and English Politics, 1621–29* (Oxford: Oxford University Press, 1979)

Rutter, Carol Chillington (ed.), *Documents of the Rose Playhouse* (Manchester: Manchester University Press, 1984)

Salgado, Gamini (ed.), *Four Jacobean City Comedies* (Harmondsworth: Penguin, 1985)

Salingar, Leo, 'Crowd and Public in *Bartholomew Fair*', *Renaissance Drama*, n.s. 10 (1979), 141–59

Sallust, *Works*, trans. J.C. Rolfe (Cambridge, MA: Harvard University Press, 1921)

Sanders, Julie, '"The Collective Contract is a Fragile Structure": Local Government and Personal Rule in Jonson's *A Tale of a Tub*,' *English Literary Renaissance*, 27 (1997), 443–67

——, '"The Day's Sports Devised in the Inn": Jonson's *The New Inn* and Theatrical Politics', *Modern Language Review*, 91 (1996), 545–60

——, 'Midwives and the New Science in the Seventeenth Century: Language, Print and Theatre', in Erica Fudge, Ruth Gilbert and Susan Wiseman (eds), *At the Borders of the Human: Science and Culture in the Seventeenth Century* (London: Macmillan, forthcoming)

——, 'A Parody of Lord Chief Justice Popham in *The Devil is an Ass*', *Notes and Queries* 44 (1997), 528–30

——, 'The Politics of Escapism: Fantasies of Travel and Power in Ben Jonson's *The Alchemist* and Richard Brome's *The Antipodes*', in Ceri Sullivan and Barbara White (eds), *Writing and Fantasy* (London and New York: Longman, forthcoming)

——, 'Seeing the Seventeenth-Century Forest for the Woods and the Trees', unpublished paper, 'Literature and Ecology' conference, University of Swansea, March 1997

——, 'The Trials of Frances Fitzdottrel in *The Devil is an Ass*', unpublished paper, Northern Renaissance Seminar, Sheffield Hallam University, November 1996

——, '"Twill Fit the Players Yet": Women and Theatre in Jonson's Later Drama', forthcoming

Sanders, Julie, with Kate Chedgzoy and Susan Wiseman (eds), *Refashioning Ben Jonson: Gender, Politics, and the Jonsonian Canon* (London: Macmillan, 1998)

Schellhase, Kenneth, *Tacitus in Renaissance Political Thought* (Chicago and London: University of Chicago Press, 1976)

Schmitt, Charles B. and Quentin Skinner (eds), *The Cambridge History of Renaissance Philosophy* (Cambridge: Cambridge University Press, 1988)

Scodel, Joshua, 'Genre and Occasion in Jonson's "On My First Sonne"', *Studies in Philology*, 86 (1989), 235–59

Scott, Jonathan, 'The English Republican Imagination', in John Morrill, (ed.), *Revolution and Restoration: England in the 1650s* (London: Collins and Brown, 1992), pp. 35–54

Sennett, Richard, *The Fall of Public Man* (London: Faber, 1986)

——, *Flesh and Stone: The Body and the City in Western Civilization* (London: Faber, 1992)

Shapiro, James, *Rival Playwrights: Marlowe, Jonson and Shakespeare* (New York: Columbia University Press, 1991)

——, '"Steale from the deade?": The Presence of Marlowe in Jonson's Early Plays', *Renaissance Drama*, n.s. 18 (1987), 67–99

Shapiro, Michael, 'Audience vs Dramatist in *Epicoene* and Other Plays of the Children's Troupes', *English Literary Renaissance*, 3 (1973), 400–17

——, *Children of the Revels* (New York: Columbia University Press, 1977)

——, 'Lady Mary Wroth Describes a "Boy Actress"', *Medieval and Renaissance Drama in England*, 4 (1989), 187–93

Sharp, Buchanan, *In Contempt of All Authority: Rural Artisans and Riot in the West of England, 1586–1660* (Berkeley: University of California Press, 1980)

Sharpe, Kevin, *Criticism and Compliment: The Politics of Literature in the England of Charles I* (Cambridge: Cambridge University Press, 1987)

——, (ed.), *Faction and Parliament: Essays on Early Stuart History* (Oxford: Clarendon Press, 1978)

——, 'The King's Writ: Royal Authors and Royal Authority in Early Modern England', in Kevin Sharpe and Peter Lake (eds), *Culture and Politics in Early Stuart England* (London: Macmillan, 1994), pp. 117–38

——, *The Personal Rule of Charles I* (London and New Haven: Yale University Press, 1992)
——, *Politics and Ideas in Early Stuart England: Essays and Studies* (London and New York: Pinter, 1989)
Sharpe, Kevin and Peter Lake (eds), *Culture and Politics in Early Stuart England* (London: Macmillan, 1994)
Sharpe, Kevin and Steven N. Zwicker (eds), *Politics of Discourse: The Literature and History of Seventeenth-Century England* (Berkeley: University of California Press, 1987)
Shaw, Catherine, *Richard Brome* (Boston, MA: Twayne, 1980)
Shepherd, Simon, *Amazons and Warrior Women: Varieties of Feminism in Seventeenth-Century Drama* (Brighton: Harvester, 1981)
——, (ed.), *The Women's Sharp Revenge: Five Women's Pamphlets from the Renaissance* (London: Fourth Estate, 1985)
Shepherd, Simon, and Peter Womack, *English Drama: A Cultural History* (Oxford: Blackwell, 1996)
Shuger, Debora Kuller, *Habits of Thought in the English Renaissance: Religion, Politics, and the Dominant Culture* (Berkeley: University of California Press, 1990)
Sinfield, Alan, *Faultlines: Cultural Materialism and the Politics of Dissident Reading* (Oxford: Oxford University Press, 1992)
Skinner, Quentin, *The Foundations of Modern Political Thought*, 2 vols (Cambridge: Cambridge University Press, 1978)
——, *Machiavelli* (Oxford: Oxford University Press, 1981)
Slights, William W.E., 'Unfashioning the Man of Mode: A Comic Countergenre in Marston, Jonson and Middleton', *Renaissance Drama*, n.s. 15 (1984), 69–91
Smallwood, Robert L., ' "Here in the Friars": Immediacy and Theatricality in *The Alchemist*', *Review of English Studies*, 32 (1981), 142–60
Smith, Bruce R., 'Ben Jonson's *Epigrammes*: Portrait-Gallery, Theater, Commonwealth', *Studies in English Literature*, 15 (1974), 91–110
Smith, David L., Richard Strier and David Bevington (eds), *The Theatrical City: Culture, Theatre, and Politics in London, 1576–1649* (Cambridge: Cambridge University Press, 1995), pp. 170–82
Somerset, Anne, *Unnatural Murder: Poison at the Court of James I* (London: Weidenfeld and Nicolson, 1996)
Stallybrass, Peter, and Allon White, *The Politics and Poetics of Transgression* (London: Methuen, 1986)
Stewart, Susan, *Crimes of Writing: Problems in the Containment of*

Representation (New York and Oxford: Oxford University Press, 1991)

Stockton, David, *Cicero the Politician* (Oxford: Oxford University Press, 1971)

Strong, Roy, *The Cult of Elizabeth: Elizabethan Portraiture and Pageantry* (London: Thames and Hudson, 1977)

——, *Henry, Prince of Wales and England's Lost Renaissance* (London: Thames and Hudson, 1986)

Sturgess, Keith, *Jacobean Private Theatre* (London: Routledge, 1987)

Summers, Claude J. and Ted-Larry Pebworth (eds), *Classic and Cavalier: Essays on Jonson and the Sons of Ben* (Pittsburgh, PA: University of Pittsburgh Press, 1982)

——, (eds), *The Muse's Common-weale: Poetry and Politics in the Seventeenth Century* (Columbia: University of Missouri Press, 1988)

Sweeney, John Gordon, *Jonson and the Psychology of Public Theater* (Princeton, NJ: Princeton University Press, 1987)

Syme, Ronald, *Tacitus*, 4 vols (Oxford: Oxford University Press, 1958)

Tacitus, *The Annals of Imperial Rome*, trans. and intro. Michael Grant (Harmondsworth: Penguin, 1971 [1956])

Tanner, Tony, *Venice Desired* (Oxford: Blackwell, 1992)

Tennenhouse, Leonard, *Power on Display: The Politics of Shakespeare's Genres* (London and New York: Methuen, 1986)

Tomlinson, Sophie, '"She That Plays the King": Henrietta Maria and the Threat of the Actress in Caroline Culture', in Gordon McMullan and Jonathan Hope (eds), *The Politics of Tragicomedy: Shakespeare and After* (London: Routledge, 1992), pp. 189–207

Traister, Barbara Howard, *Heavenly Necromancers: The Magician in English Renaissance Drama* (Columbia: University of Missouri Press, 1986)

Underdown, David, *Revel, Riot, and Rebellion: Popular Politics and Culture in England, 1603–1660* (Oxford: Oxford University Press, 1987)

Veeser, H. Aram (ed.), *The New Historicism* (New York and London: Routledge, 1989)

——, (ed.), *The New Historicism Reader* (London: Routledge, 1994)

Veevers, Erica, *Images of Love and Religion: Queen Henrietta Maria and Court Entertainments* (Cambridge: Cambridge University Press, 1989)

Waley, Daniel, *The Italian City-State Republics* 3rd edn (London and New York: Longman, 1988)

Waller, Gary, *The Sidney Family Romance: Mary Wroth, William Herbert, and the Early Modern Construction of Gender* (Detroit: Wayne State University Press, 1993)
——, *English Poetry in the Sixteenth Century* (London and New York: Longman, 1993)
Warner, Marina, *From the Beast to the Blonde: On Fairytales and their Tellers* (London: Chatto and Windus, 1994)
——, *Monuments and Maidens: The Allegory of the Female Form* (London: Weidenfeld and Nicolson, 1985)
Watson, Robert N., *Ben Jonson's Parodic Strategy: Literary Imperialism in the Comedies* (Cambridge, MA: Harvard University Press, 1987)
Wayne, Don E., 'Drama and Society in the Age of Jonson: An Alternative View', *Renaissance Drama*, n.s. 13 (1982), 103–29
——, *Penshurst: The Semiotics of Place and the Poetics of History* (London: Methuen, 1984)
Wells, Susan, 'Jacobean City Comedy and the Ideology of the City', *English Literary History*, 48 (1991), 37-60
White, Stephen D., *Sir Edward Coke and the Grievances of the Commonwealth* (Manchester: Manchester University Press, 1979)
Williams, Raymond, *Keywords: A Vocabulary of Culture and Society* (London: Fontana, 1976)
——, *Marxism and Literature* (Oxford: Oxford University Press, 1977)
Wills, Garry, *Witches and Jesuits: Shakespeare's 'Macbeth'* (Oxford: Oxford University Press, 1995)
Wilson, Jean, *Entertainments for Elizabeth I* (Woodbridge: Brewer, 1980)
Wilson, Richard, *Will Power: Essays on Shakespearean Authority* (Detroit: Wayne State University Press, 1993)
Wilson, Richard, and Richard Dutton (eds), *New Historicism and Renaissance Drama* (London and New York: Longman, 1992)
Wiltenburg, Robert, *Ben Jonson and Self-Love: The Subtlest Maze of All* (Columbia: University of Missouri Press, 1990)
Wiseman, Susan, 'The Eccho of Uncertaintie: Jonson, Classical Drama and the Civil War', in Julie Sanders, with Kate Chedgzoy and Susan Wiseman (eds), *Refashioning Ben Jonson: Gender, Politics, and the Jonsonian Canon* (London: Macmillan, 1998), pp. 208–29
Womack, Peter, *Ben Jonson* (Oxford: Blackwell, 1986)
Wootton, David (ed.), *Divine Right and Democracy: An Anthology of Political Writings in Stuart England* (Harmondsworth: Penguin, 1986)

——, (ed.), *Republicanism, Liberty, and Commercial Society, 1649–1776* (Stanford, CA: Stanford University Press, 1994)

Worden, Blair, 'Ben Jonson Among the Historians', in Kevin Sharpe and Peter Lake (eds), *Culture and Politics in Early Stuart England* (London: Macmillan, 1994), pp. 67–90

——, 'Classical Republicanism and the Puritan Revolution', in Hugh Lloyd-Jones, Valerie Pearl and Blair Worden (eds), *History and the Imagination: Essays in Honour of Hugh Trevor-Roper* (London: Duckworth, 1981), pp. 182–200

——, 'English Republicanism', in J.H. Burns and Mark Goldie (eds), *The Cambridge History of Renaissance Political Thought* (Cambridge: Cambridge University Press, 1991), pp. 443–75

——, 'Literature and Political Censorship in Early Modern Europe', in A.C. Duke and C.A. Tamse (eds), *Too Mighty to be Free: Censorship and the Press in Britain and the Netherlands* (Zutphen: De Walburg, 1987), pp. 45–62

——, 'Marchamont Nedham and the Beginnings of English Republicanism, 1649–1656', in David Wootton (ed.), *Republicanism, Liberty and Commercial Society* (Stanford, CA: Stanford University Press, 1994), pp. 45–81

——, 'Shakespeare and Politics', *Shakespeare Survey*, 44 (1992), 1–15

Wormald, Jenny, *Court, Kirk and Community: Scotland, 1470–1625* (London: Arnold, 1981)

——, 'James VI and I: Two Kings or One?', *History*, 68 (1985), 187–209

Wrightson, Keith, 'Alehouses, Order and Reformation in Rural England, 1590-1660', in Eileen and Stephen Yeo (eds), *Popular Culture and Class Conflict, 1590–1914: Explorations in the History of Labour and Leisure* (Brighton: Harvester Press, 1981), pp. 1–27

——, 'Two Concepts of Order: Justices, Constables and Jurymen in Seventeenth-Century England', in John Brewer and John Styles (eds), *An Ungovernable People: The English and their Law in the Seventeenth and Eighteenth Centuries* (London: Hutchinson, 1980), pp. 21–46

Wynne-Davies, Marion, 'The Queen's Masque: Renaissance Women and the Seventeenth-Century Court Masque', in S.P. Cerasano and Marion Wynne-Davies (eds), *Gloriana's Face: Women, Public and Private, in the English Renaissance* (Hemel Hempstead: Harvester, 1992), pp. 79–104

Index

absolutism, 1–2, 5, 16, 22, 33, 44, 49, 55, 73, 76, 82, 84, 88, 95, 103, 104, 119, 128, 144, 180, 182, 186
acting companies, 77, 93, 96, 148, 200 n16
  boys' companies, 93, 108
  Children of the Queen's Revels, 93, 200 n16
  Lady Elizabeth's Men, 93
adventurers, 108–9, 115
Agnew, Jean-Christophe, 40, 41, 43, 70–1, 84, 188 n3, 196 n24, 202 n 9, n10, 206 n26
alchemy, 69, 71, 72, 75–6, 79
alehouses, 8, 107, 115, 144–7, 152, 153–4, 156, 160
Anabaptists, 80, 88, 142, 191 n28
  see also Puritanism
Anderson, Michael, 197 n35
Anne of Denmark, Queen, 23, 49–50, 54–6, 136, 193 n26, 199–200 n16
antiquarianism, 165–6
Archer, Ian, 103, 107–8, 205 n22, 207 n40, n2
Aristophanes, 116
Armstrong, Archibald, 133, 167
Athens, 152, 197 n2
audiences, *see* Jonson, Ben, life and views; audiences
Augustus, Emperor, 11, 31, 40, 169
Ayres, Philip, 211 n20

Bach, Rebecca Ann, 145, 203 n24, 213 n4, 218 n13
Bacon, Sir Francis, 109
Bakhtin, Mikhail, 90, 204 n4, 204 n6, 214 n7

ballads, 100–1, 124, 131, 133, 212 n27
Barish, Jonas, 124, 196 n23, 216 n2
Barnes, Peter, 205–6 n23
Bartholomew Fair, 89–90
Barton, Anne, 35, 61–2, 77, 99, 119, 162, 165, 190 n17, 192 n9, 194 n2, 195 n7, 196 n17, 201 n29, n30, 204n2, 213n3, 215n18, n29, 217 n4
  see also Righter, Anne
Bate, Jonathan, 194 n2, 207 n35, 208–9 n16
Bedford, Lucy Russell, Countess of, 54–5
Beer, Gillian, 96, 206 n24
Bellany, Alistair, 212 n27
Belsey, Catherine, 194 n3
Bennett, Benjamin, 91, 99–100, 205 n9, 206 n31
Bennett, Susan, 97, 206 n28, 207 n37
Blackfriars
  region, 52, 55, 68–9, 71, 73, 83, 86, 88, 109, 121, 181, 191 n28
  theatre, 55, 68–9, 71, 82, 109, 202 n5
Bloom, Harold, 196 n17
Boccaccio, Giovanni, 59
Bodin, Jean, 4, 38
Boose, Lynda E., 199 n15
Boughner, Daniel C., 190 n16, 192 n6, n13
Braddick, Michael J., 216 n37, 220 n34
Bradley, Humphrey, 114
Brady, Jennifer, 189 n5, 221 n2
Braunmuller, A.R., 209 n26
Breitenberg, Mark, 198 n10

253

Bretnor, Thomas, 120–1
Bridge, Giles, of Hereford, 153
Brome, Richard, 122, 160, 186, 209 n32, 212 n37, 222 n13
  The Court Beggar, 122, 209 n32
  A Jovial Crew, 122, 160, 186, 212 n37
Broughton, Hugh, 52, 73, 84
Bruni, Leonardo, 13, 32
Brutus, 13, 20, 22, 32, 35
Buckingham, George Villiers, Duke of, 55, 122, 132, 134, 146, 160, 211 n23
Burt, Richard, 75, 128–9, 130, 139, 141–2, 194 n4, 202 n13, 206 n30, 211 n13, n21, 213 n48, 217 n9, 221 n3
Butler, Martin, 146, 155, 157, 162–6, 168, 170, 175, 177–8, 188 n3, 196 n25, 200 n20, 203 n25, 205 n10, 209 n24, 211 n23, 214 n10, 215n27, 216 n35, n36, 217 n2, n6, n7, n10, 218 n12, n14, n18, 220 n36, n37, n39, 222 n7, 13
Butter, Nathaniel, 134

Cadiz, 175
Cain, Tom, 191 n1
Caligula, 25
Calvino, Italo, 194 n1
Camden, William, 12, 165, 217 n5
  Britannia, 12, 217 n5
carnival, carnivalesque, 45, 90, 93, 145, 154, 170, 184, 204 n4, n6
Caroline court, 146, 155–6, 175, 219–20 n32
Caroline period (1625–42), 1, 124–5, 141–2, 162, 164, 168–9, 179, 182
Carr, Robert, Earl of Somerset, *see* Somerset, Robert Carr, Earl of
Carr, Sir Robert, 119–21
Cassius, 13
Castiglione, Baldassare, 156
  Il cortegiano, 156
Catesby, Robert, 113
Catholicism, 110, 113, 132, 191 n28, 209 n18
Catiline, 13, 14, 16, 19, 20, 22, 26, 32, 61–2, 76

Cato, 30, 33
Cave, Richard Allen, 213 n2
censorship. 34, 87, 123–8, 132, 134, 139, 211 n12, 213 n47
Cethegus, 18–19, 61
Chapman, George, 82, 200 n16
Charles I, King, 8, 65, 114, 121–2, 131–2, 134, 146, 152, 154, 160–3, 167–8, 174–9, 211 n23, 212 n37, 217 n3
  Book of Sports (1633 reprint), 178
Chaucer, Geoffrey, 154
  The Parliament of Fowls, 154
Chedgzoy, Kate, 189 n3, 191 n30, 222 n7
Christianson, Paul, 215 n28
Church, 169, 177–8
Cicero, 15, 19–22, 25–6, 32–4, 61–3, 76, 192 n11, 193 n33, 201 n31
  De Finibus, 21
citizen militia, 108–10, 152, 160
city, concepts of, 3, 34–5, 40, 46, 68–70, 77–8, 92, 95, 107–8, 196 n18, n21, 205 n17, n22
city comedies, 124, 146, 202 n8
city states, 5, 15, 32, 35–6, 68
civil wars, *see* English Civil Wars
Clare, Janet, 194 n4, 211 n12
Clark, Peter, 147, 152–3, 214 n5, n8, n14, 215 n22, n24, n25
classical republicanism, *see* republicanism
Clifford, Lady Anne, 55, 200 n26, 209 n20
Cockayne, Sir William, Alderman, 113, 208 n12
Cogswell, Thomas, 132, 191 n23, 212 n26, n27
Coke, Sir Edward, 112–13, 142, 219 n22
commedia dell'arte, 45, 197 n35, n36
common good, 3, 20, 187
Common Law, 4, 6, 165
community, concepts of, 5–11, 40, 49, 64–9, 80, 88–109, 119–22, 126, 144–7, 166–87, 203 n29, 208–9 n16
commonwealth, concepts of, 3, 8, 21, 49–50, 67, 85, 94, 98, 108, 187

Index

constitution, 2, 4, 5, 34, 95, 142–3, 158, 165
constables, 170–1
consul, consulship, 12, 20–21, 26, 169
Contarini, Gasparo, 35–7
corantos, 123, 127, 141
Coriolanus, Caius Martius, 13–14
Coryat, Thomas, 36
  Coryat's Crudities, 36
Cotton, Sir Robert, 217 n10
Crassus, 19, 22
Creaser, John, 97, 205 n15, 206 n29, 210 n2
Crew, Sergeant Ranulph (Randal), 112
Cromwell, Oliver, 210 n33
Cultural Materialism, 2, 90, 188 n3
Cust, Richard, 175, 188 n2, 210 n3, 216 n37, n38, n39, 218 n15, 220 n34, 221 n5

Danaë, myth of, 85
Darling, Thomas, Boy of Burton, 111
Daniel, Samuel, 171
Darrel, John, 107, 111, 113
Davis, Natalie Zemon, 129, 210 n7, 210–11 n11
de Certeau, Michel, 39, 196 n18
DeLuna, B.N., 192 n16, 208 n13
Dekker, Thomas, 198 n10, 207 n38
  The Gull's Hornbook, 207 n38
  The Roaring Girl, 198 n10
de Man, Paul, 83
Dentith, Simon, 204n4, 205 n16
Digby, Sir Kenelm, 207 n3
Doge of Venice, 4, 35, 37, 41, 46
Dollimore, Jonathan, 204 n5, n7
Donaldson, Ian, 44, 170, 191 n26, 197 n31, 203 n27, 209 n18, 219 n21, 221 n2
Donne, John, 51, 156, 198 n4
Dorenkamp, Angela G., 191 n4
Drummond, William, of Hawthornden, 6, 14, 120, 191 n26
Dryden, John, 61, 221 n2
  Essay of Dramatick Poesie, 61

Dusinberre, Juliet, 198 n5
Dutch Republic, 5
  see also United Provinces
Dutton, Richard, 44, 92, 188 n3, 189 n5, 194 n4, 197 n34, 200 n18, 203 n31, 205 n11, n12, n13, 206 n32, 208 n13

Echeruo, Michael J.C., 191–2 n4
Edward VI, King, 167
Eisenstein, Elizabeth, 127–8, 130, 210 n5, n8
Eleven Year Tyranny, 165, 179, *see also* Personal Rule
Elsky, Martin, 217 n5
Elizabeth I, Queen, 23, 45, 114, 138, 162, 165, 215 n30
Elizabethan drama, 14, 23, 190 n17, 207 n39
Elizabethan period (1558–1603), 13–15, 23, 82, 86, 103, 147, 166–8, 175, 178, 214 n8
Empson, William, 108, 207 n4
English Civil Wars, 146, 153, 161, 165–6, 174–5, 181, 189 n7
English Commonwealth, 187
Erskine-Hill, Howard, 191 n1
Essex, county of, 174–6
Essex, Robert Devereux, Earl of (first husband of Frances Howard), 120–1
Evans, Robert C., 113, 190 n16, n6, 197 n27, 207 n1, 208 n12, 215 n23

Feminist criticism, 51, 189 n3, 198 n11
fen drainage, 8, 50, 107, 114–22, 208 n15, 210 n33
Fincham, K., 216 n37
Fish, Stanley, 94, 129, 204 n3, 205 n18, 211 n14, 221 n1
Fiske, Nicholas, 121–2
Flesch, William, 198 n9
Fletcher, John, 92, 193 n34
  The Two Noble Kinsmen, 92
Florence, 5, 15, 35–6, 208 n10
Florio, John, 36, 46
  A World of Words, 36

Index

Forced Loan, 159, 168
forest law, 208 n15
Forman, Dr Simon, 120–1
Foster, Andrew, 220–1 n41
Foucault, Michel, 29, 31, 194 n39, n40, 198 n9
Franklin, James, 121–2
Fumerton, Patricia, 211 n24, 212 n33

Gaby, Rosemary, 222 n12
Gender Studies, 2
Gianakaris, C.J., 37, 195 n12
Giannotti, Donato, 35, 37
Gibbons, Brian, 205 n17
Globe Theatre, 160
Goldberg, Jonathan, 22–3, 27, 35, 37, 44, 190 n19, 193 n24, n25, n26, 193 n29, 195 n13, 196 n16, 197 n32
Golden Age, 85, 165
Gondomar, Count, 141
Gonzaga family, 45
Greenblatt, Stephen, 1, 35, 41, 43, 83, 87, 110, 188 n1, 195 n6, 196 n25, 197 n29, n30, 202 n12, 203 n22, 23, 204 n32, 205 n21, 208 n7, n8, n9
Gresham, Edward, 120–1
Guicciardini, Francesco, 13, 35, 94
  History of Italy 13
guilds, 108
Gunpowder Plot, 15, 113, 196 n22
Gurr, Andrew, 201 n2

Habsburgs, 5, 132–3
Hackett, Helen, 198 n11
Hakluyt, Richard, 82
  Principal Navigations, 82–3
Hale, John, 195 n8, 197 n37
Hall, Kim F., 198–9 n11, 199 n15
Happé, Peter, 113, 208 n15
Harsnett, Samuel, 110–11, 113
  A Declaration of Egregious Popish Impostures, 110–11
  A Discovery of the Fraudulent Practices of John Darrel, 111
Hattaway, Michael, 154, 155, 156–7, 214 n17, 215 n30, n31, 216 n34

Hayes, Tom, 125, 202 n11, 209 n28, 210 n4, 222 n8
Healy, Thomas, 189 n5, 202 n8, 211 n18
Heinemann, Margot, 162, 216 n40, 218 n15, 219 n25
Helgerson, Richard, 213 n1, 221 n1
Henrietta Maria, Queen, 156, 167, 215–16 n33
Henri III of France, King, 195 n14
Henry, Prince, 133
Henslowe, Philip, 202 n16
Herbert, George, 156
  The Temple, 156
Herbert, William, *see* Pembroke, William Herbert, Earl of
Herendeen, W.H., 189 n5
Herford, C.H. and Percy and Evelyn Simpson, 13, 36, 212 n34, 217 n4
Hero and Leander, myth of, 102
Herrick, Robert, 221 n42
  Hesperides, 221 n42
Hill, Christopher, 28, 194 n37
Hill, Geoffrey, 21, 193 n21
Hill, L.M., 168–9, 173, 218 n17, 219 n29, n30, n32
history plays, 202 n8
Hobbes, Thomas, 95, 215 n21
Hofmannsthal, Hugo von, 91
Holland, Peter, 86, 203 n28, 205–6 n23
Holland, Philemon, 12
Holmes, C., 208 n15
Hope Theatre, 92–3
Horace, 11, 130
Hornblower, Simon, 152, 215 n20
House of Commons, 6, 154, 183
  see also Parliament
Howard, Lady Frances, 55–6, 107, 120–1
Howard, Henry *see* Northampton, Henry Howard, Earl of
Howe, Elizabeth, 216–17 n33
Hughes, Ann, 175, 188 n2, 201 n33, 216 n39, 217 n8, 220 n33, n34, n35, 221 n5, 221–2 n6
humanism, 4, 12, 35, 192 n9

Index

Hunt, William, 220 n33
Hunter, G.K., 192 n9

Jacobean court, 20, 55, 67, 136, 168
Jacobean drama, 14, 23, 90, 94, 146, 190 n17
Jacobean period (1603–25), 1, 13–15, 23, 25, 82, 103, 107, 110, 119, 125, 147, 167, 170, 178–9, 182
James I of England (VI of Scotland), King, 2, 15, 22–4, 85–6, 92–4, 100, 112, 114, 116, 119–20, 126, 132–3, 149, 152, 154–6, 161, 167, 177, 200 n16, 203 n31, 208 n12, 217 n3
  Basilikon Doron, 133
  Book of Sports, 149, 177
James, Henry, 194n3
Jardine, Lisa, 198 n5
joint-stock communities, 72–7
Jones, Ann Rosalind, 199 n13
Jones, Inigo, 23, 103, 137–8, 204 n31, 217 n9
Jonson, Ben, life and views
  anti-theatricalism, 7, 210 n2
  audiences, 1, 7–8, 11, 26–7, 32–3, 39–40, 44, 46, 54, 69, 70–1, 79, 81, 85–6, 88–99, 102, 109, 121, 138, 144, 159, 167, 181–2, 187
  authorship, 2, 68, 79, 90, 98, 129–30, 145, 183, 187
  canon, 2–3, 7, 11, 33, 51, 89–90, 180–6, 191 n30
  capitalism, 72, 94, 109–10, 119, 126, 135, 188 n3, 212 n33
  career, 1, 125, 171, 181
  death (1637), and final years, 126, 146, 149
  education, 12, 217 n5
  elite sphere, 2, 11, 69, 89–95, 100, 103, 125–6, 129, 133, 138, 156, 180
  family, concepts of, 2, 49, 144, 176
  female representations, 49–67, 101–2, 124, 154, 184–5
  gossips, representations of, 64–6, 112, 124, 133–4, 181

  as 'King's Poet', 1–2, 167, 189 n5
  language, 1–7, 12, 32, 36, 56, 59, 69, 95, 97, 101, 136–7, 157, 186–7
  legal system, representations of, 36–9, 43–6, 94, 103, 111–12
  library, 12–13, 36, 190 n18, 198 n3, 201 n31
  marriage, representations of, 50–8, 67, 90–1, 120, 145, 169–71, 178, 204–5 n8
  metaphor, 172
  midwives, representations of, 64–6
  misogyny, 184–5, 198 n6
  names, 99, 113, 165, 176, 214 n5, 217 n5
  nostalgia, 119, 151, 156, 161, 165–7
  oral culture, 186
  parasitism, concepts of, 41–2, 196–7 n26
  patriarchy, 2, 49, 67, 73
  patronage, 42, 53–4, 100, 104, 125–6
  popular sphere, 2, 11, 89–92, 103, 128
  press, representations of the, 8, 129
  print culture, 2, 7, 123, 143
  private theatres, 8, 69
  public theatre dramatist, 1–2, 50, 68–9, 86, 89, 92–3, 100, 156, 180, 188 n1
  puppetry, 103, 124–5, 144
  religious exorcisms, 107, 110
  royalism, 16, 18, 22, 27
  'schizophrenia', 15, 20, 129, 182
  soldier in Netherlands War, 6
  sons of Ben, 122
  source materials, 12, 34, 49, 62, 68
  unities, concept of the, 71
  witchcraft, representations of, 55, 67, 112, 120–1, 126–7, 155, 184–6
Jonson, Ben, writings
  masques, 23, 49–50, 54–6, 65–7, 94, 97, 100, 103–4, 129, 132–9, 146, 149–50, 156, 160, 166–7,

171, 180, 186, 188 n1, n3, 193 n26, 200 n18, 206 n32, 211 n23, 212 n33, 213 n39, 218 n12; antimasque, 50, 186; *The Golden Age Restored*, 119–20; *The Gypsies Metamorphosed*, 122, 160, 211 n23; *Hymenaei*, 55–6, 120; *The Irish Masque*, 120; *Love's Triumph through Callipolis*, 156; *Masque of Beauty*, 49, 55; *Masque of Blackness*, 49, 54–5, 136; *Masque of Queens*, 49, 55, 97; *Neptune's Triumph*, 132–3, 137, 167, 212 n30, 212–13 n28; *News from the New World Discovered in the Moon*, 126–7, 129, 135, 212 n30; *Pleasure Reconciled to Virtue*, 213 n39

plays: *The Alchemist*, 3, 7, 26, 41, 52, 54, 68–88, 96–7, 107, 119, 145, 152, 181, 184–5; *Bartholomew Fair*, 3, 40, 52, 57, 71, 89–104, 107–8, 112, 133, 145, 147, 170, 181, 183–4, 203 n29, 205–6 n23, 207 n39, n3, 213 n47, 218 n13; Caroline drama and later plays, 3, 8, 49, 64, 97, 144, 165, 181, 188 n3; *The Case is Altered*, 217 n4; *Catiline, His Conspiracy*, 11–16, 20–36, 42, 49, 60–2, 192 n11, 201 n31, 208 n13; comedies, 11, 96, 181, 183; *Cynthia's Revels*, 136, 182; *The Devil is an Ass*, 8, 49–51, 55–60, 64–7, 107–22, 151–2, 181–5, 208 n12; *Eastward Ho*, 70, 82, 200 n16, 206 n32; *Epicoene; or The Silent Woman*, 49–60, 64, 67, 93, 97, 107, 109, 198 n6, 198 n10; epilogues, 2, 39, 46, 71, 87, 167; *Every Man in His Humour*, 15, 112, 151–2, 172, 208 n10; *Every Man Out of His Humour*, 181; frontispieces, 2, 130; *The Magnetic Lady*, 57, 60, 64, 66–7, 144, 158–9, 163, 204 n31, 205 n8, 205–6 n23; *The New Inn*, 8, 49, 64, 144–63, 165, 167, 175, 182, 184–5; *Poetaster*, 11, 113, 156, 169; prefaces, 2, 71; prologues and Inductions, 2, 57, 71, 91, 93, 95, 100, 103, 135, 164–5, 171, 183–4, 205–6 n23; quarto versions, 34; *The Sad Shepherd*, 64, 67, 144, 154–5, 183–6; *Sejanus, His Fall*, 11–34, 42, 126, 161, 169, 192 n13; *The Staple of News*, 8, 52, 54, 64–7, 73, 123–43, 165, 168, 181; *A Tale of a Tub*, 8, 95, 109, 112, 146, 155, 164–79, 184, 186; tragedies (Roman), 3, 11–12, 13, 14, 16, 21, 22, 28, 32, 34, 42, 61, 67, 91, 96, 178, 181; *Volpone*, 3, 5, 15, 19, 34–46, 57, 69, 71, 97, 107, 111–12, 118–19, 126, 148, 196 n17

poetry: 54, 110, 151, 180, 216 n39, 217 n5, 217 n10; 'A Speech According to Horace', 110; *Underwood*, 54, 179, 217 n10

prose: *Conversations with Drummond*, 6, 14, 54; *Discoveries (Timber)*, 8, 14, 190 n17; marginalia, 2, 68, 130, 190 n18

publications: Folio *Works* (1616), 2, 7, 68, 81, 108, 112, 124, 130, 183, 189 n5, 203 n25, 207 n3, 208 n10

Julius Caesar, 13, 19, 22, 25
Justices of the Peace, 94, 108–9, 111–13, 168–73, 219 n26
Juvenal, 200 n24

Kay, W. David, 189 n6
Kenilworth Castle, 138
Kent, Joan, 170, 218 n20, 219 n23
Kifer, Devra, 142, 213 n49
King's Peace, 165
see also Personal Rule

Index

Knights, L.C., 119, 209 n23
Knowles, James, 205 n11
Kyd, Thomas, 78
  The Spanish Tragedy, 78

Lake, Peter, 216n37
Lambert, S.L., 211 n12
Laud, William, Archbishop of Canterbury, 177–8, 212 n37, 220 n39
Leggatt, Alexander, 194 n38
Lemly, John, 220 n38
Lewalski, Barbara Kiefer, 193 n26, 199 n14
Lewkenor, Lewis, 36
Levellers, 63, 167, 210–11
Lever, J.W., 192 n9
Levin, Harry, 203 n22
Levin, Richard, 136, 212 n37
Liberties of London, 68, 92–3
limited monarchy, 1, 4, 95, 103, 179, 186, 213 n42
Lindley, David, 200 n17, n19, n20, 208 n15, 209 n24, n27
Lindley, Keith, 121–2, 209 n31
Lipsius, Justus, 4, 13, 27, 36, 152, 190 n16, n18, 192 n6, 193–4 n34
Livy, Titus, 4, 12–15, 192 n8
local government, 164, 168–9, 173
local history, 166
Loewenstein, Joseph, 130, 211 n19
London, 27, 34, 36, 50–2, 58, 65, 68–75, 79, 89–99, 102, 104, 108–12, 118–19, 122, 127, 151, 169, 174–5, 195 n5, 196 n17, 208 n10
Low Countries, 6, 27, 115, 141, 193–4 n34
Lyly, John, 170
  Endymion, 170

Machiavelli, Niccoló, 4, 12–16, 20, 28, 33, 35–8, 43, 60, 75, 80–1, 94, 96, 109, 152, 190 n16, 192 n10, n11, n12, n13, 193 n18, 202 n20
Machin, Richard, 3, 189 n9
Mackenney, Richard, 68, 195 n10, 201 n1

MacNiece, Louis, 211 n25
Macro, 25, 28
Magna Carta, 4, 6, 148, 157–62
Mann, David, 202 n14
Mann, Thomas, 194 n3
Mantua, 40, 43–5
Marcus, Leah, 112–13, 177, 195 n5, 207 n1, 208 n11, 210 n5, 211 n17, 213 n39, 214 n16, 217 n1, 219 n22, 220 n40, 222 n9
Margaret of Parma, 193 n34
Marlowe, Christopher, 14, 103, 207 n36, 214 n15
  'Hero and Leander', 103
  The Jew of Malta, 14
Marston, John, 82, 124, 200 n16, 205 n20, 215 n30
  The Fawn, 215 n30
  The Malcontent, 205 n20
Martin, Richard, 113
Massinger, Philip, 154, 193 n34, 212–13 n38, 215 n30, 218 n15
  King and the Subject, 218 n15
  A New Way to Pay Old Debts, 154, 212–13 n38
  The Parliament of Love, 215 n30
Master of the Revels, 82, 87, 203 n31
Maus, Katherine Eisaman, 21, 191 n2, 193 n22, n23
May, Thomas, 221 n4
McCanles, Michael, 42, 174, 197 n27, 216 n39, 219 n31
McKenzie, D.F., 128–9, 210 n9, 211 n15, n16, 212 n31, n37, 213 n42
McLuskie, Kathleen, 200 n28, 205 n13, 207 n38
McPherson, David, 190 n18, 192 n5, n7, 195 n11, 197 n3
Mebane, John S., 85, 203 n26
Medici family, 15
Merchant Adventurers' Company, 113
Middleton, Thomas, 124, 141–2, 196 n21
  A Game at Chess, 141–2
militia, *see* citizen militia
millenarianism, 85

Miller, Anthony, 25, 193 n31, 193 n32
Miller, J. Hillis, 42, 196–7 n26, 197 n8
Millet, Kate, 200 n27
Milton, John
  Areopagitica, 139, 213 n44
  Comus, or A Masque at Ludlow, 213 n39
mixed government, 2, 4, 36, 67, 71, 74
  see also stato misto
Mompesson, Sir Giles, 153–4
monarchy, concepts of, 3, 11, 16, 23, 82, 88, 90, 95, 100, 104, 131, 133, 155, 157–8, 160–1, 166, 182, 186
monopolies, 50, 75, 107–9, 113, 119–20
Moretti, Franco, 11, 23, 191 n3, 193 n27, n28
Morrill, John, 189 n7, 210 n33
Motion, Andrew, 118, 209 n21
Mulier, Eco Haitsma, 5, 190 n20, n22
Mullaney, Steven, 68–9, 78, 201 n3, n4, 202 n17
Mullini, Roberta, 194 n2

neoplatonism, 146, 156
New Historicism, 1, 188 n1, 198 n5
Newman, Karen, 210 n3
New Model Army, 158
newsbooks, 123–4, 128, 143
Nicholl, Charles, 214 n15
Norbrook, David, 123, 139–40, 210 n1, 213 n45, 221 n4
Norman Yoke, 167
Norris, Christopher, 3, 189 n9
Northampton, Henry Howard, Earl of, 15

Oldenbarneveldt, Jan van, 193 n34
Orgel, Stephen, 188 n1, 191 n29, 199 n15, 207 n30
Ostovich, Helen, 52, 64, 66–7, 184–5, 198 n7, n8, 200 n21, n23, 201 n40, n41, 209 n29, 222 n10, n11

Otway, Thomas, 194 n3
Overbury, Sir Thomas, 120–1, 209 n28
Ovid, 11, 85, 102, 156

pamphlets, 124, 127, 139, 149
Parker, Brian, 194 n2
Parker, Geoffrey, 191 n24
Parliament, 6, 63, 114, 132, 134, 139, 142, 146, 154–7, 161, 163, 165, 172, 174, 179, 182–3, 189 n7, 214 n10, 217 n3
  see also House of Commons
Parr, Anthony, 128, 210 n6, n10, 211 n22
Parry, Graham, 214 n9, 215 n32, 217 n8
Paster, Gail Kern, 200 n22, 206–7 n34
pastoral, 178, 183–4
Patterson, Annabel, 3, 27–8, 94, 179, 189 n11, n12, 194 n35, n36, 205 n19, 211 n12, 221 n43
Pearl, Sara, 135, 212 n32
Pearl, Valerie, 168–9, 218 n16, n19, 219 n32
Peltonen, Markku, 110, 189 n10, n13, 192 n9, 200 n25, 201 n32, 208 n6
Pembroke, William Herbert, Earl of, 199 n12
Penshurst Place, 54, 147
Performance theory, 2
Personal Rule, 8, 114, 122, 142, 160, 164–79, 182, 221 n5
Peterson, Richard S., 215 n19
Petition of Right (1628–9), 142, 146, 156–7, 161, 174, 214 n10
plague, 69, 77, 79, 86, 97
Plato, 8, 49–50, 156, 197 n1, 198 n3, 217 n5
  Ion, 49
  Phaedrus, 49
  The Republic, 8, 49, 197 n1, n2
  Symposium, 49, 156
Plutarch, 13, 19, 109
  Lives, 13, 19, 109
Pocahontas, 65–6
Pocock, J.G.A., 191 n23

Index

Polybius, 5, 36, 37, 190 n18
Pompey, 13, 19
Popham, Sir John, Lord Chief Justice, 113, 114, 121
populace, 11, 25–7, 30–3, 94, 97, 103–4, 127, 129, 159, 170, 213 n42
Principate, 12, 19, 42
Privy Council, 15, 23, 172, 175
prodigal son plays, 124, 139
Pullan, Brian, 195 n8
Puritanism, 51–2, 80, 94, 110–11, 115, 158–9, 184, 191 n28, 198 n5
see also Anabaptists
Purseglove, Jeremy, 115, 209 n19, n30
Pye, Christopher, 202 n8

Quarter Sessions, 153, 174, 219–20 n32
Queer theory, 189 n3

Randolph, Thomas, 122, 210 n33
The Muse's Looking Glass, 122
republicanism, republics, 1–19, 22, 25, 27, 30–50, 57, 73, 75, 81, 84, 88–90, 94, 96, 104, 107–8, 125, 139–40, 157, 162, 180–3, 187, 188 n2, 189 n10, 200 n25, 201 n32
Restoration, 93
revisionism, 182, 216 n37, n39, 220 n41
Ricks, Christopher, 193 n31
Riggs, David, 6, 55–7, 113, 119–20, 189 n6, 191 n25, n27, 199–200 n16, 208 n13, 209 n22, n24
Righter, Anne, 202n15
see also Barton, Anne
Roberts, S.K., 214 n5, n26
Rodgers, Thomas, 72
Rome, 3, 4, 6, 11–29, 34, 36, 60, 63, 206 n25
Rose, Mary Beth, 52, 198 n6, n10
Rose Theatre, 202 n16
Royal National Theatre, 196 n17, 205–6 n23
Royal Shakespeare Company, 196 n17, 203 n27, 205–6 n23

Russell, Conrad, 191 n23, 216 n36, n37, 219 n25, 220 n41
Russell, Lucy, *see* Bedford, Lucy Russell, Countess of
Rutland, Elizabeth Sidney, Countess of, 54

Sale of titles, 116, 150
Salingar, Leo, 203 n29
Sallust, 4, 12, 18, 34, 62
Bellum Catilinae, 62, 210 n31
saltpetre, 176, 220 n37
Savory, Abraham, 120–1
Schellhase, Kenneth, 192 n6
Scott, Jonathan, 190 n13
Scottish Wars, 176
Sejanus, 14, 20, 25–30, 42, 76
Selden, Sir John, 165–6, 217 n10
Senate, 5, 12, 20, 26, 28–9, 36–7, 40, 62
Seneca, 20, 149, 197 n27
Sennett, Richard, 39–40, 70, 78, 195–6 n15, 196 n19, n20, n21, 202 n6, n18
Shakespeare, William, 13, 20, 25, 28, 40, 43, 46, 75, 77, 84, 87, 90, 92, 98, 110–11, 116, 119, 160, 170, 173, 190 n17, 193 n16, 194 n3, 195 n5, 198 n6, 205 n20, 206 n30
plays: *As You Like It*, 98; *Coriolanus*, 13, 25, 40, 190 n17; *Hamlet*, 43, 160; *Julius Caesar*, 13, 20, 25; *King Lear*, 110–11; *Measure for Measure*, 173, 195 n5, 205 n20; *The Merchant of Venice*, 194 n3; *Much Ado About Nothing*, 170, 173; *The Tempest*, 46, 75, 84, 119; *The Two Noble Kinsmen*, 92; *The Winter's Tale*, 98, 206 n30
poetry: sonnets, 116
Sharp, Buchanan, 208–9 n16
Shapiro, Michael, 54, 199 n13
Sharpe, Kevin, 114–15, 172, 174–5, 208 n15, 212 n28, 214 n10, 217 n3, 219 n24, 220 n41, 221 n5
Sherwood Forest, 144, 154, 183–5

Ship Money, 157, 168, 173, 175–6, 216 n37
Shirley, James, 186
  The Sisters, 186
Sidney, Sir Philip, 54, 92, 156
  Arcadia, 92
Sidney, Sir Robert, 54
Skinner, Quentin, 15, 189 n13, 192 n11, n14, 193 n17, 202–3 n20, 215 n20
Slights, William W.E., 196 n22, 203 n30
Smallwood, Robert, 70, 77, 202 n7
Smith, John, 112
Smith, Nigel, 210 n11
Smithfield, 89, 92–3
Social Contract, 179
Somers, William, 111–12
Somerset, Ann, 200 n19
Somerset faction, 55
Somerset, Robert Carr, Earl of, 120–1
Southwark, 92
Spain, 5, 27, 132–3, 141, 193–4 n34
  Spanish Infanta, 65–6, 124, 132–4
  Spanish Match, 65–6, 132–3, 211 n24
Sparta, 152, 161, 197 n2, 215 n21
Spenser, Sir Edmund, 156, 158
Stallybrass, 204 n1, n4, n5
States-General, 5, 141
stato misto, 4, 5
  see also mixed government
Stockton, David, 193 n20
Strong, Roy, 212 n29
Stuart, Lady Arbella, 54
Sturgess, Keith, 93, 205 n13
Suetonius, 12
Sweeney, John Gordon, 206 n27
Sylla, 17–20, 32

Tacitus, 4, 12–15, 24–5, 31, 34, 56, 192 n6
  Annals, 12–13, 24, 31, 192 n6, n8, n11
Tennenhouse, Leonard, 193 n26
Thirty Years War, 127

Thurborne, James, 153
Tiberius, 14, 22–30, 42, 76, 169
Tomlinson, Sophie, 215 n33
tonnage and poundage, 161
Turner, Anne, 120–1

Underdown, David, 214 n16, 220 n40
United Provinces, 5, 127, 141, 193 n34

vagabond literature, 186
van Gelderen, Martin, 21
Veevers, Erica, 215 n32
Venice, 3–5, 15, 19, 28, 34–43, 46, 68–9, 165, 194 n1, n2, n3, 195 n14, 195–6 n15, 196 n17, 197 n33
Vermuyden, Cornelius, 121
Villiers, George, see Buckingham, George Villiers, Duke of
Virgil, 11
Virginia Colony, 82
virtù, 30, 60, 149
Vitruvius, 137

Westminster School, 12
White, Allon, 204 n1, n4, n5
Wilson, Jean, 213 n41
Winch, Sir Humphrey, 112
Winterson, Jeanette, 194 n3
Wiseman, Susan, 189 n3, 191 n30, 205 n14, 222 n7
Wolfe, John, 130
Womack, Peter, 24, 193 n29, 204 n2, n4, 219 n22
Wootton, David, 189 n7
Worden, Blair, 3, 4, 16, 24, 128, 189 n8, 189–90 n13, 190 n14, n15, 193 n19, n30, 194 n4, 211 n12
Wotton, Sir Henry, 37, 46, 195 n14
Wrightson, Keith, 147, 172–4, 214 n5, 219 n27, n8, 220 n33
Wroth, Lady Mary, 54, 198–9 n11, 199 n12, n13
  Urania, 54, 199 n11
Wynne-Davies, Marion, 193 n26